D1155492

QUONDAM

TRAVELS IN A ONCE WORLD

QUONDAM

TRAVELS IN A ONCE WORLD

John Devoy

QUONDAM BOOKS

Rosscarbery,
County Cork,
Ireland

ISBN: 978-1-9996014-0-9

Copyright © John Devoy 2018

The moral right of the author has been asserted.
All rights reserved.

First published 2018.

Dedicated to my wife SARA

and our three children,

OISÍN, AISHA, and MERIEL

Fulsere quondam candidi tibi soles….[*]

CATULLUS

[*]Bright suns once shone for you…

A tale of search and adventure,
intimacy and renewal,
landscapes and imagination
long before the tech-umbilical.

About the author

Growing up in Whitegate, County Cork, Ireland, John Devoy studied medical laboratory science and worked in Cork University Hospital until 1985. In April that year he set out on his great adventure, in which he covered more than 33,000 kilometres in two years, cycling first to beyond the Arctic Circle in Norway, then south through Europe and the Middle East to Africa, where he continued to Capetown. *Quondam* tells the story of his journey from Cairo to Nairobi. Two forthcoming books will recount the other parts of his great trek. Today he lives with his wife Sara and their three teenage children, Oisín, Aisha, and Meriel, on their organic farm in West Cork, Ireland.

PHOTO: ADORNED DREAMS
(www.adorneddreams.com)

www.johndevoyauthor.com

CONTENTS

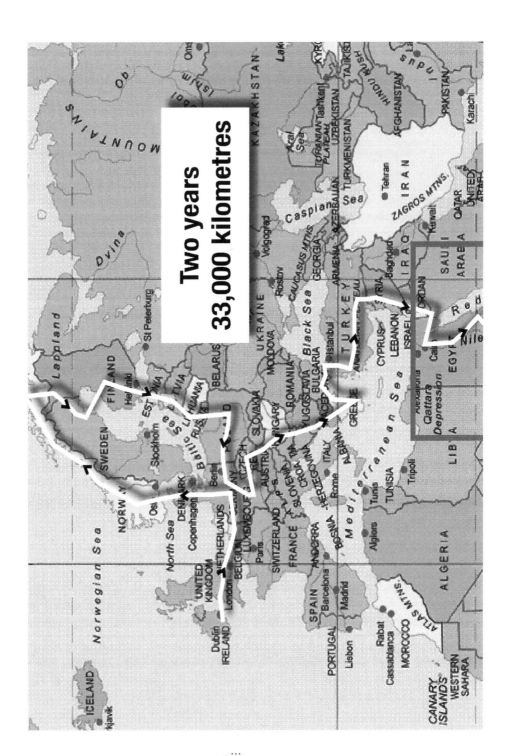

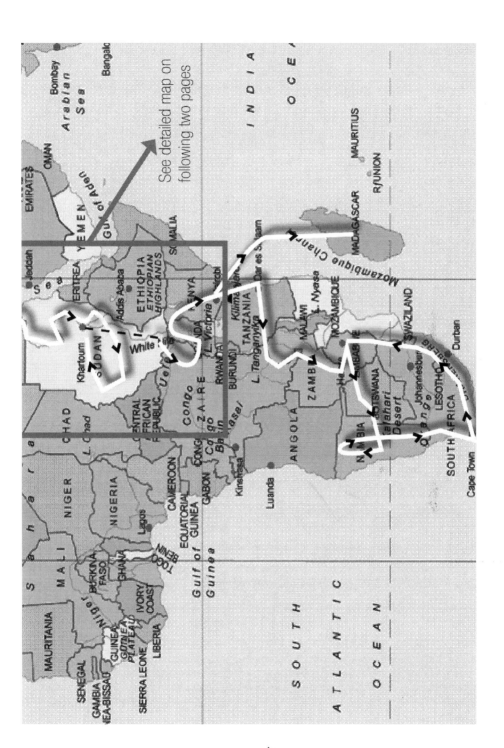

See detailed map on following two pages

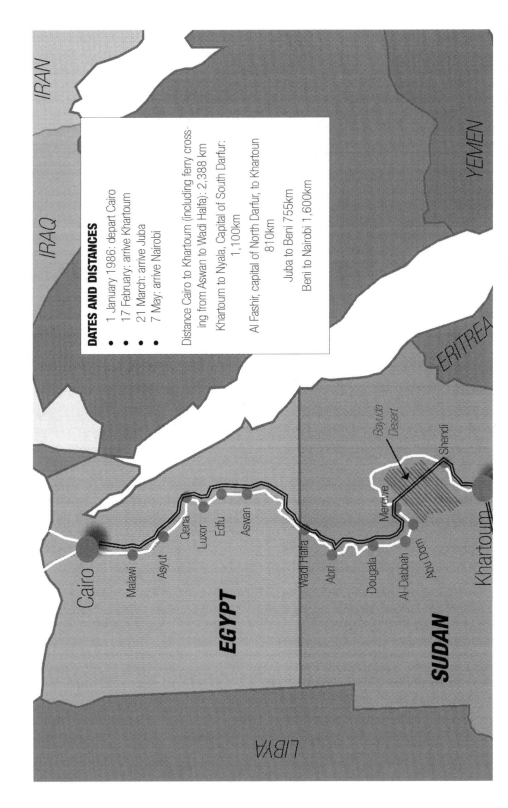

DATES AND DISTANCES

- 1 January 1986: depart Cairo
- 17 February: arrive Khartoum
- 21 March: arrive Juba
- 7 May: arrive Nairobi

Distance Cairo to Khartoum (including ferry crossing from Aswan to Wadi Halfa): 2,388 km

Khartoum to Nyala, Capital of South Darfur: 1,100km

Al Fashir, capital of North Darfur, to Khartoun 810km

Juba to Beni 755km

Beni to Nairobi 1,600km

IRAN

IRAQ

YEMEN

ERITREA

EGYPT

SUDAN

LIBYA

Cairo

Malawi

Asyut

Qena

Luxor

Edfu

Aswan

Wadi Halfa

Abri

Dougala

Al Dabbah

Abu Dom

Merowe

Bayuda Desert

Shendi

Khartoum

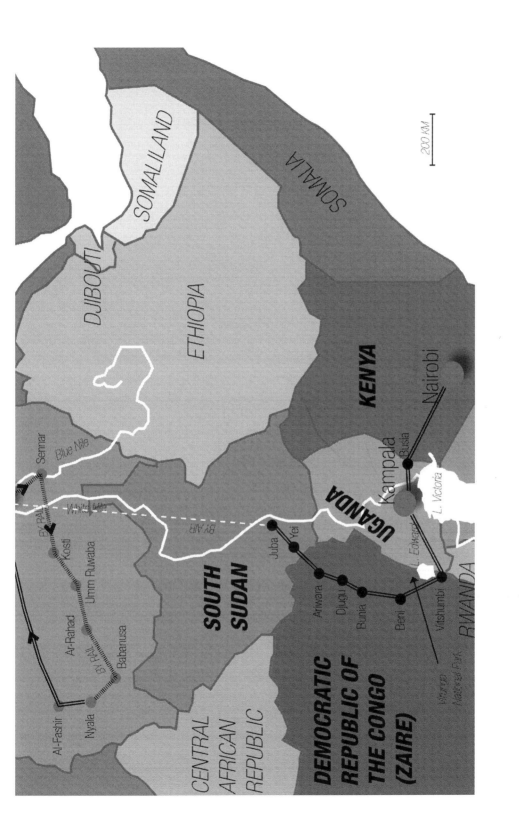

Foreword
by Dervla Murphy

QUONDAM gained an unwelcome topicality on 9 April 2018. Grim news came then from Virunga Park: five Rangers had been murdered by poachers—a too-common tragedy. These very brave men dedicate their lives to protecting Virunga's mountain gorillas who were cherished for twenty years by Dian Fossey, herself mysteriously murdered in 1985.

For the Devoy family this latest crime was especially shocking. Perhaps they'd met one or all of the five men a year previously, when John took them to Virunga. There he had enjoyed one of the most memorable experiences described in *Quondam,* and thirty years later he was determined to share this special place with Sara and their children. Virunga, because of its 'protected' status, was among the few areas where he could expect to find a landscape and people almost unchanged. However, its charming changelessness is also sinister. As you read these chapters you come to understand some of the severe pressures and complicated motives behind the harrowing events of 9 April 2018.

On page 1 of *Quondam* we realise that this happy cyclist has already spent nine months pedalling through nineteen countries on his way from Finnish Lapland to Cairo. His perception of the tourist/traveller dichotomy is congenial to me. What he most values is 'The daily engagement with ordinary life…When you travel slow and solo, you are exposed to the rich intensity of humanity as old as time.'

John Devoy's impressive saga could not be repeated today. The intervening decades have transformed travelling as a way of life, making it very difficult (impossible?) for anyone unselfconsciously to immerse themselves in the countries through which they travel, learning something new every day. From my (born 1931) viewpoint, globalization in all its manifestations inevitably diminishes a journey's excitement. Unpredictability used to be an essential ingredient, giving savour to all else. Admittedly, it could on rare occasions cause minor problems. But in general one rejoiced, at sunrise, to start another stage through unfamiliar terrain not knowing where one might be at sunset. Sadly, modern communications have made such voluntary isolation from kith and kin seem artificial—even cranky.

John's advice to young travellers is 'Do it alone, quietly, on the back roads and, yes, without technology.' I, too, urge the abandonment of technology but in general youngsters' reactions suggest alarm at the prospect of coping with a tech-free world. And in fact they couldn't attain it unless they confined their wanderings to uninhabited territories. For this reason alone John's narrative, describing a wide variety of peoples and their customs met along the way, has a particular value. It records how things were on the very eve of globalization-by-technology. Were he or I to retrace our wheelmarks in 2018 our relationships with most of those peoples could not be the same. Internettery has profoundly changed all societies. Communities which in the 1980s lacked running water and electricity (never mind telephones) now organise their personal and business lives through the skilled use of smart phones - and waste much of their time watching 'globalizing' films designed to promote consumerism. (I'm told this is known as the leapfrog effect.)

In Cairo John shrewdly noted that 'an Egyptian's primary source of identity is in being Egyptian rather than being Muslim.' On the road to Harare he spent his first night as the guest of a Nile valley farming family—the first of many such nights. Everywhere he was spontaneously made welcome, one of the many advantages of being a solo cyclist. However, finding oneself at the centre of a village's excited attention, after a long strenuous day, can be rather exhausting; at intervals all John wanted was a secluded campsite where he could relax in solitude and silence. (I mean of course a 'wild' site; neither John nor I ever travelled in African regions afflicted by commercial sites.)

One of the most gruelling stages of John's journey, 900 kilometres. on a rough sandy track from Wadi to Khartoum, has since been transformed by Chinese 'developers' into a smooth, tarred motorway. In 2016 John read about the numerous cycling groups (often escorted by a 'health and safety' motor vehicle) who now zoom along that road 'in a cultural bubble', unaware of what they are missing. As he observes, a new breed of cyclist has evolved, quite distinct from the traditional sort. Evidently these would-be record breakers are inspired by the Tour de France and have no time to appreciate the landscapes they traverse. For them cycling is a quasi-professional sport rather than an enjoyable and sometimes challenging form of transport. Therefore they are easily persuaded that cyclists need to *spend*—money as well as energy. John and I set out to cycle thousands of unsponsored miles wearing everyday clothing without any of the risible garments and aids (electronic and dietary) foisted upon the gullible in recent decades.

Simplicity used to be an integral part of the joy of cycling; all you need is a standard machine and a normally healthy body. In what was once called the Third World, touring cyclists fitted in: we rode loaded bicycles as did the more affluent of the locals. The 21st-century hybrids would have seemed almost as alien as foreigners who arrive in 4x4s.

In conclusion, what is it about the Mountains of the Moon? En route to Virunga, John's fifty-mile ride parallel to that range felt 'really, really good'. In 1992 my ride on the other side of the same mountains felt equally elating. Must be something in the atmosphere, a something the lycra-clad speedsters might miss....

Dervla Murphy's account of her journey by bike from Ireland to India in 1963 launched her as an internationally acclaimed travel writer.

Foreword
by Ted Simon

AS ONE who rode around the world on a motorcycle, reading John Devoy's overwhelmingly rich story of his bicycle ride through Africa is like repeatedly pushing the plus sign on a Google map and watching blank areas spring to life in ever denser detail.

The book is crowded with events both painful and exhilarating, with intimate observations, interactions, conversations and wide-ranging reflections, all strung like beads on a thread of relentless physical effort. Even though the journey was made more than thirty years ago I don't for a moment doubt the authenticity of the account. I know how the details of such a culminating experience are stamped in the mind forever, and he conveys this sense of heightened awareness very well.

This is a traveller's banquet of passion, youthful enthusiasm, and hard-earned wisdom, flavoured with a dash of erudition. I am proud to have played some small part in its genesis. I once wrote that all I could hope to do on my bike was to make a narrow track around the globe and extrapolate. John Devoy is The Extrapolator.

Ted Simon is the author of the internationally best-selling books Jupiter's Travels *and* Dreaming of Jupiter, *which recount his circumnavigation of the world by motorbike on two separate occasions.*

Prologue

Sometimes the beginnings and endings of journeys grab all the attention—the excitement of departure, the euphoria of return—so that the juicy bit in the middle, the marrow in the travel bone, remains untouched. This book tells the story of that raw 'marrow' time and thus begins not at the chronological beginning of the journey, but rather nine months *after* our traveller has left home, when those first few thousand miles of delight are well burned off, when life on-the-road has settled down and, of course, long before our traveller begins his descent home.

★★★

Two pot-holing friends, Eamon from Kilkenny and John from Cork, left everything—jobs, potholes, girlfriends, everything—to cycle in different directions out into the bigger, wider world that was then. Eamon went around it, John from top to bottom. Riding together was never an option. 'Solo or bust' was their credo, and anyway they reckoned that the years of crawling on their bellies in tight, wet, pitch-black caves had done just enough to prepare them for a more full-on, outward-bound adventure. How right they were and how wrong. They cycled off into a pre-tech world, a time when leaving on a long trip meant exactly that…leaving! Bar the odd postcard, there would be little or no communication, for once that inevitable bend in the road was rounded, that was it, you were gone. Those were the days.

In Dublin, in a Hare Krishna restaurant because money was tight, they took off their shoes and teased out the only bit of a mutual plan they had—a rendezvous six months later outside a backstreet bike shop in the centre of Athens. Six months was what John reckoned he needed to complete the first part of his own journey: to ride 5,000 kilometres to North Cape, 700 kilometres beyond the Arctic Circle, then turn to face a zig-zag route south through Scandinavia, Central Europe, the Yugoslavia that was, and on to meet Eamon in the Greek capital. A Greek friend had translated a letter to explain to George, the owner of a bike shop there, to expect two Irish guys outside his shop at precisely 4pm, six months to the day later. George wrote back in perfect English, which he understood and spoke very well. 'Your arrival date is circled on my shop calendar,' he wrote. 'and there is a nice cafe opposite my shop.' Perfect! On the street outside the Hare Krishna restaurant the friends shook hands.

'Right so,' said Eamon, 'see you last day in September, okay, and don't be late!'

'Take care, buddy. See you in six months give or take a few minutes.'

John set out on April Fool's Day 1985, which seemed fitting to those who asked, 'What?…He's cycling to where? Cape Town? Geez, the whole thing's a joke!' Others, knowing he was 'no cyclist', whispered that he'd never get beyond the village pub. But he took the backroads, bypassed the village and reached Lismore where, riding past the gated laneway where Dervla Murphy lived, he raised his right fist in a silent salute.

A couple of months previously he had visited her and they had sat for a while in her study with the wood-stove busy, and books, especially the travel kind, running around the walls and from floor to ceiling. 'Oh yes,' she half-joked, 'they come into their own at this time of year…great insulation, you know.' He spied a few that he had read and a few that he had attempted. He was young and in awe, for he had never sat for so long with such well-travelled company. She had received his letter, but he guessed she received many such. 'Now, remind me again about your trip,' she said.

He was barely six when, in 1963, she left her home to cycle to New Delhi, a solo journey that lit the beacon for many to follow. *Full Tilt: Ireland to India with a Bicycle*, the book born of that journey, certainly fanned his own desire for adventure, and now, perhaps unconsciously, he had come to hoover up some imagined wisdom in handling those imagined back roads. She, however, was more eager to hear about the beauty of the wintry looking local ones, those he had just taken between Cork City and Lismore. They sat at opposite sides of her desk and at opposite ends of the travel game. She had distilled down her years to the present things, to nearby and ever-present wonders; he was already half departed, dreaming of the remote and the exotic.

'Well that sounds a grand adventure,' she said, looking for something on her desk as he waxed on about his 'plan', like the novice who had done it all before doing anything.

'And how will you cook your food,' she asked.

'Oh, that will be easy,' he said with an air of confidence, thinking how he had at least that particular nut cracked. 'I'll use a Sigg petrol stove.'

'Ah, I see. No, I'd never use petrol, too much of that stuff around the place, don't you think? We just light a campfire and cook on that…much nicer too.' She spoke of the joy of campfires with a black pot simmering, and he got the message.

'Well I don't have much to say really,' she said. 'You sound as if you have it all well organised, just don't forget you'll have to come back sometime…I presume you plan to come back?'

'Oh yes,' he replied in deadly earnest, 'I'll come back for sure.'

'Well that's good, that's good. Come back with a good story to share…sure that's half the reason.'

After he had cycled away from Lismore that winter evening, he had pondered for a mile or two about what Dervla Murphy had said, '… don't forget, you'll have to come back sometime', but her words had no hold, they couldn't stick. With just eight weeks then to departure, the force of an idea to ride to North Cape, Norway, then turn about to ride to Cape Point, South Africa, was altogether too all-consuming to let the notion of 'coming back' have any traction. It would be years, long after the journey was over, before he could

3

understand fully what she might have meant, but she was right, '...the story, sure that's half the reason.'

★★★

On that April Fool's Day in 1985 he rode onward to Carlow where his uncle's alsatian bit his thigh badly, then to Wicklow where he got completely lost, and to Dublin where a double-decker bus missed him by inches and then, to the Dun Laoghaire ferry where he watched a drowned woman being hauled up in that tight space between ship and quay. Even before getting out of his own country, that safe secure life he had known was being torn up and shredded; and it was only the beginning.

On the far side of the Irish Sea the occasional Union Jack and those yellow registration plates reminded him he was now definitely pedalling on foreign soil. His destination was Coventry. On the second floor of its Transport Museum, his hand rested for a while on the weather-worn saddle of a 500cc Triumph Tiger 100 motorbike—the very machine that in 1973 carried Ted Simon on his four-year odyssey across all continents. It was a mode of transport he would never have chosen but, to see it there, leaning still and silent on its stand was inspiring and motivating.

From Harwich to the Hook of Holland, time was spent tweaking his machine, after which it glided along the dykes, into a bitter north wind. Battling too was an old man cycling in bright yellow clogs. Without exchanging a word they took turns to wind-break each other. 'These Dutch,' he thought, 'they know about cycling.' He followed the yellow clogs towards Amsterdam, until the man suddenly waved and turned right, leaving him to the bitter wind with a tightening crick in the neck. Head bent, he watched the gravel cycle path disappear beneath the front wheel and tried hard not to dwell on what a hell of a long-way it seemed to an island off the north coast of Norway. Up there, 4,800 kilometres away, the summer solstice of North Cape awaited him; there at 71 degress north was the real, dreamt of starting point of the journey.

★★★

Six months, 9,000 kilometres, twenty-two punctures, two tyres and one crappy pair of cycling shoes later, he pulled the brakes at 5.05pm in downtown Athens. There it was, George's humble bike shop, and there waiting in the café opposite, strumming his mandolin, was his friend Eamon.

'Your an hour late!'

'Sorry…got stuck at the Berlin Wall.'

George stepped across the street, shook hands and called for three ouzos and a plate of baklava. He was not the plump greasy-old bike mechanic they had envisaged, more a tall, dark handsome actor-type with the culture to appreciate a few Irish tunes. He insisted on paying for everything and without giving anything away, tricked his Irish guests into leaving their bikes in his shop the following day.

'Go to the Acropolis early,' he had advised, 'your bikes will be safe here.'

When they returned that evening both bikes gleamed with the overhaul they had received—'a gift to both your journeys,' he said. George has never been forgotten.

Joining forces, they rode on and off with each other through Bulgaria's beautiful leafy autumn, across the open steppe of Central Anatolia, then south into Syrian hospitality. In Amman, the Jordanian capital, they would part company, for that was the plan. Eamon would ride east through Saudi to Pakistan, Nepal, Tibet, China, Australia, John south, through north and central Africa to Botswana, Namibia, Cape town, Lesotho and back to Zimbabwe. Yes, that was the plan! They entered Amman in twilight, just a few hundred metres apart… and then, lost each other! The following morning John climbed slowly out of the bowl of the city centre, wondering where his friend had got to, imagining he would not see him for several years, yet thinking, 'Well, we were going to part here anyway.'

On the crest of the final hill before the road straightened south to Aqaba, he pulled over and turned back, 'Take, care mate where ever the hell you are. Have a great trip.'

Five days later Eamon had enough of banging his head against Saudi intransigence. They wouldn't let him in so, true to form, he thought, 'What the hell, I'll pedal to Egypt instead.' He tracked John all the way to Cairo and three weeks later, in a suburb of that vast city, he finally caught up with him. A doorbell rang at 8.30am on Christmas morning. 'Bloody hell, what are you doing here? Thought you'd be in Karachi by now!' It was a wonderful and totally unexpected surprise to see him standing there, outside the door of the Embassy secretary's place, and in perfect time to tuck into a very Irish Christmas breakfast. On the Christmas tree hung two small gifts from the hostess, a bar of scented soap for each of them. The hint was graciously taken, but later on that Christmas night, back on Talaat Harb street in their hotel-hostel, the shower had no water; at least the soap smelled good. There we meet them, late on New Year's Eve, the day before their final farewell.

Chapter 1

The Nile is Egypt, Egypt is the Nile

The window on the top floor of the Oxford Hotel that I wanted to open wouldn't. Layers of old paint had sealed it, but then, with one final sharp pull, the chill air suddenly rushed in, and I stuck my head out into the last day of the year. Dusk was sweeping fast over Cairo. Down below, on Talaat Harb Street, the busyness of the day was almost done and, bar some traffic and the occasional honk of a taxi, the street was emptying itself. The city's foot-soldiers, Egypt's urban fellaheen, were drifting home. Across the street, in another window one floor lower, a small plastic Christmas tree blinked its white lights in an otherwise darkened building—off-on, off-on, off-on, a lone token to Christian tradition but enough to make me think of home, until the umpteen minarets called out to prayer and a Quranic rhythm wafted over us all.

The sprawl of lights stretched as far as my eye could see, fanning into a wide arc. I let myself sink into it, into that megacity scene, savouring its very personal significance. Cairo was both end and beginning. Timing dictated that somewhere here, a Christmas of sorts would be spent, but above all it would be a place to rest and recalibrate before cycling on into the awesome bulk of Africa.

I had climbed a creaky back-stair to the top floor of the Oxford Hotel, as much to reflect as to get a better view…and of all nights, New Year's Eve was apparently a good one to do so. Nine months riding through nineteen countries and now here, gazing at a lonely Christmas tree in a sea of city lights, the memories came all by themselves, from the high points to the low, from that April Fool's day departure to North Cape's longest day, from the diabolical hoards of midge and mosquito in Finnish Lapland to the warmth of Syrian hospitality… it had been kindness through every country, along every back road, every farm, every village, every down-stroke of the way. The ferry from Aqaba in Jordan to Nuweiba on the Sinai coast felt like a mini-transition in itself. Being ferried under the Suez Canal felt like another, but to ride, unbelievably rain-sodden, on the shortest day of the year into Egypt's capital felt truly an end and beginning all rolled into one. But all that was over now. On the morrow I would ride out of Cairo into the pulsating heart of 'real' Egypt.

The Oxford Hotel, what a lively cheap dive it was, full of transient long haulers and long-term inmates who had 'got stuck' in Cairo. In and around its smoky reception area there were more shady deals done, more swapping tales and rabbiting-on about rodents, fleas and cockroaches than in any downtown tea house, but wasn't that exactly what overland warriors wanted, to pretend to be toughened and seasoned by such 'never could you forget' places? Certainly, for Eamon and I, the Oxford was another mini-marker to broaden the mind.

I descended to him, to our cruddy fourth floor room using the rickety old lift, which one long-term American aptly described as akin to a 'vertical coffin stained for eternity with nicotine'. It shuddered as it trundled downward, making me look up through a hole in its ceiling, imagining a single fraying cable and a sudden snap…and 'my coffin' falling freely to burst me open at the bottom. Had it happened, after the week we'd had of parties and Christmas over-indulgence, I would have had no complaints!

The Irish Embassy staff were good, too good, bringing us to that traveller's heaven where wine, breads and cheeses, even foods from home, were placed before us; with beer into late nights it created a widening and dangerous gap between life on the perpetual hungry edge of cycle-travel and that rarified ephemeral paradise. Even caviar was taken, by a giggly secretary, out of the Chargé d'Affaires' fridge, on my friend's skinny behalf.

'You lads, especially you…,' she looked at Eamon, 'you must be fattened up for your ride! Here, eat this, no one will mind.' There was a burst of laughter at her choice of words. Months later, at the Irish Embassy in Nairobi, when I nonchalantly enquired about her, I was informed that she wasn't in Cairo any longer. I wondered had she paid a 'caviar price'? In Nairobi they weren't about to take any chances. They'd been well forewarned about letting anyone near fridges.

But it was understandable, of course, that some excited fuss was being made of us. We were an out-of-the-ordinary passing treat, and it was Christmas after all. How could anyone resist two fellow-countryman making their parting 'X' on the world map right there in Cairo. When the staff got wind of our respective journeys we were wheeled from one party to another. But travellers on a mission tire fast of heaven; it doesn't have what they seek. Despite the angelic ladies, the wine, banter and good craic…as potholers we would never get stuck, like some in the Oxford had.

When I re-entered our room, Eamon was map reading on his bed, his greasy forefinger still traversing Saudi Arabia, as if in hope. Even had there been some sort of collective Cairo New Year celebration, neither of us would have bothered. That feeling of one's cultural umbilical being slowly cut was almost pleasurable. All afternoon we had worked on our upturned bikes, with bits and greasy bobs strewn across the floor. 'These rooms are a mess,' he had said. No wonder. Indeed anything and everything happened in those Oxford boxes. We even heard of a guy who pitched his tent in his, to keep the insects out, then lit his stove and nearly burnt the building down while visiting the bog. It was that kind of place.

I took up where I'd left off an hour before, gripping the rear wheel between my knees, rotating it slowly, pulling a dirty cloth between each spoke, making the rim shine. Not since sitting outside Ali Bozdag's carpet shop in Kaymakli, Turkey, had I given the wheels such attention. 'No point riding out of Cairo on a dirty machine,' or so I thought, but of course I wasn't fooling myself. This cleaning had as much to do with preparing my mind for the next stage as with getting the bike right. Nine months riding done and dusted, and now the eve of the next stage.

★★★

There had always been three points of departure, three stages which I could hold onto: leaving home, leaving North Cape and leaving Cairo. The first two were easy on the mind. There was always someone somewhere along the way to sweeten the journey, and though I could never know what the road would throw up, I imagined whatever came would be familiar and manageable, but leaving Cairo for Sudan was somehow different. It was, to a certain extent, unknown and *that*, ironically, felt good. After Cairo the next friend-of-a-friend contact was in Harare, 6,000 kilometres away. Not exactly down the road.

With a dirty rag wrapped around my forefinger, I rubbed meditatively along the edge of the rim. Eamon, lifting his curly head out of Pakistan, suggested I was taking this 'cleaning thing' a bit too far. He was right, of course, but I didn't care. I was letting the previous months settle, waiting for my mind to play catch-up. I spun the clean wheel and took the odd look out the Oxford window and felt focussed again. I looked at him, kneeling on the floor. He was giving a final adjustment to a brake pad. We were gladiators then, sharpening our weapons, preparing for battle, a solo battle, experienced, as it must be, alone. These journeys we undertook were long and extraordinary and were hardly if at all understood by our nearest and dearest, let alone anyone else. More often than not they were hardly even grasped by the one in the saddle. They were simply too long and complex in time and space for most heads to comprehend. Much easier to take in a tight singular expedition like climbing a mountain or trekking to the Pole.

Eamon slid off his bunk and muttered something about 'hope' and 'visas'. Could he get across Saudi and on to Pakistan to India to Tibet. Visas? I didn't want to get involved; I'd my own problems but neither of us wanted a repeat of the cock-up that was getting into Syria. It was strange to see him there, flatmate and friend from potholing days when we crawled on our bellies in damp, dark limestone chambers. A year and a half before he had dozed in the back of that old Land Rover, coming up through France after our expedition to Sardinia, when in the sunshine I quietly nodded my decision to 'do it'. That sunny decision of mine had woken a yearning in him too and had set us both in motion. We had soldiered together, had lost and found each other several times on the road and now, tomorrow, we'd say a final farewell. In a half-hearted attempt to honour the approaching midnight hour he took out his penny whistle and played a few tunes while I sang the 'Rocky Road to Dublin', which he despised! After that brief outburst our efforts dissolved away, and at the stroke of midnight he was back in his map and I in another letter to my girlfriend ,'J'.

On New Year's Day we raised a glass of guava juice outside a fruit stall and said our 'adios'. I would send him a postcard care-of Poste Restante, Karachi, and he one to me in Nairobi. There are goodbyes of all kinds but this was as good as you could get between a pair of close but fiercely independent travellers. To-day one can say goodbye to a friend and be Skyping them on another continent a few hours later. Then a 'goodbye' carried a different weight, and for us it was laden with potential finality. Eight and more hours per day on the road...we had had enough near misses to know what could happen in an instant. One's end could lie round the next bend or even on a dead straight stretch. Eamon went on in the time-honoured fashion of the Buddhist monk, accepting all that came his way with minimum resistance, even, I often thought, his own potential demise. I, on the other hand, had a Samurai-like spirit, a bring-it-on-whatever attitude, and whoever wins, wins. If I die then so be it, Amen. So we finished our guavas and I rode out of Cairo. I did not see him again for three years.

★★★

'Giza, Giza?' I called to an old man who quickly pointed to a cart just ahead. 'Zoo, zoo," he replied. It took me a second to get it. To paraphrase what he said, 'Look, fellah, follow that cart and it will take you to the Zoo and from there you're almost out, okay.' The cart was driven by two youths and carried three headless bullock carcasses, blood dripping from their necks. The youths were unaware that I was now in tow, moving at the leisurely pace of their pony but slightly to the left of the dripping red line. The pace of my unknowing guides allowed me to relax, and in the sunshine I daydreamed of Eratosthenes.

I imagined him jogging beside me and told him that what he did back then was real cool and that I'd be remembering him all the way to *Syene* (Aswan), 800 kilometres down the road. I had convinced myself that to travel through a country with one of its heroes, long dead or not, was a good idea. They would always help with perspective, with another angle to understanding how culture and topography have merged and intertwined over the millennia. Strictly speaking, Eratosthenes was a Greek, but there was no point splitting hairs; Egypt was his adopted country.

Years before, J had given me Carl Sagan's book *Cosmos*, and from its pages

Eratosthenes' simple genius leapt. What a guy! Chief librarian in the Great Library at Alexandria and today acknowledged as the 'Father of Geography', he was the first to give the subject a name and the first to originate the concept of longitude and latitude. Every map I looked at, that vertical-horizontal grid, reminded me of his dedication to his science. Yet even this was not why I remembered him. It was his childlike experiment using a bit of basic trigonometry, shadows and sticks in the sand, which changed our understanding of our planet Earth forever. That's what got me.

In that great library he read what was for him an ancient papyrus scroll, how in Syene the Sun cast *no* shadow at midday on 21 June, the summer solstice. He knew that at that same hour the Sun *did* cast a shadow in Alexandria. What was going on? According to Sagan, Eratosthenes paid someone to walk the 800 kilometres to Syene to get an accurate measurement of the distance between his two 'sticks', the one in Alexandria and the other perhaps on Elephantine Island opposite the Aswan of today. From his calculations he deduced that the Earth must be round, not only that but he arrived at a circumference pretty close to what we know it is today, about 40,000 kilometres. As Sagan put it, '…not bad for someone in the third century BCE using naught but sticks and shadows and a bit of grey matter.' It impressed me at any rate, and I promised myself before leaving Ireland that I'd remember his work when I got to Egypt.

Now I was there, observing today's Egyptians going about their day. I imagined one of their ancestors being tasked with that onerous walking honour. Did someone actually walk the whole way or was a camel used? Whatever about walking or camel riding, it would take me ten or eleven days cycling to reach Aswan and there I'd reflect again on all that flowed from one man's endeavour.

Passing the Zoo, the big crowd pullers were at the back, well away from the road. Only birds and gazelle could be seen for free just inside the perimeter fence. Passing them, I couldn't help wondering if would I really see big game—lion, elephant, giraffe, rhino, hippo, buffalo—all free of charge further down the continent. I had no idea, but the thought excited me. In hindsight, would I have been as excited if I'd known that on one day alone in Tanzania I would be charged by an elephant and pass within sixty metres of a male lion, while in Zaire—now the Democratic Republic of the Congo (DRC)—I would be lucky one inebriated night to be stopped by a local from walking in front of an old female hippo?

Crossing the Nile at Giza, I turned to see a blanket of smog hanging over the vast city. It was good to be out of it but the air was still heavy. I was now on the Cairo-Aswan agricultural road east of the Nile, hoping it would be less busy than its parallel conduit. In most countries when you ride out of the capital, sooner or later you enter the spaciousness of the countryside. Departing Cairo, there was no such space bar the nearby desert; it was congested sprawl all the way. 'Don't ride here if you wish peace and quiet!' I later wrote to a cycling friend.

As I passed a school at break-time the children ran to the fence and gleefully called out. I waved back, dodging a male duck as I did. He had no interest in the rules of the road, just wanted to join his mate for a splash in the nearby canal. There they dipped and washed and appeared unperturbed by a large raft ferrying people over and back. On the other side, a man in a white *jalabiya* yanked hard on the pull cord of a water pump. It chugged to life, spitting black smoke. Behind him, camels, donkeys and water buffalo all chewed together in the corner of a yard. Then, like a bat out of hell, a hoopoe shot across my path...*oop-oop-oop, oop-oop-oop*. It nearly took my head off, but I loved its Mohican crown and its low undulating flight across the water. The sun was high and hot, and my blue hat, shrunk as it was through various washings, barely covered my head, yet it all felt good, that first proper day's work in real Egypt.

By late afternoon the iconic step pyramid at Saqqara, Ancient City of the Dead, came slowly into view. I walked the bike towards the tomb of Pharaoh Djoser, built 2,700 BCE, and on top of a mound of excavated rubble I clicked my little Rollei camera. There was hardly a soul about. Newgrange came to mind, for as boldly captivating as the Pyramids are, indeed Stonehenge also, the working realness of that older County Meath astronomical temple-cum-tomb struck me then as even more impressive. I said as much to a pair of middle-aged American tourists. They had been to Stonehenge, had marvelled at the Pyramids, but had never heard of Newgrange!

'Yes, you can actually go inside," I explained, 'down a passage, into a chamber. If your lucky you'll even see its real function".

'Gee, sound's amazing, where is it again?' They began note-taking as their

13

taxi waited. 'Well, young man, goodbye and thank you so much,' she said. 'And good luck with your cycle to Aswan,' he added.

'Aswan', I thought, '…if they only knew.'

I watched them walk to the waiting car, bound perhaps for a four-star in Cairo. With their spotlessly clean outfits, slung cameras and guide books, they looked all of the archaeological part. Indiana Jones came to mind, on one of his good days.

Four-star, three-star, one-star, no star at all or all the stars above, for me the choice was quite simple, crash-out at the back of the pyramid or push-on into an unknown evening. I threw my leg over and was gone in an instant, with the world-apart worlds of tourist and traveller flip-flopping in my head. Hardly five kilometres along that dusty road it was I who entered another world, and indeed another time.

From my diary: I am listening to the banter in Egyptian Arabic between two young boys, perhaps nine and eleven. They found me earlier trying to camp incognito and hauled me to their humble home. They, their father and I are sitting on mats by the canal, giving our all to communicate. Like me they too practice Shotokan Karate, so we have something in common. Their father nods and smiles at them and at me. He gestures to the food and says something, then points towards the open door of their home. I do not understand but take his hint and eat some more. The light from the fire spreads over the bread and cheese and turns the large metal platter into a fiery gold. The boys talk quietly now, as their father stands to face Mecca. 'Allahu akbar,' he continues his prayer, now bowing, now kneeling. He's on my left, a kitten plays before me, and to the right his sons sit in the glow of the fire, and in the half light I write the diary.

The old donkey stands still, tethered to a post. A waning moon rises between palm branches. The donkeys foal is free to move and comes to nudge its mother, comforting her. The dog barks as the woman of the house comes from the open door bearing more food. The bread and cheese was just a starter, for me I guess. On a low table she places rice, soup, chicken, pitta bread and tea. She disappears. We men eat and attempt to talk until the boys are told by their father to sleep. School in the morning. On the open porch they continue to mutter under the blankets, bubbling with a good story to tell their friends.

Sleep is elusive. It's not the tea, or any concern past or present, I am simply *too alive. The dog barks one last time into the dark, then comes to lie between the father and me. Mosquitoes come to torment and the young ass comes to sniff my head. There are stars. My thoughts drift to J and home but I tell myself the best thing I can do is to let that go. The old donkey turns. The moon rises and I sleep…eventually.*

The day began before six. From my bag I peep to see a young girl's face glow beside the flames of a new fire. She tends it, in its wok-like basin, carefully placing more wood. Her father is already half way through his Fajr, God's most favoured prayer, when others are still asleep. His donkey stands close-by, exactly where it has stood all night. The animal looks as if it too is in deep meditation. The air is chill and I warmly accept the hot tea offered me. Soon thereafter our hands shake in farewell, 'Ma'as-salaam,' they say. 'Shukran,' I repeat several times. We wave and I push off into the morning. My host is surprised to see me leaving in shorts for they are all well wrapped, January being the coldest month. Yet I know pretty soon I will be sweating and that by mid-day the temperature will be like a summer's day in Ireland. I am alien here.

It was beautiful before dawn, the road surprisingly quiet. The air was crisp and clean, and I stopped to pull on my fading red windcheater. There was no wind but it would take time before I warmed up. I noticed how my clothes were also beginning to look the part…rough, like Indiana Jones after one of his bad days. My right foot effortlessly flicked back the pedal to slot into the open toe-clip, ready for the off. For fun, I did the sums. I reckoned that foot-flick had been done over 4,000 times—flick back, slot in, flick back, slot in—or should it be flick back, slot in, push down, oh what the hell.

I rode past men riding donkeys to the fields and I thought of that burdened animal. That donkey stood there all night like her mother before her, and before her and before her, all the way back to those who built that step pyramid, incredible. It was about then, 3,000 ago when the donkey was first domesticated right here in Egypt. They dragged the stone, the rubble, the food, the tools and were on their own in doing so, for camels did not enter Upper Egypt for another 2,000 years. No doubt Imhotep's desire to build for the Pharaoh sped up the donkey's domestication, and the rest, as they say, is history: 3,000 years of burden, 3,000 years of standing still in the night down all those nights.

Never had I considered the role of the donkey. The only one I was aware of was used by an elderly entrepreneurial farmer in Ballyvaughan, County Clare, on the west coast of Ireland. There, beside a well-known village road sign, he would stand by his beast, while his old dog stood on the donkey's back. All this to call attention to himself and have 'the Yanks' and other tourists take their cameras out, and, of course, their wallets. By all accounts he did nicely. Ireland has moved far away from donkeys, but here in this land, this culture birthed by the Nile, and indeed everywhere where life is subsistent, where people live their daily grind to just get through the day, one will find the donkey either working or patiently standing for its next task.

On a parallel track, on the canal's other side, a plump man in a brown *jalabiya* reminded me of Friar Tuck in Robin Hood. He whipped his mule while yanking a second mule behind. The towed one was weighed down with drums of water, or perhaps diesel for some remote water pump. He kicked the ribs hard and tugged sharply at the pulling rope. The animals responded. They'd seen and felt it all before. A drum of diesel today, a basket of rubble thousands of years ago, it was all the same to them. He turned away from the canal toward the desert and I went straight on. Not ten minutes further, I came within a whisper of losing my life.

A multicoloured dress caught my eye. A girl, nine or ten, sat on a rock, arms resting on a stick like an old woman. She appeared indifferent to her flock, perhaps bored, watching nothing but traffic all day. Her goats were scattered along the narrow busy road. There seemed nothing for them to eat, yet they were all busy nibbling at something. I stopped just across from her to pull off the red windcheater. She stared at me, no smile, just blankly stared. I saluted her anyway and flicked the pedal to go. It is strange what we recall when we are nearly wiped off the map…those wide-open eyes from across the narrow road. Did she see the truck coming? Did she want to call out? It came so fast as if out of nowhere, catching the rear pannier, and I was blown away. It was gone a hundred metres by the time I stood in anger, cursing and shaking my fist, 'You bastard, you fucking bastard,' I yelled out.

The girl stood, confused, her goats scattering. For a split second I saw her and then, very shaken, I went about checking the damage. Some men came running to see if I was all right. A nasty grazed right hand and a pair of bloody knees seemed the sum of my bodily scars but later that day it would be the shock which struck hardest. Someone brought antiseptic, at least that's what I presumed it was. No one spoke English or French, and I could not read Arabic, but it stung like hell as the guy daubed it to my wounds. *Bulees, Bulees*, said another man. 'Yeah, a bully, a stupid fucking bully,' I agreed, knowing they could not understand my words, but the guy was insistent. '*Bulees, Bulees*,' he said, pointing back the road. It was then I realized, he meant the police. 'No, no,' I protested as he was about to run off. 'No *Bulees*, please, *shukran*.' There were no broken bones, and stupidly I just wanted to move on. The *Bulees* would have played with me for the rest of the day. With a few kilometres under my belt I'd feel fine again, or so I thought.

I stood the bike. It looked okay, so I mounted. Everyone watched. I wobbled a few metres then abruptly stopped. 'Shit…ah shit,' I bellowed. It was too much to hope the bike had come off unscathed. The '48' ring was bent. It could not move the chain. When I looked closer I saw that the bottom bracket was loose. When your transmission system is up the swanee, you ain't goin' nowhere! The crowd gathered round, and as always in this classic kind of bike-travel hiccup, someone came up with the goods. My nurse with the stinging antiseptic gel explained that his friend was 'mechanic, mechanic'. Now when a cyclist hears this, it does not, unfortunately, give the same rosy feeling as it may do for the mechanised traveller. Yet beggars can't be choosers, so I was led away. Pretty soon the smartest school kid in town was dug out of his books. The poor lad arrived confused, feeling the pressure from his adult escorts. He was told to put his English to the test and, like the real *Bulees* might have done, he began with the obvious 'Where you from? Where you go?'

Over the following three hours of laughter, sweet teas and talk of trucks and how green Ireland *really* was, the boy grew in confidence and in stature. The 'mechanic' straightened the chain-ring…almost, and together we did the rest. A crowd of youths piled in for a final photo, the boy put centre stage, the 'nurse' in the rear and the older mechanic standing sombre to the right. I had been saved and not a *Bulees* to be seen. The young lad, now hero in his own right, translated the mechanic's blessing, 'May Allah guide and protect you,' he said. 'Amen to that,' I answered. The nibbling goats and the wide-eyed girl were nowhere to be seen, and as I rode off I wondered had it all been just a dream.

Running with the bulls, I called it. It was a nervy last few hours back on the road. Ears became antennae, tuned now to the various engine sounds looming like beasts from behind. I became more sensitised to my safety, negotiating the chipped and broken edges of that narrow busy thoroughfare. That normal unconscious cycling confidence was shelved and I rode in a state of heightened sensory awareness. Frequently, to let the monsters pass, I'd pull-off to the side, making progress slow. At five or so, my ears had had enough and my eyes tuned into potential tent-pitching spots. At 5.10pm the bike swung off the road down an embankment and braked hard beside yet another canal. 'This is it for the night' I told myself….

Behind an earth bank I kept a low profile, watching silhouetted people walk homeward. After the day I'd had I wanted to be quiet, to get into the tent, close my eyes and sleep. It was 5.20pm, the sun had set, darkness would soon come, then I could pitch. While waiting I rummaged quietly in the panniers for food. Out of nowhere it seemed, a flock of goats appeared and, as goats do, halted above my head. 'Scram, will ye,' I muttered, but the herdsman either heard or saw me or both and called in my direction. I wished he'd shoo off too, but in Egypt…forget it!

The universal sign for 'A-okay' had no effect on him. He shouted to some boys flying by on their bikes and I guessed told them to talk some sense into me and take me to their home. The game was up, resistance was futile. Hospitality to strangers is 'king' in Egypt and one dare not disobey the 'king'. The excited teenagers watched as I packed up, feeling utterly exhausted. The aftershock of the truck's hit had come home to roost, sapping reserves, but that was only the beginning! The boys had yet to decide which of their homes I would go to. 'Oh, sweet Jesus,' I thought, as they began to argue. For a moment I considered saying 'good luck' and riding on into the night, but finally I got them to agree to let *me* decide. So I tossed a coin for my fate and that was how I ended up sitting on the carpeted floor of Moshin Fangary's home, watching ballet on a small black-and-white TV dumbstruck while he and his friend thumbed through their school English book. But Allah was watching. Moshin's father came in and switched the ballet off. I was never into ballet. The entire left half of his face was covered by a purple birth mark. His children's faces were clear and beautiful.

'*Ahlan wa sahlan* (You've arrived as part of the family),' he said. His eyes told me he had long passed beyond impressions and calmly welcomed me as if I was a stray dog he had found himself. He could see I was beyond tired so led me to a bedroom and there I was blown away for the second time that day. It was obvious they were not a wealthy family. The house was typical mud and wattle and badly in need of maintenance, but the bedroom was extraordinary. Beautiful wall hangings with Quranic inscriptions, deep carpets on the floor, bright brass candelabras, pictures, memorabilia of all kinds and in the centre, a double hand-carved four-poster bed with a richly embroidered canopy. His wife came with a smile and a glass of sweet milky *helba* (fenugreek), a wad of cotton and another 'magic' bottle. She had noted my bandaged knees and the black plastic handlebar tape wrapped around my right hand. She left the room, leaving the bandaging to me. I taped the wounds tight, not wishing to stain her bed linen, while listening to her husband trying his best to explain how the furnishings and hangings had come from the home of his deceased parents in Iraq, all most interesting but I wondered why I was given *helba*. It's often given to women to improve lactation or increase contractions during labour!

The day had begun under the stars on an open lean-to porch, outside a simple home, and ended in a four-poster, in a family museum. In between was eventful, to say the least. My body ached, and sleep once again took its time. I replayed the near miss, the fifth serious one of the trip. The first in Dublin, a bus, the second in Finnish Lapland, a huge logging truck, the third in Zagreb, a tram, the fourth in central Turkey, a lorry. I sank into that four-poster feeling like a king but suspicious that my hosts had given up their own bedroom. This was no museum. There were too many tell-tale signs of regular use.

Stiff and sore, I woke early and rested on my best elbow. To greet the day, a bed bug fell from my mop of hair onto the clean sheet. I watched it with complete indifference, a blood-bloated pest, as it crawled over a crease. Was I becoming too filthy even for a humble bug? 'So you're jumping ship, my friend, ya little bugger.' I wondered had I carried it there, or had it lain in waiting to find me? Regardless, I squashed it on the floor with my thumb nail, so as not to mark the sheet with blood. If the bug was indeed part of the furnishings, I didn't mind. There was always a price for comfort. Outside, in the long drop I squatted, waiting. Dehydration makes life a little difficult. The ox on the other side of the latted partition entertained with its one, two, three, ploop, plop, ploop. Finally my own contribution arrived, but nothing as loud.

Young Moshin entered the room with a cup of warm *chai haleeb* (milk tea).

A bright-faced lad of about 13, he wanted to ride with me to the end of the street where it met the main road. His father frowned, but when Moshin's friend arrived he relented. The two boys took off down shortcuts and back alleys, not to the end of the street but to the outskirts of the town. Several times I was tempted to turn them back but they were having so much fun. Nothing out of the ordinary happened and hardly a word passed between us. They led, I followed, just an escorted bike ride with a wave at the end, after which they turned homeward, planning their excuses.

Back on the dusty road my rotating knees were painful but it was my right hand which annoyed most. The cut across the pad at the base of my thumb meant gripping the handlebar was sore. I pulled over to pack a sock with the cotton wool I'd been given. With the hand inside it acted as a glove. A Toyota pick-up passed, pushing out a wave of chill morning air against my bare legs. In the rear two burly men sat either side of a big bull camel no doubt being taken somewhere to sit on the ground and sire, for that's what bull camels do, sit and sire. They saluted, I waved back. It promised to be another eventful day on the way to Aswan.

I often thought of those boys racing home. So many times youngsters would want to join in the adventure, if only for a few hundred metres. All they wished for was to pedal a while with a stranger, or to be part of something big, something many of them could never even imagine. For my part, it took time to grasp what was really going on. It was the beginning of the realisation that *this* was only partly 'my' trip. I had presumed always that this was my plan, my execution. How could it be otherwise? Something you spend years pondering and stitching together. Now, in the slanting beams of sun-up as I rode toward Asyut, a new sense came. I no longer owned it. I, the traveller, was in essence just a bit player in a mega-drama and I felt the first tinge of a letting go, which would deepen over the months ahead—letting go of my ownership of what I thought was solely mine. It may have been blatantly obvious to everyone else, but it came to me as a revelation. The yin and yang of a journey, 'mine' and 'not mine' together on the road.

Wary of vehicles now and the whizzing by of commerce, I crossed a footbridge to the canal's other side, across to a parallel world of natural noises. Here, an older Egypt sounded its various choruses—a water pump chug-chugged, donkeys brayed, hoopoes hooped, dogs barked and ducks scuttled in the water.

Children chatted school-ward, and their elders likewise on their way to work. An old man, his eyes closed, was carried in slumber or meditation, his jennet knowing where to go. It felt too as if my own wheels knew where to go. They whooshed through the warming air of morning with that smooth well-oiled sound to make any rider smile. A line of women sitting or squatting outside their homes watched whatever there was to be watched. Their heads turned as one as I glided by, while their lines of white round loaves, laid neatly out on mats at the edge of the road, rose gently in the rising heat.

Out in the field, white cattle-egrets followed a big brown ox, steam rising from its back. The animal seemed to pull both plough and farmer effortlessly as the sod turned and crumbled. Behind a mud wall, where I took a pee, I leaned for a while, watching the pair work together…like the thousands of suchlike pairs throughout the world at that very moment. 'Whoa, whoa, whoa,' came the farmer's call, and the big beast slowly turned, pulling now in the other direction.

The mud wall formed a square compound, within which a second ox walked blindfolded, round and round an eternal circle, through its own manure. It turned an old wooden shaft, tipping bucket upon bucket of Nile into irrigation channels. The water flowed away into those productive fields, leaving me looking deep into Egyptian history. That brownish water spilled over into 'agriculture', as it has always done and as for *agriculture,* there was no escaping it. When cycling, its constantly in your face. I rode past fields of cotton, then maize, then clover and beans, then sugar cane, water melon, then a vast field of onions, and I was reminded of how we keep alive, how we thrive…or not. Yet things were strained, were pushed to limits, making me question just how long this can this go on, how long can we all survive?

Nearing Asyut, agriculture seemed more intense. Fertiliser was being used where it hardly was before. Later, while on Lake Nasser, I would be told where much of Egypt's fertility lay, but I was still stuck in my old schoolbooks, telling me how the Nile flooded to fertilize the land. Once upon a time it did, but in 1970 that flooding, which pulsed through every fibre of the ancient and not so ancient Egyptian psyche, came abruptly to an end. The Aswan dam saw to that.

How many farms had I passed between home and where I was? Thousands, I guessed. Yet right here what struck home was the precariousness of that most basic of life efforts, the growing of food. I was to see it forcibly while high on a hill above the Valley of the Kings. While the tombs below were full of tourists, my eyes were fixed on that snaking blue strip of water with its attendant green aprons sandwiched by vast yellow Sahara sands. I felt that many in urban Europe and beyond took it all for granted, but there beside the Nile the links in the chain were so blatantly plain to see—water, soil fertility, crops, climate, pests, disease and people to do the hard graft. Egypt of old did not take it for granted; although they could set their calendar by the flooding, nothing was a given. Every year they walked the line of possible crop failure, hunger and famine. 'Food security' is not a recent term; it was understood long ago, and perhaps we need to understand it afresh.

I reached Asyut, a sizable city, and negotiated it easily. On its southern outskirts laziness drew me to a simple café. I'd had nothing to eat since leaving Malawi and the two boys who had escorted me. As usual the tea was sweet, and I reached for the crusty end of yesterday's bread hoping no one would mind me dipping it. Through cracked patched-up shades I watched people come and go, wearing their well-worn winter *jalabiyas* of white, brown, blue, grey, even pink. Men's heads were scarf-wrapped, and some looked curiously at my small blue hat, my red bushy beard, my filthy shorts and sweaty T-shirt. To their welcoming eyes, I was surely a peculiar and most decrepit sight.

One is rarely alone when riding in Egypt, and that can be pleasant or not. On the way to Qena a bunch of bicycle boy-racers zoomed alongside, crossing in front and behind. It didn't take long for annoyance to rise in me. I looked at my last two sugar cane sticks and considered flinging them at the pack leader. 'No, not wise,' I thought, so I tried to out-pedal but they were unburdened and fast. In the end I simply looked ahead and ignored their calls. They tired and turned back. I rode on, until a hunger pang and an open burial ground arrived together. 'What better place to eat in peace,' I thought, so in full sun among the raised mounds of the dead I ate my crust and no one bothered; two boiled salted eggs, cold beans and bread, a peaceful, life-affirming nosh. I rode on again, with a full belly and my mind preparing for Luxor.

Preparing? I'd been warned that Luxor would be having its usual January deluge, and it would not be rain! A week out of Cairo, I longed to slip quietly under a rock to rest and sleep. Every night as a guest in someone's home, it was expected I gave an account of myself, my views, my country and of course I did, and did gladly. But, tired as I was, I could never say, 'Well guys thanks for the meal, now I'm off to *that* bed you have prepared for me and oh, by the way do wake me gently at seven. Now, good night!' After seven nights chatting into the small hours I was fairly shattered. Hospitality would kill me! That night, the night before Luxor, I was determined to find that 'rock', but yet again it was not to be.

Nineteen kilometres north of Luxor City, in his own village, Muhammad rescued me from an unruly mob. It had all begun with an innocent puncture. A puncture can be hazardous in Upper Egypt, not for any other reason than it stops you and, once stopped, you are open season for all and sundry to descend and descend they did, like the midges and mosquitoes of Lapland. As if a circus had come to town, excited children danced around, first one, then two, then the floodgates opened. A little girl came first. 'Bye-bye, bye-bye,' she said. I wasn't going anywhere but it was the only word she knew. Stripping the bike, I foolishly looked down at her. She grinned, I smiled and mumbled something pleasant, to which she loudly exclaimed 'Baksheesh, baksheesh.' From nowhere the hordes came, but the puncture was repaired, or so I thought. I was about to flee when it deflated again. 'You bloody idiot, you rushed it.' It was too late. Twenty-five, thirty, forty, who knew how many kids, encircled me. Some wanted to grab whatever they could, some wished to genuinely help, but it was useless chaos and I was in the dead centre.

In his mid-twenties, Muhammad was a sizable, not-to-be- messed-with kind of guy. Whatever magic words he said would have put Harry Potter to shame. The kids vanished and I saw it was too late to ride on, so I graciously accepted his invitation. Before we arrived at his home he asked if I'd put my *pantalon* on. In the bowels of the pannier I rummaged for the khaki-green trouser and shook it out. Stains of chain-oil, honey, one clearly of tomato from a sardine tin and what I thought was beer all reminded me that it was due a wash sometime, somewhere.

Before we sat with his family, he also asked if I'd wash my face and hair. In a courtyard, his sister placed a basin on the concrete floor and like Jesus I knelt. From a multicoloured earthenware jug Muhammad poured warmed water over my head. It flowed away brown, then very brown, then almost black. As I was to discover, in his worldview cleanliness was definitely close to godliness, and it seemed obvious to him that I was far removed from that divine state. I would require a thorough cleansing. His sister was requested to fetch another jug until the water ran clear.

We sat on mats, propped with cushions, and I noted that all the women were present—his mother, sisters, even his grandmother was brought down from an upstairs room. A platter piled high with *aish* (pitta bread) was placed centrally, followed by *baba ghanoush*, *felafel*, hummus, olives and soft *gebna* (cheese). The smell of good wholesome food settled everyone, and every last morsel was delicious. Through Muhammad's interpreting, his father told of his *hajj* almost forty years before. His soft eyes looked directly at me as I looked from him to his son. 'My father says you are on your *hajj*,' said Muhammad, 'and he wishes you to go and come safely.' I nodded to him, reached out and shook his hand. In the warmth of his smile there came a feeling of being blessed by a man who had seen a lot.

In Egypt, Islam is not the sole source of identity. An Egyptian's primary source is that he or she is Egyptian, yet despite this somewhere along that long road through the Arab world, sooner or later one bumps into a dedicated devotee to the Prophet, ready to attempt the conversion of any wayward passing soul. I'd got off lightly through Turkey, Syria and Jordan but here in Upper Egypt, Muhammad was waiting for a soul just like mine. How could I blame him? To any righteous follower, I surely appeared a wild-looking infidel from the far end of Europe.

Like most Egyptians he was Sunni, and when it came to Islam he was a gently persuasive character. Before I knew it I was standing in a tiny mosque waiting for evening prayer, along with his father, brothers and, I presumed, every other male in the village. He had saved me once and was determined to save me twice. In the tiny six-by-five metre space, the men lined up. I was on my own in the fifth line which filled up quickly. Not knowing the procedure, I followed what was happening in front of me. If I'd been told that one day karate experience would be put to use in a mosque, I'd have laughed. I followed the flow of movement as if I was learning a new 'kata', only easier. 'Gee,' I thought, 'if Sensei Harte could see this.'

When prayer was over I was motioned to remain. Muhammad returned with a copy of the Quran. He sat close beside me while all the other younger men sat in a semi-circle. There was no escape. All eyes were on me, the first non-Muslim to enter their mosque. In truth, as he recited the beginning of the book, I felt relaxed and I waited for the question, knowing it had to come sooner or later.

Probably since puberty I'd given up on formal religion and did not believe in the god of the Quran or the Bible, old or new. Yet there are times when in company one must deftly tread that belief-non-belief thin ice. I knew enough to know that our belief or not in a god was only one aspect of our nature but, if allowed, it had the power to negate all the other aspects connecting us. I did not wish that to happen here. There was no point. So I decided to tell no lies and tell no truth. Thankfully, my flatmate Paul's parting gift of a New Testament was at the bottom of the handlebar bag, which I carried everywhere. I was already reaching for it as Muhammad formed his question in his rudimentary English. 'John, you believe in the God, in Allah?' he asked.

They say a picture paints a thousand words; so does holding something in one's hand without opening one's mouth. I pulled the little black book from its plastic rice bag and held it up for my audience to see. I told how it had been carried all the way from Ireland but never mentioned that I could not recall having ever opened it! I told them that on occasion, in the morning, I would bless myself before stepping on to the road, how I had entered both splendid and lonely churches en route, how in Istanbul the Saint Sofia mosque left me peaceful, how the call to prayer throughout many lands was strangely comforting, and that 'truth' in its many guises was challenging me along the way, and so on. All of it true, but more to the point, Muhammad now felt assured I was no *kafir* and would not go to Hell after all.

With God out of the way, a tea house beckoned and we relaxed under a strip light to talk about more worldly matters. My views on travel, Israel, the plight of Palestinians were all probed, along with the looming World Cup (neither Egypt nor Ireland participating) and, of course, whether or not I had a girl-friend. From the latter subject it was but a stone's throw to the trickier topic of marriage. As one would expect with a group of young males in this part of the world, that got them all more focused than all other topics put together. Not marriage of itself but, as Muhammad put it, the difficulty for the average Egyptian male in 'attaining it'. This sad point was unanimously impressed upon me, as if I had some magic wand. All the marriage issues that I could think of back home seemed insignificant by comparison.

Regardless of the topics and the near blinding light of the strip, it was a privilege to be chilling out with them after the intensity of the mosque. Later, on a couch in his family's front room, I couldn't find the light switch. For some reason, probably me, it was left on all night, but despite it I slept. I dreamt I was with a group under date palms. Faces and flashes from the journey came in and out, and even a sense of Muhammad and his friends was there. An older man spoke but I could hear nothing, like I was deaf.

Outside the family home, the family minus grandma stood for the photo. Muhammad's father, in a deep brown *jalabiya* stood centre, with a compassionate smile to the camera, but Muhammad wanted a private photo. So, with his young brother, he took me to the edge of a sugar cane field. The ten-year-old clicked but I wondered did he get us; his aim seemed off. 'Would I send a copy?' asked Muhammad. 'Yes, of course I will,' I replied…but I didn't, to my shame I didn't. His little brother took a good photo; his aim was good after all. I see it now…perfect. How much it would have meant to them had I sent it. So many photos never sent, lost addresses, forgotten promises, too long ago, lame and weak excuses. But people remember; Muhammad remembers; I know he does, I know he remembers exactly. He is older now, like me, and if I could find him he would tell of the night I stayed with his family, how his father spoke to me of Islam and the journey he took to Mecca. If he could see that photo, he would also nod and smile at our youth. At the edge of that dusty road he held the hand of his young brother and waved as I rode away, heading to a part of his country he'd never been to. I may not have sent the photo but still I hold him in my mind and in the long run I like to think he might prefer that.

The bike was oiled, greased and tweaked to the last, which made the riding smooth. The nineteen kilometres to Luxor whizzed by. The ride, though short, was made all the sweeter with a feeling that I could now handle whatever Egypt would throw at me. I even smiled, seeing youngsters scurry late to school, their bluish pyjama-like *jalabiyas* making them look like a bunch of Wee Willie Winkies. They moved in and out behind the palm trees on the other side of an irrigation canal. Some had their book-parcels clutched tight to the chest; others had them tied with a leather thong and slung coolly over the shoulder. For a few innocent minutes we paralleled each other. I wanted to wave but they could not see me, then suddenly they disappeared behind a wall. I cycled on, on automatic, to the northernmost limits to Luxor, chuffed to have my own school days dredged up.

★★★

Freewheeling into a vast bus-park, I knew immediately I'd got my timing all wrong. Before me lay the organised chaos of touts, taxis, camels and bus loads seeking the Valleys. The tourist deluge was a shock to the system, and I came close to riding on. 'Therein,' I later reflected, 'lies a dilemma for the traveller. No longer a tourist, yet at times those same tourist desires are there to be filled.' Straddling the bike, I looked at what lay before me through the still raw fresh memories of the preceding days and genuinely asked myself, 'Do I have to do this?'

I wished to see the tombs too (the famous Valleys of the Kings and Queens) and to absorb their antiquity as much as anyone. However, the daily engagement with ordinary life, ordinary Egyptians and the grinding out of movement had shifted my perception. I felt caught between real life and a stage set. It was visceral and, no matter the wonders that lay in those valleys just beyond the dunes, I had to resist the urge to leave. Along the engaging way, in and out of peoples lives and homes, I had felt *part* of something but now I felt corralled like an animal to merely *look* at something. The paradox, of course, was that I really did wish to look at hieroglyphics and gaze upon the mask of Tutankhamun but, oh, did I have to share it with hundreds of others?

The dreaded 'traveller arrogance' pursued me to the nearest campsite and as I pitched the tent in the coolest corner I wrestled it round and round until quite abruptly, it was cut short by a yellow bolt of lightning—a sunbird! The tiny little bombshell shot straight into a grove of papyrus reeds. I had never before seen a sunbird but now thanked it, for its green phosphorescent head and fiery yellow belly shook me from a vicious circle. 'Yes,' I thought, 'a walk above the tombs would be good.'

The well-worn track was obvious and within the hour I could see a line of tourists like ants entering dark openings at the base of the opposite hill...the Valley of the Queens was below me. The following day, I too would be a tourist and would descend that narrow dimly lit corridor under tons of rock and sand, but until then I continued upward. From the height came the first real view of the Nile, threading itself into afternoon haze. When you see it, there is no doubt how it gave birth to so much over the millennia, from the ever-waiting donkey and the eternal turning of the ox, to the chug-chug of a water pump, to modern vertical farming—and who knows what into the future. There could hardly have been a better place to imagine the long history of Egypt than high above the tombs of its ancient dead with that bluish lifeblood flowing away to

the north, just as it flowed during the lives of those who lived here before the
Pharaohs.

★★★

Mahmud was the old campsite owner's son. In the late morning I helped repair
his nephew's bike, so we chatted. 'No one stays to talk anymore,' he said, 'they're
not interested, they treat us like dirt…snobs they are.' Thus he summarized
twenty years in the business, seeing thousands come and go. His command of
English was good due to tourists and time spent in America. He asked why I
did not go to the sound-and-light show in the Valley of the Kings the previous
night. Indeed I had heard the noise and had seen the lights hovering above the
temple of Karnak. 'It's not my cup of tea,' I said, 'and anyway I'm on a tight
budget.' Explaining those quirky idioms gave us a few laughs, as he poured
sweet *chai* from his grandfathers exquisite old teapot. It had that Aladdin's cave
look about it and if he had told me it had been plundered from Tut's Tomb I'd
have believed him.

That afternoon I learned more from Mahmud about 'King Tut', Seti, Nefer-
tari and ancient Egypt than I did that morning listening to an overstretched
guide. 'They (the tourists) think the Pharaohs were wonderful…to be revered.
Huh! Tutankhamun was just a kid,' he said, 'they married each other…had
children with their sisters. Incest was of no concern to them.' He leaned back
on his chair, raising his arms upward. 'If you believe you are descended from
the gods, of course you will breed with your sister or your mother. They had
many health problems because of this. Even today, royal families marry royal
families, no?'

'Yes,' I agreed, thinking of the so called royals of Europe down through
history.

'You know, my friend,' he continued, 'those tombs were never meant to be
visited but I make my living from them. I should not complain too much, eh?'
He laughed and I saw the same big smile beaming out from the hundreds of
photos up and down his office wall.

Mahmud was correct. They were never meant to be visited. Howard Carter's
break-in in 1922 opened the door to the millions. They shuffled through from
every corner of the world, with their coughs and sneezes, their splutters and
spores, and now I too had gone down that narrow corridor to Tut's famous
chamber. It was like an Irish wake, everyone queuing to take one last look at

the deceased and offer condolences to the next of kin, but of course there were no next of kin and the deceased had been dead for 2,347 years. Unlike an Irish wake, young Tutankhamun's gold sarcophagus gleamed and the paintings and hieroglyphics glowed in the subdued light. Inevitably there has been irreparable damage and today the tombs are sealed once again and one visits a replica a mile away.

Beyond the honey-pot of tourist Luxor, sugar cane became my riding ritual. Young guys would run alongside the bike to sell their short sticks. We'd do a deal, I'd slip a coin and like a relay runner grab one. Then we'd shout to each other 'Shukran, shukran', waving our sticks in the air. With front teeth I'd tear at the tough bark, exposing the succulent sweet inner fibres. Kilometre after kilometre, ripping, grinding, sucking, then chewing the sugary cud like a cow and swallowing the sweet saliva. The remains would be spat to the ground and after hours I was as good as the locals in the art of blowing the gob as far as I could. There it would lie with a billion others, fresh and long desiccated, like an endless crumb trail from Hansel and Gretel. No surprise then, that my abiding memory of Egypt is not the Pyramids or the Sphinx, Cairo, Luxor or even the *fellahin* but spitting those fibrous gobs with gusto to the roadside. And perhaps no surprise to the traveller when I report that not even a wonder of the world could compete with the sweaty life of a journey. Even the awe of Pyramids and Tombs was no match for the daily grind on the ever-morphing road.

Occasionally a tour bus would pass by and I would wave my sugary baton at those faces looking down. They would wave back and smile, quickly pointing me out to another until it seemed like everyone was up snapping their cameras. The driver, seeing me in his big wing mirror might beep, happy that an oddball on the road had given some entertainment to his group. He would drive on, leaving me in dust, and I'd stop to let it blow away or settle. Still chewing, I'd watch the receding faces in the rear window and would *feel* for the certain few in that air-conditioned bus who really wanted to be out here in 'real' Egypt. I knew they were in there, feeling trapped by age or circumstance or maybe even a friend.

I had met them many times at border crossings, at village markets or a tourist place...like that first time, that night in North Cape. The laden bike leaning against a wall would attract them and, when I would return, a brief but telling

29

conversation would ensue. It would always be much the same. 'Oh, I'd love to do what you're doing but....' or 'Yes, I cycled from "someplace" to "someplace" when I was your age. I'd love to do it again.' or 'If I had the energy I'd....' Yet there would be one or two who said little but whose eyes said it all. They would wait until the others had gone and then quietly confess, 'I'd prefer to be out here, not on that bus. I'd rather do something like this. How did you begin?' Usually there was too little time to say much; the guide would call her flock and that potential traveller would be whisked away to the next stop. I'd shout 'Go for it,' or 'Do it, you won't regret it,' or some such. The response would be a certain nod or a thumbs-up as they found their seat.

I recall when my little travel bubble began to burst. It was in Konya, central Turkey, where a tour guide woke me to the obvious fact. 'Some on my bus,' he had said, 'will never do such a thing but they want to imagine that they might. They want to dream. You are out here living their dream. Believe me, mister, they are willing you on.' I've never forgotten that guide. He began the turning of my journey from inside to out. Thank you 'mister', wherever you are. Others were too old to jump on a bike, but by the time I got to Luxor I felt I was doing it for them too, just like young Moshin racing home to his father.

There were times between towns when I mused a lot. Egypt gives much to muse about. Yet, with almost its entire population of over eighty million squeezed along the Nile strip, musing will always be a fractured affair. Someone had told me jokingly how 'Egypt is full to the brim with Egyptians'! Ride it and you'll discover it's no joke. Of all the countries between the far north of Europe and the bottom of Africa, Egypt, bang in the middle, will teach you things fast. One such is to let go. If you resist, then the waves of its wonderful people with their enthusiastic and overwhelming embrace will exhaust and pulverise you in the sweetest possible way. When you travel slow and solo, you are exposed to the rich intensity of humanity as old as time. Egypt will squeeze and suck at you, then squirt you out at its tail end and, if you've walked or ridden to there, well done indeed.

★★★

Leaving Luxor behind I felt the heat rise, as if an oven had been turned up a tad more. The Western Agricultural Road was a dusty devil but it shot me past villages and food-growing life all the way to Edfu. 'Take your break beyond the town. Okay, buddy?' I accepted my own orders without a blink and let the road take me right to the centre. Unexpectedly, a temple caught my eye, and I hung a right towards its huge entrance. For two millennia the Temple of Horus entrance was almost totally buried by desert sands. Perhaps because it was not on my agenda, perhaps the fewer tourists, perhaps how the light seemed to stick to its sandstone walls, whatever it was, as I reached an inner courtyard, all the while gazing at carved reliefs of Ptolemaic kings three times human size, a sudden tidal wave of deep culture hit me. It was different to what I'd felt at those other well-trodden places, the Pyramids and Luxor. If they were theatre, this felt more a conjunction, a kind of ordinary-yet-extraordinary co-existence between long separated times. I felt the privilege, right there and then, to be able to travel through a nation-culture whose antiquity and present-day daily grind could be witnessed so cheek by jowl, the one enlivening the other.

Sweat drip dripped on a sandstone slab beneath an intimate relief of some royal woman breast-feeding her baby, watched over by her man. The gap of time dissolved. If they had stepped off that wall to saunter arm in arm toward the river, I'd hardly have batted my sweaty eye, for the slow steady pace of bicycling down from Cairo through all the welcomings and all the imagined history had closed the gap between the 'then' and the 'now'. It allowed an interweaving of past and distant past and present and even future into a tight double-helix of culture and identity. Little escapes here. The bonds are old and strong, and, to cap it all, I had the steely eyed granite statue of falcon Horus himself to myself for a short while before a bus-load of Japanese arrived to click their way through and blow me back on the road.

It was a sun-scorching Friday, a sabbath day, a mosque day, a prayer day and a supposedly non-work day for man and beast. Four hours in the saddle had passed, and the thought of a decent shady break just wouldn't go away. 'Shade shade, where is shade? Can't take a break without shade.' So went the mumbling. Looking left, looking right, I rode on, seeking that perfect spot...then there it was, a clear clean place under old palm trees beside a railway line. The bike leaned against one tree and I another. My hands reached high on the rough bark, body arched, feet back, Achilles pushed into the dust, stretching legs... then came that deep, pleasurable 'Aaaah'. It was that good. In the skin folds behind my knees the sweat was salty-sticky so I took the rag from under the saddle, sacrificed some water from the warmest bottle on the down-tube and washed them both clean. Everything I did, my every action—stretching legs, rotating arms, twisting the body— was watched by nearby curious sugar-cane workers.

On the far side of that open space they were loading goods-wagons with long shafts of cane. In the shade of the train, a long line of camels and donkeys waited, their backs burdened with the bales. Women and men worked hard, lifting the bales to others on top of the wagons. Although it was the sabbath, they worked hard. It had to be done. Perhaps on their tea break, a few men came over to discover who this guy was and, of course, to chat. Seeing my bare legs, one made a shivering gesture, enquiring if I was cold. I laughed and mimicked a wipe of sweat. They laughed and thus we settled easily into some sort of communication. In the end they insisted, with typical Egyptian-Arab generosity, that I take as many sticks of cane as I could. I rode off looking like a porcupine with twenty batons protruding from every nook and cranny.

As I departed I was joined by two boys on their bikes. Two became four and pretty soon I had an entourage. There was no hassle from them until from behind one came too close and caught my rear wheel. Down I went and with that there was a pile-up. The boys thought it was great fun as they picked themselves up but I just sat there, elbows on my knees. Unlike before, I was not angry, pissed off or even bothered about body or bike. I just sat there smiling, thinking nothing. The young lads gathered themselves and headed away, looking back, surprised that there was no display of crossness. I watched them riding off, then slowly picked myself up. There was no damage to the bike. The right-side pannier took the impact, though I was unaware that inside it my only orange had got mashed. 'This is what happens, buddy,' came the thought. 'Spend time on the road and sooner or later you'll end up on your ass. No point losing the head, pick yourself up and get on with it.' Yet there was something else; something had shifted or softened as I sat there, but I couldn't say what just then.

The sun was strong, hitting a hot right cheek, and my cracked, taped-up sunglasses annoyed me. Shoved into the front bag, they would be dumped somewhere and I made a mental note to buy another pair in Aswan. Oh Aswan, Aswan…a few more hours of riding and I'd be there, towards evening. 'The cul-de-sac of Egypt', as Arie the Dutchman described it. It was the third of my dreamed of pit-stops. I had long imagined it as a half-way house between North Cape and Cape Town, a cool place to chill before the rigours beyond. The gradient increased, and I dropped to the '38', surprised to meet hills but remembered how Egypt's southernmost city, at 120 metres, is 100 metres higher than Cairo. I glided up the gentle gradient with the energy of anticipation. There were fewer people now, less traffic, more space between the towns. At last, the squeeze of Egypt was easing.

Twenty kilometres north, the road hugged the river. There was no one around, no house, no village, nothing. The scene was too inviting. I pulled over! It was the first time to be up close to the real Nile and not some canal off it. There it was, without *feluccas* or tourists, monuments or even agriculture. Down went the bike and I stretched a stiff back while taking in the arid scene of browns, yellows and patches of green growth along the bank. On my side just a dry and dusty road, on the other the timeless desert dunes stared back at me. Sandwiched in between was the span of blue water, its motion barely noticeable, an old-timer cutting through its own silt to keep moving, descending barely a metre in every ten thousand. I wrote a few pages of diary, then shut the journal to look blankly at the water. I tried hard to imagine where I was heading, crawling so slow over the landscape like the river before me, up-river to Khartoum, up-river to Juba, to Zaire, into Uganda and on and on, but the names of places felt too remote, too distant. An ant crossing a continent—yes, that's how it felt. 'Don't let go, hold on to it, you must.' The dream, now so brimful of sweat and reality, still had to be cherished. 'There's only going forward, yeah?' I mumbled the rhetorical question and answered with an annoyed 'Yeah, yeah, okay, okay!'

A steamer broke the self-absorption. It was an upstream dot but grew steadily. It took fifteen minutes to draw opposite, and its cargo of tourists waved. I waved back. It glided on toward Luxor, churning the water like a Mississippi paddle-boat from Huckleberry Finn. It became a dot again, then on a bend it vanished and I was moved to write to J, to continue a letter begun in Cairo. I needed to tell her about this, about all of it. I needed to share.

Chapter 2
Syene, beautiful Syene

I had always imagined the Nile Delta as the open head of a funnel, narrowing at Cairo, then straight south for 1,400 kilometres to end in Aswan. Geography is always right, but sometimes it gets it perfect. At the bottom of Egypt, Aswan bestrides the Nile like a last outpost. There could hardly be a better place to unwind before embarking into Nubian sands. In mid-January its climate is more than pleasant and its intimacy with that great river makes both feel more alive. As anyone in Cairo would testify, the Aswanians are easy going. There is Nubian ancestry here, you can feel it. The proximity to that older kingdom is not for nothing. There will be places on every journey where one takes time out, to pause, reflect, recalibrate. For the trip I was on, Aswan was such a place. Five days to give bike, body and soul, whatever was required. Though I knew its name well, Carl Sagan had long before won me over to its much older title—Syene. As I rode down Egypt, this beautiful old-world word lay quiet in the back of my mind, too full of historical magic to let go of, and anyway part of me was always going there.

★★★

Opposite Elephantine Island I pulled over and looked about. It was late afternoon. Buildings faced the river, traffic on the street, people strolling to the evening bazaar, feluccas still plying their trade, some ferrying locals and others tourists. The *hantour* or horse-drawn jaunting carriages stood waiting for business, their drivers chatting to one another. Seeing them brought me straight to Killarney, County Kerry, where the jarvey-men do the same work and could so easily identify with their Aswanian cousins.

I easily found the felucca skipper and handed him a package given to me by some Germans in Luxor. He was surprised and thanked me enthusiastically and welcomed me to Aswan. 'If you have problem, I help. You find me here... every day.' I knew he meant it. Then my name filled the air. 'Hey John, John.' I looked to the sound but saw nothing. 'Hey, up here,' and there he was, Arie Baas, with some other guy on the third floor of the Continental Hotel across the street. Suddenly Aswan felt like home. As independent as we all think we are, it is good to meet a fellow traveller and it was good to see Arie again. We renewed our acquaintance from that first meeting on an Aqaba beach. The other face on the hotel balcony was of Alain, from France, a squat muscular rugby type, intending to cycle to Nairobi...on one kidney, as I was to discover. They helped lift the gear up, and I took the corner bunk.

Stretched on the beds we debriefed, like soldiers after battle, and like soldiers we shared our stories, knowing only we would understand. Our journeys needed release. Each of us knew how the experience of cycling was altogether different to that of any other mode of travel. Only those who chose to walk long distance could nod the head in mutual appreciation. We agreed that a cyclist could only go so far in the sharing of experience with those who take buses, trucks, jeeps, cars, motorbikes. The intensity of being on the road, riding day after day, week after week, month after month, is different, and to get to some dreamed of distant place by one's own effort is more than mental satisfaction, it's a muscle and sinew *knowing*. Every metre is fairly and squarely met with, even directly gazed upon, and many are remembered intimately. The slow pace allows more to be seen, to be felt, to be absorbed, for the absence of speed means the absence of a kind of protective barrier to the extraordinary detail which one is open to when moving at 10,15, or 20 kilometres per hour. Yet this is but the half of it. The flip-side is the ease of going within, cocooned in the slow meditative rhythm of steady movement. There, a pearl is formed for the future, out of a billion bits of the seen and unseen stuff of one's passing.

★★★

The 'Magnificent Seven' was the name we gave to our little group of cyclists: Alain from Paris, Arie from Aalkmar, Henrik and Helle from Copenhagen, Heinrik from Munich, Tom from Kiel and yours truly from Cork. We had all poured out, one by one, at the end of the Egyptian funnel, well, one by one bar the much-in-love Danish couple who travelled by tandem.

Aswan, wonderful relaxing Aswan, end of the road for some, pit-stop for others, but for either it was a relief from the thronged solo roller-coaster ride from Cairo. Young Tom was the last to arrive and seemed delighted to meet fellow cyclists. That first evening we sat together sipping *chai*, swapping tales, basking in evening light from the other side of the Nile, each of us proud of the other for making it thus far. We had known each other for only a few hours but, like all who travel by bike, we had already gelled into a band of mutual supporters. Gradually the conversation came around to the next step—who was bound for where?

Four of us would continue to Sudan and for the next few days we unconsciously hung out with each other. No one needed reminding of the challenge taking a bike beyond Lake Nasser. Sand, grease and ball-bearings didn't mix, and that was just for starters. Everyone had an opinion. 'I'm going this way.' 'Ah, okay, I'm going that way,' and as always someone would chip in, 'Did you hear that... such and such and blah, blah, blah?' It was all good fun but also deadly serious. It pushed each of us to re-assess our 'way', which direction to take and how best to manage. It was good too that our personal vision for what we were about came under the fresh spotlight of each new fellow traveller, for at times that vision had to be charged up and re-focused. In the easy ambiance of Aswan, we exchanged and teased out these plans. This was the launch pad for those going on, and to go on you had best not be dependent on anyone but yourself and have absolute trust that everything was already all right—to know in your gut that you'd be just fine.

Arie and I sat by the river. He voiced his concern about Tom. In his early twenties, he was the youngest and had stretched himself emotionally to get this far alone.

'He wants to see the tropical fishes in Lake Tanganyika,' Arie said.

'As good a reason as any to ride down Africa, I suppose' I replied.

'Yes, but Sudan will be different; he will want to go with one of us.'

'He's already asked about my route after Wadi.'

Arie wasn't surprised. His opinion was that Tom should take the train direct to Khartoum. 'He could hang out there, and let his confidence build,' he said. I agreed.

Tom had the physique of an athlete, yet this was not about physical tough-ness or cycling long hours, not that it ever was. From Sudan onwards cycling was secondary. I remembered wanting to set off at 22 but circumstances prevented that, and in hindsight it was a blessing. I would not have believed it, of course, but I wasn't ready, hadn't matured enough to go. The subtle and not so subtle differences between 22 and 28 or 29 made all the difference in the end. I knew how he felt and that's why he was drawn to me. He knew I knew and hoped I'd allow him join me. (To this day I still believe that although one can, of course, do a major journey in one's early twenties, there is a different capacity to witness and to absorb things at the other end of that important decade. Best, I believe, to get some of the turbulence of the twenties out of the way, but then again when one has to go, one has to go....)

Arie and Alain would depart first for Sudan, followed a few days later by Tom and I. We all agreed to go our separate ways on arrival at Wadi Halfa—'on the other side,' as Arie described it. I rode with them to the ferry beyond the New Aswan dam and there in full sun the waiting game began. The formalities of customs and police were slow but thankfully steady, giving plenty time to savour a few flat bread rolls stuffed with aubergine and *falafel*. While chewing, a strange feeling came, difficult to describe, as if my present had passed out my future.

I had imagined the scene before my eyes a hundred times or more, had played it out, up and down: the officials doing their jobs, the throngs of Sudanese with their bags and boxes, the Caucasian faces here and there, the ship, the port, this launch-pad to Sudan. This imagined scenario had been, for that long prepara-tory time, always in my future, in a kind of limbo space to be reached one day, some day...but now it was here, right there before me. Although I was sitting eating an aubergine *falafel* sandwich, drinking *chai* with the boys, in my mind I had not yet reached that place. It was still in the dream world of speculation, way off down the road. I told myself privately, 'Hey buddy, you're here', but it felt as if the reality around me did not have the power to neutralize a deeply embedded 'future image' which I had carried for so long. Like a cat creeping in the night, you see and hear nothing until, without warning, the experience has pounced. You are caught, caught in a split, time-warped-world of your own making. I was there but not there.

I truly felt as if I was in my own future. I could express none of this to Arie or Alain as I could barely understand it myself. I recalled a tinge of similar feeling at the Pyramids and the Sphinx. Was this what Alan Moorehead meant in *The Blue Nile* when he wrote, 'It's a process of recognition, the Pyramids and Sphinx are prefigured in the mind long before they meet the eye.' Was this the reason I had such a strong *déjà vu* feeling when I saw them first? Was it something similar here in Aswan port? My mind had worked hard to make it all 'real' long before I got here. Riding back over the dam I stopped to watch the ferry pull away into Lake Nasser. High in the thermals above, the black kites soared and circled, and I shook my head at the oft-times unexpected, mysterious wonders of travel. Then, flicking the pedal, I returned to my four-by-four metre box-room in Aswan.

I had the room to myself. E.M. Forester's *A Room with a View* had been released as a film a few weeks before. When I eventually saw it, I thought nothing of its story, but it did take me back to that room, Number 25, with its square-window vista. It had everything one could dream of in a room with a view, bar the romance. I could have shared it with a pair of Aussie backpackers but paid the extra to hold it as my own for the three nights before departure 'to the other side'. I dragged the bed closer so that, propped up, I could see everything. The picture was simple, a street, a river, an island and a desert beyond. Simon and Garfunkel's 'The Boxer' filled the air,

Lie-la-lie, lie-la-lielie-lie-la-lie, lie-la-lie.

Then I'm laying out my winter clothes

And wishing I was gone, going home.

From the café directly below, the song was overlaid with Arabic conversations. Then I remembered where the music was coming from— the barber shop three doors down. Catching a fistful of curls I knew it was that time again. The previous haircut was in Yayladagi, a Turkish border town halfway between Antakya, Turkey and Latakia, Syria. A haircut not to be forgotten, not for the cut, which was great, but for what came after at the Syrian border. However, that was long gone and here I was again with a massive red mop and even thicker bushy beard. I savoured the appearance, this wild-Celtic-look which I was certain had sometimes smoothed the way in tricky situations, but it would be crazy to take such a mop and beard into Sudan—I'd sweat like a pig. 'Tomorrow,' I told myself, 'tomorrow, I'll go sit in that barber's chair.'

Mid-afternoon, as I looked through the window, the tourists were still out on the river in that classic postcard scene of Aswan—those curved white feluccas gliding across the Nile—but postcards could never deliver the smells of sizzling aubergine and *falafel*. They wafted from the restaurant, overlaid with the subtler aromas of spices, horse shit and desert. Standing on the quay, three *hantour* drivers in their grey winter *jalabiyas* chatted while awaiting business from two approaching *feluccas*. Further along, another driver assisted tourists up and out of the craft and over to his jaunting car. I wondered did the *felucca* men and the *hantour* men work together? They probably did. They'd be fools not to.

Behind Elephantine Island the dunes beckoned the imagination away from all activity. Was it over there in the mid-day sun, where Eratosthenes placed his stick and took note of its 'absent' shadow, or did he come down from Alexandria to see for himself the sun's full disc at the bottom of a deep well? I pondered the imponderables, knowing of no other small city simultaneously sitting under the Tropic of Cancer and astride a noble river. Was it a fluke of geography that the Tropic lies just downstream of the first cataract where this ancient town of Swenett, then Syene, then Assuan, then Aswan, grew up? The first cataract was as far up the Nile as the ancients could sail, 1,200 kilometres from the Med. Here they settled, and here, in this frontier garrison town, they saw something strange.

Every year the sun would travel north and stop directly overhead on the twenty-first of June, the summer solstice. On that day, at mid-day, a stick would cast no shadow, but on every other day it would. With no obscuring clouds, this phenomenon was dutifully noted on a papyrus parchment which ended up generations later in the Great Library of Alexandria. There my guide came across it. He did his calculations, which others used to explore the world. Columbus deftly approached Queen Isabella with a calculation from a rival of Eratosthenes.

It was but half the true Earth circumference. Did Columbus hope this would persuade his benefactors to break open the kitty and send him off? Were they reluctant because they knew well about Eratosthenes' more accurate measurement? Who knows, but Columbus got his money and his ships. Perhaps he set sail with a wry smile, knowing he had pulled a fast one.

Such were the musings which filled Number 25, the room with the wonderful view. I lay back on the pillow and closed my eyes. Six months had passed since that solstice night as bright as day, when the bike leaned against the iconic globe monument at North Cape. With others I had stood in the chill air and, at the stroke of midnight, we all turned northwards to where the sun should have been but sadly it was obscured by cloud. We had all travelled there, seventy degrees north to witness a day without sunset. Some were noticeably disappointed, but I had already turned to face south, trying as hard as I could to grasp the enormous journey which lay before me. The fact that the solstice sun did not show its face was, for me, a lesser matter, given what was on my mind. It was enough to reflect that at midday on that same day, the sun was high over Aswan, beaming directly down out of a probable cloudless sky, down on the heads of the *hantour* men, the *felucca* men and everyone else in town.

Eyes closed on the pillow, I imagined North Cape and Aswan from out in space, picturing the Earth's tilt, the angles, the stream of light blowing past. To see our planet from far away, that was Carl Sagan's vision. Thankfully he had the foresight to convince NASA to turn the famous 1977 Voyager satellite around and face it back the way it had come, back towards Earth. Whatever 'click' sound its camera made, it clicked the single most important photo ever taken in the history of humanity. From six billion kilometres we are indeed 'a mote of dust suspended in a sunbeam'. We *are* that 'pale blue dot'. On seeing this incredible photo, where Earth is but 0.12 of a pixel, Sagan wrote:

> That's here, that's home. That's us. On it everyone you love, everyone you know, everyone you have ever heard of, every human being who ever was, lived out their lives…every king and peasant, every young couple in love, every mother and father, hopeful child, inventor, explorer, every revered teacher of morals, every corrupt politician, every superstar, every supreme leader, every saint and sinner in the history of our species…lived there, on a mote of dust suspended in a

sunbeam ...Think of the rivers of blood spilled by all those generals and emperors so that in glory and triumph they could become the momentary masters of a fraction of a dot.

To cycle down the tiniest fraction of this 'dot' felt immense at times, but with perspective I knew it was miniscule. I knew also I could not get above myself for the distance travelled, for the story lay in the daily stuff happening between the lines of the miles, not the miles themselves. I imagined bringing these explorers together from their vastly different eras to talk to each other of their work—Sagan and Columbus telling Eratosthenes where *his* work had led them both—but my imagination was getting carried away! Outside, here and there, one by one, the lights of homes came on. I closed the shutters and ventured down to the souk with nothing more on my mind than a new pair of shades.

From the diary: With money belt tight beneath a light shirt I melted into the throng. The souk felt the heart and soul of the place and I felt sharp and awake but then forgot to follow my own money-changing golden rule—walk the full souk first, get the rates, then decide. Stupidly I went for the second guy at 1.75! Hardly fifty metres along I could have got 1.80. Ha! So you think you're sharp, eh...but the sunglasses seemed worth the money and with a bag of dates I returned to the café beside the barber shop. The shop was busier than before with men and boys out for a clean cut in the cool of evening. Donovan's 'Donna, Donna, Donna' played and I sipped cay and watched older men sipping and smoking their water pipes while their shoes were being shined to radiance under the tables. One shoeshine boy finished his job, stood and silently watched my trail of words across the diary page. He looked at my shoes, which made me look at my shoes. Indeed they are a sorry sight! I smiled at him and pointed at my feet making a sad mouth. He shrugged his shoulders in complete indifference, then walked to another table, wondering, I'm sure, how a 'wealthy' tourist could go out in public in such wrecks!

The once-upon-a-time, state-of-the-art, cycle touring ventilated shoes were indeed but a patch of their former glory. The ventilation came now through big holes along the sides, and the only reason I kept them was for the soles. Surely,

I thought, ten 'mil' of moulded plastic would get me to Nairobi? Okay, then maybe Khartoum! I ordered another *chai* and tucked my feet under the chair, reminding myself that apart from a visit to the barber I had to visit 'that doctor' to be injected with a final dose of gamma globulin.

Hepatitis A always lurked for the off-guard traveller. One slip-up with a gulp of unhygienic water or an unwashed salad prepared with unwashed hands and, in a few weeks, there might be no appetite, just a nauseous feverish fatigue. Then jaundice would set in with yellow eyes and yellower urine. In that pre-Hep A vaccine era, all one could do was boost one's immune system with an injection of gamma globulin. I had one before leaving home and another in Athens. The vial I had carried since there was to be administered here in Aswan—my final boost. (Note: this was the passive form of protection that travellers used and it continued until the hepatitis vaccine was introduced in 1995.)

★★★

It was the last night in Egypt, the last night in Room 25. I got on with packing with the vaccine coursing through my veins. As always, imagination was ahead of the game, and thus I stuffed the panniers with some consideration as to the way onward. Impossible questions tumbled through a tired mind. Should I ride out of Wadi Halfa, away from the river, out into the desert between the train tracks, or should I follow the river, ride where possible and drag where not? Would it not be a more sociable journey through the villages? Would there be food and clean water on the way to Abri? How many litres should I, or could I, carry? Would young Tom be on the ferry? How long before I'd feel rain again? Finally, fully clothed, I crashed on the bed, falling into fitful dreams of rain, sea mist, drizzle, dew, home, jumbled up places, faces from everywhere all mixed up amid a flood of Egyptian scenes—all playing hide-and-seek in my psyche.

In the morning, a few cupped handfuls of cold water woke me fully, followed by stretches on the floor, a quick shower, then downstairs to have my pan filled with *ful muddamas* and *falafel*. The guy knew I was leaving, so he tossed in an extra *falafel*. '*Shukran*,' I said, bounding back to the room, skipping every other step, letting a wave of excitement rise. 'You're leaving for Sudan,' I told myself. For the last time I shoved my head through the open window. The first *feluccas* were already gliding on the river, the black kites were circling. I took one long last look, up and down the street, breathing, absorbing, remembering for the future. It was time to go. I paid the six pounds, and with panniers bulging with food I rode towards the dams.

'Understand our dams and you'll understand us more,' were the parting words of the well-heeled gentleman who spoke to me at the café. It was a curious piece of advice, I thought, as I rode the first hill to the old dam, which is two kilometres of masonry rubble piled up to an eventual height of thirty six-metres. Half way over I stopped to take it in. The morning light was intense, even behind my new 'Polaroids' which I was beginning to have doubts about. As sizable as the old dam is, I was assured it was but a dwarf to Nasser's 'baby' six kilometres down the road. Leaning the bike against the parapet, I walked along, looking down on the river for the first time. The Nile seemed naked here, flanked by rock and sand. Naked, at least to Irish eyes programmed to see rivers draped in greenery. Above the dam the kites swirled round and round in great circles, their jagged wing tips gauging the thermals, while below a pair of white storks stood in the shallows like an elderly couple and then, as if they sensed my gaze, leapt to flight. I watched them glide after each other out over the tail waters to a tiny mid-stream island.

Why would Britain have build a massive dam at the 'bottom' of Egypt? Altruism? Hardly. Not since the building of the pyramids had such a massive project happened in Egypt, with perhaps the same number of men working on both, 20,000 give or take a few. In 1882 Britain invaded the country on the pretext of supporting the Anglo-French controlled government of Khedive Tewfik against a military revolt, but some suggest it had more to do with protecting British bondholders who had invested in the Suez Canal, than anything to do with securing it or putting down revolts. But there was another possible reason: cotton.

Just twenty years before, in 1862, the American civil war had stymied the flow of cotton to France and Britain. Britain needed cotton like a drug. Cotton in the nineteenth century was as oil in the twenty-first, big, very big business. Cotton production, slavery, civil war politics and the accruing of vast wealth were all bedfellows. The British textile industry had to be protected. All those textile mills in Lancashire and Derbyshire had to have their raw material to make garments for the empire and of course to keep people employed. Where money was being made hand over fist, minds focused on how to keep it flowing. I imagined the conversation between the textile barons and Gladstone's government:

'Minister, we need to secure other sources of good workable cotton.'

'Well, surely the American supply will continue.'

'Minister, we suggest we secure another source…from Egypt.'

'Egypt?'

'Yes, Minister, we suggest Britain build a dam to provide water for a continuous supply of Egyptian cotton.'

Perhaps such a conversation never took place, but then again who knows? Sixteen years after the invasion, in 1898, dam construction began. Nothing of its scale had ever been attempted. When the red ribbon was cut before Christmas 1902, it was the largest masonry dam in the world. It was not high enough to store sufficient water for more than a season but it did have the benefit of numerous gates which, when opened, allowed the sediments to flow out, as they had always done, to fertilise the fields. Today the old dam just catches the tail waters of the High Dam built in 1960, just six kilometres upstream.

I rode on, immersed in history until, quite abruptly, 'Nasser's baby' came into view—the Aswan High Dam. A rush of excitement welled up, outweighing some sadness, for Egypt had given me more than I'd bargained for. I would miss it. Up on a hill past the police station, the hospital and the African University stood the Lotus Flower monument like a huge Olympic flame holder. Built after the Russians completed the High Dam, it symbolized the Egyptian-Soviet friendship of the day.

It is difficult to know where the High Dam ends or even begins. Almost four kilometres across, 980 metres wide at the base, 111 metres high, it does indeed dwarf the old. It was General Abdel Nasser's dream-child. He knew Egypt had to be in control of its own destiny and its own section of the Nile. Thus the new dam had to be built within Egyptian territory. He also knew that Egyptians were growing hostile to the British presence in their country. Attacks on them and other foreigners grew until finally on Saturday 25 January 1952 the hairspring was sprung at Ismailia. Fifty local police were killed by the British in a heavy-handed tank-versus-rifle skirmish. That was the tipping point. If Ireland has her 'Bloody Sunday', Egypt has her 'Black Saturday', the day the nation erupted.

Nasser seized the moment on 23 July 1952 when, in command of his 'Free Officers', he took control of the country. King Farouk was calmly escorted to his yacht in Alexandria and pushed off to exile, thus ending a monarchy that had

45

long worked hand in glove with vested western interests. A typical example of that relationship had been King Farouk's shelving of a forty-year-old (1912) plan to build a dam within Egypt. Farouk believed in the old British idea of storing water further upstream in Sudan, but Nasser's military mind blew the dust off this old visionary project. He had no desire to be held hostage to the shifting politics of upstream governments. Unfortunately for him and Egypt, it wasn't the best time to go looking for construction money in a Cold War world, but he had yet to play his trump card—the Suez Canal.

On 26 July 1956, Nasser announced the nationalization of the canal with the intention of paying compensation to the previous owners. It was his plan that the revenue from the canal would help defray much of the costs of the construction of the dam. The United Kingdom and France saw Nassers's action as a threat to their interests and invaded Egypt, seizing the canal and the Sinai with the support of Israel. Extreme diplomatic pressure, however, from the US and the USSR at the United Nations and behind the scenes forced them to withdraw ignominiously.

The Americans had at one stage considered providing funding for the dam but had dallied, and in 1958 Nasser accepted the support, both financial and technical, of the Russians, who were only too happy to gain an important foothold in the Middle East. The dam opened in July 1970.

Some say Egypt today is held hostage to this superstructure across the Nile. If the dam was breached and all 132 cubic kilometres of Lake Nasser roared through the Nile Valley, is there another country that would lose as much in a single calamity? Yet what really focussed global interest in this part of the world, as I learned from Sudanese fellow travellers that afternoon, was the upriver social consequences of the dam's construction, along with the biggest international archaeological manoeuvres ever undertaken. Everyone of a certain age will remember Abu Simbel but who recalls the Nubians?

★★★

Midway along the great curve of the dam, under the bluest of skies, I stopped and straddled the bike to look out at Lake Nasser sitting so still and stretching 550 kilometres south to Sudan. I had long been fascinated by this mammoth construction beneath my feet and the enormous man-made landscape before my eyes. A tingle of satisfaction rose in the veins. I felt it, and knew it had to do with the months of sweat in slowly getting there and I knew too how cycle travel was all about 'that tingle'.

Did I look too suspicious? A security jeep approached, its headlights flashing. I got back on the saddle, my right palm pleading innocence before the co-driver ushered me on. As they sped away I realised it wasn't me they were interested in and I felt ordinary again. Just an ordinary guy, freewheeling down to the ferry terminal, relishing the onrushing warm air in his face. Down to the chaos of customs, police, fellow passengers and jumbles of Sudanese-bound paraphernalia.

Journeys begin afresh many times along their path. Journeys within journeys, butting up to each other as waves to the shore of experience. Sudan? It pulled like a magnet. It would be its own journey, separate and totally distinct, of that I was certain. Of all the countries on that Christmas-like string of lights in my head, Sudan was the one place friends had advised me to skip. The civil war was ongoing in the south, with no end in sight. (Since independence in 2011, that conflict continues). Yet my thinking was simple: if I could get in, I'd travel on. Despite some trepidation outweighing the lightness of adventure, I trusted all would be well. In the end, years after I returned home, Sudan still played in my dreams.

At the ferry terminal, Caucasians were thin on the ground, outnumbered a hundred to one by Sudanese. It did not take long before we knew each other. Ben from NY, Peter from NZ, Tony from Munich, and Tom from Kiel. Tom saw me, beamed a smile and approached. 'He will want to stick with you,' Arie had said…and Arie was right. For some unknown reason, as the only two using pedal power, we were kept back until everyone else was on board. By the time we made the main deck every inch of walk-space was strewn with bags, suitcases, boxes, blankets and all kinds of stuff. Shouldering thirty kilos across this sea of jumbled belongings and up to the second level was the first real test getting into the country. As we lashed our bikes to the rail and staked out our 'camp' for the two-night trip, Tom told how my old friend Eamon had made it to Luxor, along with a nasty chest infection. It would be three years before I learned what had happened to him, but, now that I know, I can tell the story.

After our farewell guava juice, he decided he would also like to bike to Luxor. Reaching it, he about-turned to Cairo. A day later, on his way to the Israeli border he unwittingly took an innocent break near a secret military installation. That was enough. The roll of film in his camera was destroyed and he was unceremoniously dumped out of Egypt to Israel. There he was refused a visa to Saudi, so like in a bad game of snakes and ladders he ended up in Cyprus and thereafter back in Athens. In frustration he took a flight direct to Karachi to continue his bike trip to North Pakistan, Nepal, Tibet and China and on to 'Oz'. Naturally, in those pre-tech days, I was oblivious to all this but I well recall leaning on that ship rail, gazing at a receding Aswan and thinking of him, wishing him well. In a strange way, I didn't need to know where he was. He was a caver and potholer, wiry-tough; one thing I knew, if he could worm his way through a tight key-hole in a wet Burren cave, nothing would stop him. He'd be just fine. (Strange to say, that today, like the author, he too farms an organic farm. Yes, strange what a long trip can do to one.)

★★★

There were seven years between Tom and me, and, quite apart from a desire to ride down through Africa, we both shared a love of astronomy. He was the first guy I'd met who didn't think anything odd about looking up…just looking up into an awesome night sky. We spoke about the subtle changes happening above our heads as we moved ever southward. Yet, aware of what he hoped for, I knew in my gut that sooner or later I'd have to tell him that he had to go his own way.

Three hours out of Aswan, in the cool of late evening, the ship dropped anchor. We didn't know why, but the Sudanese lads seemed not surprised and most got on with their food preparations. Wanting to break gently with Tom, I accepted an invitation to join three of them, Ali, Sabri and Hassan. Onto their big bowl of *ful mudammas* and chopped onion, a fistful of shredded green leaf was tossed, then vegetable oil poured over the lot, Ali, the 'chef', complaining all the while that there was no lemon. 'I need lemon, I need lemon,' he wailed. With strips of flat bread we scooped up mouthfuls while watching their Muslim countrymen, face Mecca in a straight line across the deck. They were quick to let me know how not all young Muslims were so devout. Over on the starboard side, dark-skinned Sudanese from the deep south also chewed and also watched the *salat* (prayer) unfold. There on that ship deck and for the first time, Sudan's Muslim north and Christian south were laid out before me.

Night drew in and, as one does on ships, I leaned again on the rail. Directly below on the lower deck, Tony, Ben and some South Sudanese guys played cards in the yellowish light above a stern door, their convivial chatter peppered by the odd laugh. To the north, back the way we had come, a yellowish halo hung over Aswan and to there, in memory, I went. Recalling that well-heeled elderly gentleman, having his shoes shined outside the café near the barber shop, I realised how he had opened my mind to another bit of history. 'Right to the end,' I thought, 'Egypt offered the unexpected.'

His shoes and his command of English told me he was a well educated man. When he learned I was Irish, 'the British' rose in his conversation. All I could do was nod my young head as he spoke of historical parallels. 'Egypt, India and your country were thorns in Britain's blind vision of Empire,' he said. 'Sa'd Zaghloul, Mahatma Gandhi and your Michael Collins made them negotiate. Those men were visionaries for their countries. You should be proud.

'Do you know, my friend, it took time for the British elite to understand our nation's desire for self-determination. Gandhi wanted them out, Zaghloul wanted them out and your Michael Collins and de Valera wanted them out… and out they slowly went.'

I was amazed he knew so much and was more than pleased that he felt pleased to have met, as he put it, 'a real Irishman'. Our conversation was lengthy, and in the end my several *chais* were paid for without question. He wished me a safe eventual return to my home. The only thing he had offered of himself was that he had once taught in a university. History, I presumed, but then it could have been anything. 'Sudan will test you, my friend, but you will be fine, you are young and strong…you will be fine. Remember, like us Egyptians, they know how to look after a guest. Bon voyage et bon chance.' Those were his parting words. He was the last person I spoke to in Egypt.

That chance occurrence got me reflecting on other interactions over the previous months where, on finding out I was Irish, people became, in a subtle way, more welcoming or engaging or responsive or whatever. I could not put my finger on it but in relation to 'British', it would be another six months before a Dave from Nottingham nailed it by saying, as we discussed our respective 'welcomings'…'You, mate, you would be brought into the kitchen. Oh, I'd be welcomed too but only to the parlour.' I got no better summing up of the difference in those days between travelling with an Irish passport and a British one.

★★★

Tom arrived a bit flustered at the poor quality of ship grub but his mind moved on when we engaged with the stars. He pointed to where he thought Aquarius should be. Halley's comet was crossing it about then. We scanned the southern sky for the constellation's zig-zag pattern. He knew the mythology, the Greek story behind Aquarius. Zeus, deciding to flood mankind for 'something or other', tells Prometheus to tell his son Deucalion and wife Pyrrha to build an ark to escape. The flood story is an old one indeed. '... and here we are,' I said, 'on a boat in the middle of a man-made lake rather than a god-made one!'

Star by faint star, Aquarius revealed herself, and Tom did his best to show me the hard-to-see Norma Nilotica, the 'stick' in the heavens with which the ancient Egyptians used to measure the flood level of the Nile. Sooner or later every big river floods, and it would seem there is a flood story around every corner of the world. We saw the 'stick' but not the comet. Halley was nowhere to be seen. In fact, most comet watchers were disappointed that year as Halley decided to zoom in and out like a stealth bomber as it catapulted back to the depths. Every seventy-six years it pays us a visit from deep space. Its next call will be in 2061. Wind the clock back in seventy-six years jumps and that 'star' over Bethlehem was more than likely Halley. Certainly, in 1066, it scared the living daylights out of those who fought at the battle of Hastings and apparently swung it for the Normans.

★★★

It was 17 January, another boring blue-sky morning! I peeled out of the bag like a snake shedding its skin, the sun already warm on my face. To the fore, the bulk of Lake Nasser stretched away, to the rear, an entourage of gulls glided effortlessly. Their ease seemed carefree but their downward eyes were deadly focussed, swooping at scraps from the galley or a propeller-minced fish thrown to the surface. Tom had gone below to eat, but surprisingly my first coherent thought was not breakfast but rather the Tropic of Cancer. During the night, somewhere out there on the lake, we had crossed this imaginary line at 23.5 degrees north—this imaginary circle around the planet. It would take five more months of planet tilting before the Sun would shine directly down on where we were—at noon on the longest day of the year.

Circles: the Arctic had been the first, now Cancer the second, and the Equator I would cross somewhere in Zaire (DRC), then Capricorn in Namibia. Whatever about Zaire, Namibia may as well have been on another planet. Way down there, at that very moment the sun was climbing high above the Namib desert and, all going well, I would cross that desert at the back end of the year, when the sun's heat would be waxing there and waning where I was in the middle of this man-made lake.

Hassan and Ali came over to chat. 'Would we see Abu Simbel?' I asked. 'If we are lucky, towards evening,' they said. Both studied agricultural science in Cairo and were an engaging pair, rambling on like tour guides about old Wadi Halfa before the deluge, the town being now under the waters of Lake Nasser. They spoke proudly of its gardens and wonderful buildings and, though from Khartoum, were aware of the heartache of their northern Nubian cousins on that inaugural day in 1970 when dynamite blew a hole in the rock wall which had held the Nile back while the dam was being built—*that* moment, when the Nile surged forward and rose and rose then stopped, then spread backward for 500 kilometres filling the valley all the way to Wadi Halfa. It was the day when farm lands, fishing villages, the homes of 50,000 Nubians, countless ancient temples and Wadi Halfa itself were submerged forever. So a flood did come to pass. Zeus had his way and 'arks of a different kind' had to be built for both man and monument to save both from destruction.

As to the price of progress, they were unsure. They turned to each other and in the privacy of their own language debated the pros and cons. Then Ali faced me, pointing to the waters below. 'The fertility is down there,' he said. 'And so is the food for the fish,' added Hassan. 'Go ask the fishermen in Alexandria. They catch nothing now.'

I had never considered the millions of tonnes of sediment on Lake Nasser's bottom, trapped and unavailable. 'Why would the good nature be halted after so many millennia…do you believe some better way could have been found?' Ali had posed the question, looking at me as if I had an answer. I didn't, of course, but we agreed that the sediment below us told a sad reality about human-centred endeavours…that not enough of us know that we really don't know, and that too many with power still believe that they know all that there is to know to do anything they please. Dams are built, jungles cut, oil extracted, waste dumped and all kinds of things are done, only to discover later, often too late, that, though the idea was brilliant, even genius, it only added to our bigger woes.

Today Egypt imports artificial fertilizer to fuel its ever-expanding agriculture, while lying at the bottom of that man-made lake with their hero's name is a sizable chunk of what they now need. We wondered what the Pharaohs would have thought, and played with fanciful ideas about sucking it up and piping it down to the Egyptian farmlands. Ali laughed about going into business together, an Irish-Sudanese consortium selling Ethiopian sediment to the Egyptians!

★★★

I first saw Abu Simbel through a un-openable, paint-encrusted toilet porthole. The smell in that tiny below-deck 'bog' was abominable, but that's exactly where I was, innocently doing my business when the Great Temple came into view. I finished in double-quick time and shot up the metal stair to join the others. Peter was there, sharing his knowledge with his all white audience, and in his soft New Zealand accent explained how the east sun would creep along the engraved walls of the passageway to enter the innermost chamber. There the light would illuminate the face of Ramesses and two of his flanking gods, but not the face of Ptah. Poor Ptah, god of the underworld, he was deliberately left forever in darkness, not that he minded. Oh what supreme precision engineering from 1244 BCE.

If UNESCO had ignored the Egyptian request to rescue these Nubian temples, the waters of Lake Nasser would have submerged the lot in perpetual underwater darkness. Ptah would have won the day, and one would have to don a diving suit to see them. In 1964, 2,000 engineers and archaeologists from fifty countries descended on the banks of the Nile to engage in what was the most amazing engineering-archaeological rescue ever undertaken—*anywhere*. In a race against time they raised the 250,000-tonne temple and many others to higher ground above the projected level of the lake. A monumental Lego-like operation and, once again, engineering of the highest order, fit for a pharaoh.

Ramesses may have seen himself as a god and built his temple to recall his prowess at the battle of Kadesh (in modern day Syria) but his temple is today named Abu Simbel, the name of a lowly shepherd boy who led an archaeologist to the site when it was half-buried in sand in 1817. Did Ramesses' spirit return to ensure his temple would once again be open to receive the sun? A temple built out of a war now acts, or should do, as a symbol of the first proper peace treaty in the world, written between the Egyptians and the Hittites in 1259 BCE. Ironic, as so many Middle East peace treaties have come, gone or been torn up since.

Chapter 3

'The sun has got your brain'

What follows refers to the Sudan that existed before the 2011 independence of South Sudan. At that time it was the largest country in Africa, approximately four times the size of France.

The captain slowed the ship almost to a stall so that this ancient and indeed not so ancient history could be witnessed as we passed by, but as evening darkened he ploughed on again, crossing into Lake Nubia, the Sudanese section of Lake Nasser. There we anchored for the night. The Sudanese passengers were returning home, but for the rest of us, we were entering one of the high points in our separate journeys. In the years following our respective homecomings, Arie, Ben and Peter all agreed that Sudan was special; for myself, what occurred in Khartoum alone made it unforgettable, but that is getting ahead of the story.

The ship came closer and closer to the tiny ferry port of

Wadi Halfa. Beyond lay the desert wastelands, and I was surprised to feel a wonderful sense of readiness and a *joi de vivre* at being there. Those who have been before, especially those who have come with bike in tow, will know that feeling. Indeed, that other word for bicycle, 'pushbike', would take on a whole new meaning throughout the weeks that followed.

Tom and I *pushed* our bikes onto dry land, an understatement if ever there was one! The four kilometres to Wadi centre was sandy enough to forewarn of what was to come but we reached the *chai* shack where everyone was chilling out. The shack boasted a shiny new siding of corrugated tin and there, amid bowls of goat stew, bread and tea, us Caucasians re-grouped along with our Sudanese friends. No one, not even they, wished to hang about Wadi. Bar Tom and I, everyone awaited the Khartoum train. It came in the night, bringing passengers for the return voyage to Aswan and was due to return to Khartoum at 2pm, then 3 then 4, then finally the bell rang at 5.07pm. It pulled away with hundreds on the roof and arms waving from every window and, like in a scene from a wild west movie, those with no tickets sprinted along the track to catch the rear carriage.

Tony's head protruded, followed by Ben's. 'See you somewhere down the road, John,' they shouted. I waved, imagining how that was distinctly possible, Africa being such a small place for the traveller. I watched the train until it passed beyond the *jebels* and felt like the last soldier in the outpost. Tom and I were now the only non-Sudanese in town and as to where he was I had no idea. I felt good, at ease, so out of curiosity began to walk into the desert to take a look at the road to Dongala. Maybe, I thought, just maybe it would be all right to cycle.

Only for John Azambi from Uganda I would have continued heading in the wrong direction. 'Ah no, no, no, no,' he laughed, 'this is not the way to Dongala.' So we sat on the sand, warm from the heat of the day, like old friends and he spelt out his name with his finger. He had come north to work on the railway, '...at Station 14,' he said. Station 14, it sounded quite a pleasant little place, until you realize it's in that category of 'most remote rail stops'. In fact it isn't a stop at all but a maintenance 'x' on the map, although the detailed map I carried for north-east Africa only showed an 'x' for Station 6. 'Ah, Station 6, yes, that would be a promotion,' he assured me. It had water.

'Is it possible to cycle between the tracks, John?' I asked, knowing a French guy had done just that some years before, well, at least said he did. The idea of riding a bike along *his* track to *his* station brought him no end of mirth. He was a big man, and his laugh boomed out over the sand. 'Ah no, no, that would be bad, very bad.' Enough said. Though I felt sure it could be done, it would have meant missing out on the Nubian villages along the Nile. Meeting people had now become more precious than slogging it out alone. I wasn't out here to break records, and anyway there had already been, and would be, plenty of slog to come.

The sun was golden as we walked out in the right direction. He let his home-sickness pour out of him, how he missed his wife, his two children and, just like me, missed that spectrum of shades between yellow and blue. 'Oh you will like Uganda,' he offered, '…it is beautiful, everywhere green like your country and so, so different to here.' John would have walked on as long as I wanted but, when I'd seen enough of fine sand to know I could never ride here, we about-turned. From a deep pocket in his long trench coat he produced a jam-jar of *aragi.* Out of politeness I took a sip. Like a rough gut-rot *poteen,* it had the kick of a Kerry mule but I held my nerve and half-choked a compliment which brought a grin to his face and tears to mine.

We sat on a sand bluff above the flat-roofed sprawl of Wadi, sipping *aragi* in silence while minute by minute the feeble street lights gained a foothold against the fast coming dark. What an odd sight we were, I thought, like a Vladimir and Estragon . . . he in his heavy black coat, I in red T-shirt and khaki shorts. Oh how Beckett would have smiled at the surrealness of it. I hoped he'd get back someday to be with his family and that, yes, I would go to his country. 'Maybe we will meet there,' he said. 'Maybe,' I replied, 'maybe.' The tail-end of his long coat swayed from side to side as his big frame took off down a shadowy alley, 'to meet someone,' he had said. I imagined where he might be going and how lonely it surely got out at Station 14.

Dogs barked and Wadi felt like a place with its throat cut after the departure of the train, a ghost town. On my way back to base I stopped to watch a pair of donkeys copulating. The pair were silhouetted by one of those dim street lights and I almost laughed out loud. Not at the donkeys but at how things just roll on, how they 'happen' . . . one minute waving to guys I hardly knew leaving on a train, the next, a mile out in the desert sipping illicit alcohol from a jam-jar with a lonely Ugandan six inches taller than I, and he, wrapped in scarf and ex-army coat against an apparent chill, I bare legged.

The 'base' was an abandoned mud-wall bunker, barely two metres square open to the sky. Therein I began cooking. A candle struggled for a moment against the gentle breeze but then settled into a feeble glow. Tom arrived and, as I had guessed, presumed we would travel together. 'It just wouldn't work, Tom,' I said. 'But in Aswan I thought you said we might…,' he replied. So began a long chat, or rather I began a long chat. He stood leaning at the entrance in the half-light from the stove. I was blunt at first, told him what the others thought, that he was a bit young to head to Africa on such a trip; that I never suggested we might travel together; that he wasn't the first and wouldn't be the last to take to the long road to work through his demons; that to do justice to himself and what he ultimately wanted from his efforts, he had to … just had to do it alone, there was no other way. He could not lean on me or anyone else and that, yes, we would both get on a truck out of Wadi but I would jump off as soon as I could, and he best prepare to carry on alone.

'Hey, you couldn't have picked a better country to be supported. Sudan is okay,' I said. 'Safer than Germany, I bet. You'll be fine, these people are great. Ask anyone for anything and they will help.' He said nothing, just stood in the doorway like someone taking unpalatable medicine. I held out my hand and he shook it and then told me he was glad of what was said and that he needed to sleep. I spooned cold rice, watching him brush his teeth in the light of a locked-up kiosk across the sandy street, trusting that I had spoken the truth. In silence we bivied in our bunker, the wind whipping sand round the corners to pitter-patter on our sleeping bags. I hardly slept but knew that at least tomorrow we would head out of town . *Insha' Allah*.

Insha' Allah took its time, but towards evening our convoy of three Nissan 103-horse-power trucks finally revved engines and powered out of Wadi. Seventeen souls in all sat on top, among them Tom and I, with our bellies full of a dubious goat stew. As to my plan? Use the truck to get beyond the first ten to fifteen kilometres of soft sand, then jump off and go it alone. Like amateur to professional, I felt more physically and mentally ready than at any other time, even the day I left home. Time and miles had honed a new awareness, and just as well, for the following two months were to test every sinew and ounce of attitude.

Ali's back was to mine. We did our best to get comfortable. Beneath us lay sack upon sack of beans, flour, rice and who knew what else, all of it having come off the Aswan ferry just like ourselves. Every square centimetre of cash-making space was utilised. For me it was a mystery how such over-laden trucks could move at all across the sands but Ali and Hassan smiled at my 'European naïvety', as they bluntly put it. They were heading to Dongala and I enjoyed their jovial company. Close by, Tom engaged with someone. He was breaking free.

For a few hours, as darkness deepened, we were thrown forward and back, side to side with sudden bursts of power as our driver revved through soft sections of sand. He had his two prime paying passengers beside him in the warmth and light of the cab, while his two 'turn boys' leaned on the roof above, heavily wrapped against the cold, waiting for the shout from their boss. Once they saw soft sand ahead, they would leap like commandos from the cab roof, one either side, grab the metal running boards and sprint alongside the truck to position the boards in front of the rear wheels. Their job was simple but tough, to keep the truck moving through the softer sections. That done, they would grab the six-foot-long boards and strap them back while keeping pace as the truck could not stop. Pulling themselves up with a rope at the rear, like sailors out of the sea, they would climb over everyone to resettle again on the cab roof and wait for the next shout from the boss. This was done in great humour and as matter-of-factly as leaping on and off a bike.

Tom leaned over the edge, and above the engine whine I heard the plate of goat stew go swiftly to the depths below. Even out in a Lake Nasser storm we would hardly have suffered such seasickness but, as Ali joked, at least if you fell off here you would not drown. Whatever about drowning, I had a decision to make and fast. I had noticed that, two kilometres beyond where John Azambi and I had stopped, the desert floor was firm…well, an on-and-off firmness, but it was enough to get me thinking of jumping ship.

We were the middle truck of three. To our left, about 200 metres behind, the headlights of the third truck bounced up and down in the dark as it too fought for traction. There was no road, no certain way. Each driver literally ploughed his own furrow. Then unexpectedly the convoy stopped. Passengers climbed down to relieve themselves, and I took the opportunity to talk to the driver. Hassan and Ali gathered round as did others, including Tom. As Ali translated my plan to the driver, he looked at me bemused, then shook his head. 'He says the sun has got your brain,' said Ali, laughing. The driver spoke again, pointing ahead, pointing at me, then Hassan explained, 'John, we are nowhere here. The driver prefers you wait until he gets to Akasha. I think that would be better for you.' So it was agreed, I would get off at Akasha in the middle of the night, along with the return of half the fare and I was happy with that.

Huddled under blankets, four heads facing three, we continued with a bitter cold wind whipping the edges. No doubt about it, it was exciting for us westerners but torturous on our backs and shoulders. For the Sudanese lads it was just a bus ride home, no big deal, though they too felt every twist and chill. We bounced over yet another corrugated section, the engine revving to fever pitch. To take my mind off the discomfort, I pondered on the bike and which nuts might be loosening.

At 1.30am the three trucks stopped before a simple three-sided open pole and palm-frond shelter, and our collective suffering ended. Like any shelter in the middle of the night it was welcome. During the heat of day it offered shade to the Bedouin women who made their living bringing sustenance to the passing trucks. From the dark, they appeared, two black shawls carrying tea, flat breads and beans. They stoked the fire, poured the tea and administered the sugar, in silence. The drivers and their cab-paying clients sat closest to the flames but in reality the fires gave little heat, merely kept the dark at bay.

For the last time I joined Ali, Hassan and Tom, around a communal bowl of beans. Tom listened as they suggested I go to their friends home in Dongala— 'when you arrive there' as Ali confidently put it—but I was less interested in contacts as in my fellow cycling companion. He was anxious. In the flickering light of the fire, his forehead was tight. He would now be on his own, not what he wished for. The sharp blast of the truck horn got everyone's attention but most were already on top. 'Good luck, Tom, take care. Things will be okay, you'll see.' The words sounded hollow but what else to say? Before Hassan climbed aboard I pulled him aside and asked him to keep an eye on 'my cycling friend'. 'Do not worry about your friend,' he said in a reassuring tone. 'We will take care of him.'

The trucks revved onward, due south, into a star-studded night, the sound of their engines fading away to a distant purr. Not a soul was around; even the black-shawled women had melted away, and with each crackle of burning wood the silence grew louder. As the red tail lights receded there came a sense of splendid isolation, along with an old school poem…

I am out of Humanity's reach.
I must finish my journey alone,
Never hear the sweet music of speech;
I start at the sound of my own.

William Cowper's 'The Solitude of Alexander Selkirk' is supposed to record the words uttered by Selkirk (the real Robinson Crusoe) as he stood on the beach of his South Pacific island in 1704 watching his ship depart. Four years and four months alone on a volcanic tropical island—now that, I thought, *that* was an experience! I called out the lines of the poem into the dark, listening to the sound of my voice and felt alive . . . tired but strangely very alive. Then, turning towards the shelter, that rose-tinted 'alive' state disappeared in a flash. 'Oh shit, *shit*!' I roared. The front pannier was gone. It had the tool kit and spares, as well as petrol for the stove and two tins of sardines. Looking in the direction of the trucks served only to compound the imagined loss. They were then distant dots on the horizon. 'Fuck, fuck, fuck it!'

Calming down, I wondered if Selkirk had lambasted himself, forgetting some vital thing as his ship disappeared over the horizon. Had he too wasted energy screaming after it? I convinced myself that Ali or Tom would surely see the pannier and would keep it safe somewhere. Resigned to the loss, I turned again towards the shelter and there, out of the corner of my eye . . . *there* it was, propped up in the shadow side of one of the structural poles. One of the others must have placed it there. What sweet relief! That night, gazing into the dying embers, I was forced to look at everything— my tight little world of two wheels and battered bags, tent, stove, pot, scraps of food—all the bits and pieces grown precious with the miles. In the glowing ash I saw how I lived . . . in not one but two personal worlds, one open and vast like the desert with its lofty quests and visions, the other tight with attachment and fear. It was a moment that burned as hot as an ember.

★★★

Chewing dates before dawn, I took in the scene...sand! Sand, sand, sand, a truck-rutted sand-track over a hundred metres wide. That was the way we had come, and onward it weaved like some gigantic scratching across the desert. I spat the last stone out and got ready. Nine months of asphalt was over, for a while at least. It was 1,800 kilometres to Juba and from there into Zaire, sand and dirt track for most of it. Indeed, that felt a long way as I dragged bike and baggage along a sand-rut, one step at a time. 'It's a whole new ball game, buddy, better get used it.'

The 'new ball game' began before I even got beyond Akasha. Twice I was beckoned to take tea. I accepted the second offer from an old man sitting outside his home in the shade of his *mastaba*. What a lovely idea, a *mastaba,* a sort of brick-built seat recessed into the shadiest thick wall of a home. While sitting in there drinking tea with the old man, a group of teachers passed on their way to their school. One of them insisted I wait where I was. Minutes later he returned with at least a kilo of *kissera* (flat breads), explaining how they would not go hard in the heat. Though every extra kilo I would have to push, I simply could not refuse. I pushed that 'generosity' for the next fifteen kilometres or so, savouring the breads with the dates and the tepid water from the plastic bottles.

On-again-off-again was the best way to describe the first day's ride. From Akasha to Farka was superb wilderness. Those who have manoeuvred their bikes here before the road came will know the story—trying to ride, falling off, trying again, then pushing, dragging, sweating, stripping to the waist, absorbing the scene while gulping tepid water with a squeeze of lemon to offset the taste and a drop of iodine just in case. It did not take long to realize there was no need to carry five or six litres. From Farka to Kosha to Abri there were plenty of people living along the river, and thus no need to worry about water. All settlements had at least one large earthenware urn in an open public space and beneath its own shading roof. Akin to a well, these ingenious pots offered the coolest water, and I felt the luckiest man alive if I arrived at such urns in the full heat of midday. To stretch out on cool shaded sand and let a mouthful of chilled water cool the inside of my head was a pleasure difficult to describe. I'd rest my forehead against the urn's unglazed side, remembering Mr Cremin, a school science teacher. How proud he would be of me, I reflected, for here at last I experienced intimately and gratefully how evaporation cools.

Further on a flock of quail-like birds flew up in unison, surprised at being surprised, then landed just metres away. I clapped hands to see the reaction. Up and over a rock they swept, chattering angrily at being disrupted for a second time. Their chatter took me straight to Norway, to those willow grouse of the Lofoten Islands. I shut my eyes to tease out the memory; my brother Alan and friend Paul were there also as we watched the grouse-pair flap over a lichen-covered bluff. Similar moments from far-removed places felt as a singular occurrence and this, I realised, was one of the unsung pleasures of travel, that of its fourth dimension, when such happenings would give rise to the same feeling. I stayed in the memory for some time, then slowly opened my eyes to see where I was, as far from Lofoten Peaks and watery inlets as was possible to imagine.

My stronger right arm did the bulk of the work, dragging hour after hour. There were days when it ached but, to be honest, it was the finger creases which fared worse. The constant pressure of gripping the rear of the saddle and pulling forward made my perennial dry skin crack and open. At the end of a dragging day I'd 'talk' to an arthritic looking hand, pulling at and massaging the bent fingers. Gloves would have been great, if I'd had them, but even when wrapped with a ripped T-shirt those right-hand fingers were sore. Switching hands brought some respite, but not the power or efficiency. The irony, of course, was that the places I imagined would be the most challenging were the places that, unsurprisingly, gave the greatest satisfaction. The temptation was always to overstate the case, to over-dramatize such memorable and hard-fought days, but the reality was…it was exhilarating.

A man on a camel waved. I returned his gesture as if it was routine for camels and bicycles to pass each other out here. He had seen me sitting on the dirt, removing sand from my shoe, but swiftly moved on, rising and falling with the stride of his beast. His head was draped too like mine, and I wondered was it also to avoid the dreaded midge? They were becoming intolerable. The Sudanese called them *nimitii or nimta,* the green midge as opposed to the black. For generations in the homes along the river, their dead desiccated bodies caused asthma and respiratory problems. Out here in the open, they drove me nuts. No orifice was sacred. Eyes, ears, nose, mouth, they sought entry to one and all. Not as bad as in Lapland, but bad enough at times to want to scream. I dug deep in the pannier for a muslin cloth donated to the journey seven months previously by a Rovienemi family on the Arctic Circle. Up there I had wondered would I ever, ever make use of it, but lo, how merciful and unwittingly mindful it was to keep it. The sight of a man pushing a laden bike with his head draped in muslin, like a lost bee-keeper in the desert, must surely have looked ridiculous. Certainly the galloping kids on their donkeys, bearing bags of *balah* (dates) as a gift to the passing stranger, thought so, for as they turned back to their village of Kosha they burst into fits of laughter. I laughed with them, for such were the littler joys of traversing this fraction of Sudan.

Where to put an extra kilo on a fully laden bike? Somehow I did. This generosity repeated itself so many times on the way to Khartoum that a bike-trailer would have been required to carry the donations, and though my calorie requirements were probably off the chart, many, many offerings had to be declined. I pushed on (literally), conjuring up other ways to consume dates, bar popping them into my mouth like sweets. Cool yogurt came to mind…and then I remembered Eamon and that cool Greek yogurt we had in Kalamata. 'Oh Christ,' I mumbled, 'to dip a date in a chilled pot of yogurt. Wouldn't that be nice?' I continued torturing myself with those sweetly impossible culinary mirages until, sated and drooling, I turned to the river. There in a sandy depression facing the water I rested for the night, praying the *nimta* would not smell me.

Despite ten months of almost daily use, the Sigg petrol stove still worked well. A litre of water bubbled in minutes and in went a cup of rice and a fistful of lentils. On the pot lid, an okra, a red onion, and half a bulb of garlic were chopped and added, along with a pinch each of salt and cumin. Letting the pot simmer, I walked a short distance, attempting to dig a hole by hand in the free flowing sand. Not easy! Closer to the river the sand was damp and dig-able, so there I squatted and in that traditional evacuating position it struck me that in all I had ever read of others who had rode bikes hither and thither across the world, none, to my knowledge, had ever mentioned another of the 'littler joys' of wild camping…the humble act of squatting to aid the bowel to release its load!

With my load buried I continued to squat, mesmerised by a sun setting in absolute desert splendour. Venus took hold of the western sky before it too dropped behind a sand dune. Later, Orion the hunter climbed from behind another, and without looking at my watch I guessed the time. 'Yes!' I exclaimed. I was just a few minutes out. To tell the time by looking at Orion's position had become a personal sign of the *real* progress of travel. It felt good, though there was a way to go to hone the skill.

It was a wondrous peaceful evening-cum-night as I scooped and chewed my mix with the *kissera* while listening to the great river pass. The green terrors did not come, but were there crocodiles? I had no idea and didn't think to ask anyone. To feel more secure I moved camp twenty metres back (for all the good that might have done) and lay down to watch the nightly entertainment. I had read five bike travel books before departure, with hardly a mention of the night sky in them. Where were these guys, I had often wondered. Did they have a blind spot or a crick in the neck? Perhaps they got more seriously into cooking than I had, stirring their pot with due diligence to avoid being struck dumb by the scene above their heads.

Could one travel through such a place and not look up? To the Romans it was the *Via Lactea*, to the Greeks before them it was the *Galaxias Kyklos,* the 'Milky Circle'. I would have preferred that, but by whatever name, it is an awesome and humbling sight. The majesty of our 'milky' galaxy arcing over and turning us all is surely the grandest scene that can be witnessed by the human eye, and where better to see it than in the dryness of a desert. Wherever in the world one travels, that sight above one's head comforts and gives direction in more ways than one. The Plough pointing to Polaris, its handle to Arcturus, Orion's belt to Sirius, and so many other asterisms and constellations familiar from home made me strangely comfortable. The slow-shifting patterns of their turning embedded themselves within my head, and despite months of nightly wonder it was always difficult to let that enthralling sky vista go and close my eyes to sleep.

But before rising to the stars I had teeth to brush, and as I did there came a longing to slosh out my mouth with a chilled bottle of Irish spring water. During the heat of day the water in the plastic bottles became tepid and just about tolerable, but at night, when my world became private again, that water which had soaked up the sun was…well…bloody awful. I would spit the staleness out, shake out the sleeping bag, climb in and, like Houdini, wriggle to form a comfortable depression in the sand. Fluffing up a pile of sweat-filled clothes as a pillow was the final ritual act; only then was I ready.

I had sat in planetariums, but the real deal is truly something else. No simulation here—real satellites, real meteorites, real-time motion across the dome. The pointers of the Plough, that most recognisable of all asterisms, gave its direction to the North Star, then on to Cassiopeia, queen of Ethiopia. Below the queen, stretched her daughter Andromeda with her lover Perseus holding the severed head of Medusa and his horse Pegasus ready to fly. I spent a good hour trying to join the twinkling dots of this piece of mythology. Whose were the minds who put the stories up there? Were they shepherds or shamans, artists or seers, pharaohs, philosophers or…maybe even children? Some are as old as the last ice-age, begging an unknowable question in my mind, that ancestors of both desert Bedouin and Arctic Innuit may well have used the same asterisms to guide their respective ways over ice and sand.

Inside the 'empty' square of Pegasus I tried to spot some point of light, then hop-skipped to the real Andromeda, our closest galactic neighbour, once presumed to be inside our own galaxy until Hubble proved otherwise and blew a great hole in our collective grasp of where we thought we were. Tolerating the chill air on my naked right arm, I stretched it upward and took aim with a forefinger at that woolly smudge, 2.3 million light years away, not even a stone's throw in galactic terms. I was flying now, high on location. Surely in that fuzzy blob of a trillion stars there were thousands of travellers, travelling across their own planets, just like the thousands here on Earth. Everyone travels; if there is life there is travelling and there must be life. Are they gazing up too, up and out of their own versions of night, wondering, as we do, who is out there? Who knows? (Ten years later, in 1995, the first of many, many planets was discovered along that very edge of Pegasus.)

We travel to *travel,* to lie or sit in odd places and look beyond 'home'…to look through the given of our times into the ordinary-extraordinary that awaits us when we are ready. It was one of those nights I imagined I might never forget…nights that we all know, nights that take hold of something we cannot name, something old beyond our telling, nights when all philosophies pale to dust. I thought of Eamon, wherever he was, upper Pakistan probably. Knowing him, he was probably gazing up there too just like me. I thought of Arie the Dutchman and the sleepless nights he said he'd have, imagining snakes under his tent, scorpions in the bell and charging female hippos. Yes, that night, there may well have been scorpions under my karimat, but it was the Aries, the Leos, the Scorpios and other mysteries in the infinite night which, perhaps foolishly, held my attention.

In the early morning the pot was scrubbed with river sand, bits of encrusted rice and lentil floating down the Nile. Suddenly the sound of an engine made me turn: a Toyota pick-up was bearing down fast toward my apparently hidden location. Making camp the night before, I felt sure I was unobserved, but from half a kilometre distance Ismail's young cousin had spotted me, just as I was slipping down to the river…imagining no one could possibly have seen me. How naive! Unfamiliar with the terrain, I stuck out like a sore thumb. Knowing full well I was there, Ismail simply drove his pick-up to my 'secret' spot and invited me to his relatives' wedding. He had arrived from London the night before but as it turned out the wedding was cancelled, which didn't seem to bother anyone too much. 'Maybe next week, *Insha' Allah ,*' said Ismail, as his first wife brought out a most decorative pot of Indian tea, a bowl of Sudanese cane-sugar cubes and a plate of dates.

If chewing sugar cane was the abiding memory in Egypt, drinking tea and sucking dates was that for Sudan. We sat on a spotlessly clean date-palm mat under a date-palm awning under a date tree outside his large thick-walled, spotlessly clean Nubian home. The awning was wisely placed to protect the mat and the heads of all who sat there from the caustic droppings of palm turtles above. On a branch a pair of them cooed like lovers while through an open window Ismail's wives made cooing sounds of their own, excited by my unannounced presence. They certainly sounded happy. On the mat, under his grandfather's palm, Ismail regaled me with his family's long relationship with date palms. His voice was full of proper pride, and it was clear that while his head had to work in London, his heart was right there on the dry banks of the Nile, where his roots were as deep as the trees he cared for. I'd eaten enough dates to be more than interested in anything he had to say about them.

'This tree's mother is over there,' he said, pointing to tall palms near the river. 'My grandfather planted them.' The tree we sat under was propagated from an offshoot of the mother tree rather than a seed, '...to keep the quality,' he explained. Apparently it took seven years for a date palm to be planted into its final position, with ten more to reach full production. A serious lead-in time for a date but worth it to be rewarded with big juicy berries. 'We keep bunches on the tree for as long as we can,' he explained, '... then they get sweet but we get more than *balah* from this tree.' He called to his wife. She came bearing a variety of baskets which another, older wife had made. He proudly pointed to aspects of the intricate design as if he had made them himself. Every part of the palm was utilized in some positive way: fibres and mid-ribs for baskets, boxes and ropes, timber for construction and fuel, leaves for shade or mulch, sap for medicine and wine, date pits for animal consumption. Never again did I look at a date palm the same way.

He would have talked on about palms but I wished to know about crocodiles. 'Ah yes,' he explained, 'yes, yes they are there but they are only four or five feet long.' 'And snakes?' I enquired. 'Oh yes, yes, but only pointed heads are dangerous, round heads are harmless, do not worry.' On the ground he drew the respective shapes of snake heads to allay any concern on my part. Worry? I was not worried. I reckoned the chances of being hit by a 'box', the Sudanese name for Toyota pick-ups, was far higher than being bitten by a snake or mangled by a small croc. I bade Ismail farewell and, laden with yet more dates, I dragged and rode, where I could, onward to Abri.

(Today, 2018, there is a smooth tarred road from Wadi through Abri to Dongala and all the way to Khartoum. Nine hundred kilometres without a bump, wow! How different the experience must be for the cyclist or driver. Those who travelled here before the Chinese did such a great job should be grateful and those who may travel here today should spare a thought for those who crossed before the road was even dreamed of. No doubt about it, such infrastructure brings immense advantages. Yet a road that takes you too fast, too easy, robs you of a certain emotion which inevitably wells up when there is no other way to go. It whips the traveller too fast past people...and people like Ismail give travel its depth, its memory and its cultural colour.)

That evening, before the sun had set, I sat at a table outside an eating house in the small town square of Abri. I guess I had dived too hungrily into the big bowl of *ful mudammas* and had licked my spoon too intimately front and back, for I had been closely obsered. With spoon still in hand, I felt my shoulder being gently tapped. A tall man in a spotless while *jalabiya* stood there, his arm motioning me towards another table to join three others and an even bigger bowl of *ful*. I was duly instructed to tuck in, and their conversation continued as if I wasn't there. I liked that. 'Lads, ye don't know it, but ye've picked the right boyo to tuck in here,' I said to myself. Our evening ended after a tray of straw-coloured chais was quickly dispatched, as they wanted to re-enter the restaurant to listen to the radio.

Night descends fast the further south one travels, and thus 'the plan' to leave Abri and camp wild beyond the town was duly scuppered. I looked around. In the shadows behind the Dongala truck, my spot for the night was plain to see, a wooden bench against a wall and there I crashed, full to the brim with fava beans and sleep.

The restaurant radio filled the little square, and by the tone and timing of the voice I presumed it was the evening news, which kept the all-male clientele

in silence. From my bench in darkness I could see them, in their whiter-than
-white *jalabiyas*, brilliant in the bright strip-light of the eating house. Then the
voice changed. It must have been a comedy for they chuckled and laughed until closing time. The men went home, the lights went off and the truck driver
snored in his cab while his partner snored on the ground. The bench was hard
so I took the hint and got off for a more comfortable sleep on the sand. A dog
chased a cat across the square, one side to the other, in and out of shadows, then
all went quiet bar the muffled sound of music from the radio.

At five am I woke to hear it again. Had it ever been turned off, I wondered?
In there a silhouetted figure was already sweeping the floor, swaying his brush
to the high tinny-sounding notes of tambura strings and the dull rhythm of
drumming. The sound bounced off buildings still cloaked in the night, but
dawn was coming fast. Above the rooftops an orange glow spread, as if a distant
volcano had become suddenly active. It was cold, surprisingly so, so I remained
in my bag until six, then rose with the Dongala driver and his helper, and with
several other ordinary working souls I took two *chai-lebans* and hunkered down
outside with a few of them, letting the glass warm my hands while wondering
what the day would bring.

What would the day bring, indeed? If I had been told that by afternoon
between the villages of Chala and Soloman Ali I would be offering a placebo of
a vitamin pill to a young teacher's father as he lay ill, that I would hardly sleep
that night in an adjoining room listening to his raspy cough, that the following
day I would push the bike a mile to the teacher's school and read *Kidnapped* to
fifty pairs of ears before leaving with, yes, another bag of *balah* ...well of course
I would have believed it!

The teacher's name was Akasha, and he insisted I meet him and his friends
in Kermah, a town one day's 'push' away. I pushed on, thinking of Dongala,
playing a game of spitting the sucked date stones out of my mouth in front of
the bike as far as I could, just like the sugar cane gobs of Egypt. With two bags
of *balah* in the panniers, I was practically living on those sweet morsels and I
swore my energy levels were due to their juicy sugars.

Before I left Ireland, an all-round cleaning and filling of teeth was advised.
How insightful my dentist was—his deft hand in my mouth probing gently to
the point of barely being felt in there at all. From Turkish *locums* and *tulumbas*,
to Syrian *halva* and *baklava*, to Jordanian honeyed *katayafs*, Egyptian honey balls,

'umm ali, basbousa, syrupy figs, sticks of sugar cane and now, here in Sudan, *balah* by the bag full, what would he have said, being anti-sugar? I would send him a postcard, yes, and tell of the sweet treats that had powered my legs to crank the pedals through the Levant and beyond. Yes, and book an appointment on my return. He'd enjoy that.

'Get to Dongala, there you can rest. Get to Dongala, there you can rest.' I mumbled the words like a mantra as I dragged the bike, knowing how a journey always becomes in the end more a mental game than anything else. Mine had, by then, broken down into small baby bits, '... get to Dongala, there you can rest'. Towards late afternoon the soft sand gave way to firm track and I had energy to burn. I made the most of it into twilight, and then the reward came.

Moment by passing moment rose the motion of the spheres, with Earth, piggy-in-the-middle between the setting of a stunning sun and the rising of a luminous moon. I dropped the bike and stood to watch. The sheer scale and beauty of distance was amplified further as Venus and Mercury stole the show like twin eyes in the east. That word awesome, much favoured by Americans and often for things that hardly deserve it, here was wholly justified. More than half a mile from the Nile in dead flat terrain, I let the night settle all around me, knowing I had witnessed another reason for the travels. If there is some cosmic music to the spheres I did not hear it, but surely it was there. Such moments have effect beyond words, times when you know in your gut that it might not ever get better.

Buoyed up, it was all too easy to ride on in moonlight into another unforgettable night. An hour or so later the sound of an approaching vehicle made me pause and weigh-up the options. If I stood still or rode on, they would stop, pick me up, take me to their home and that would be that, a wonderful but predictable outcome. Did I want this to happen, now, tonight? 'Not really,' was the answer. So as the truck lights bounced closer I dived off the track. I lay beyond range and watched it pass by, imagining what friends at home would think. Would they, or could they, understand. 'You what...you hid from the locals, why would you do that?' How could I ever explain about 'self-preservation'?

Perhaps those travelling for a month or two or even three would more than likely have jumped onto that truck, gone to wherever and had a great night, but after ten months on the road, countless invitations, some wonderful, some not, there came a point when I needed time out to preserve something in myself, time away from the social exchanges. 'Conserve your head-space,' Brian Murphy had said, '…oh it'll be a marathon for sure. Whatever drives you on, protect it, don't be projecting it willy-nilly.' His advice sounded esoteric mumbo-jumbo back home, but now I began to get it. He may not have travelled to faraway places but he understood, so I settled for the night, right where I was, while looking at the tail lights recede. What a day! It began reading *Kidnapped* in a classroom and ended lying on my belly, hiding behind a sand bluff, feeling as free as a shooting star.

Deserts can be cold at night and damp at dawn. I woke with the usual condensation on the karimat and sleeping bag, knowing pretty soon it would turn to vapour as the sun dried all before it. Those first sunbeams streamed from the very spot where the moon had risen. We had all turned safely again, and a new day spread out as open as my imagination. A truck passed, going the other way, its topmost passengers waving as I forked mackerel from a tin. That was exactly how the day began. How it ended though, was a crazy, hazy blur. The day carried on as wonderful as before, with Sudanese hospitality pouring out from every door, across every field of *simsim* (sesame), onion and pumpkin and over every house being built. I had more cups of sweet tea than I could recall and more invitations to remain on than I could possibly entertain.

By late afternoon my progress was halted by a simple wooden direction sign. The script was in Arabic, two arrows pointing in opposite directions. Which way, left or right? Surely both ways led south and one had to be to Dongala but which? Flipping the pages of my diary, where someone had written my name in Arabic, I looked at the sign again, searching for similarities with the shared letters of my name. Nothing matched. In the end I let fate decide, recalling a quote from somewhere that if one was generally facing the right direction, just keep on going. I turned to the right. As it turned out it was wrong, at least for it not being the shortest way.

In those elemental moments, straddling at forks in the road, where those 'two roads diverged in the yellow wood', I often wished I could split myself so as to 'travel both and be one traveller', as Mr Frost had wished. But life and travel allow just one slice through, that's it. There's no escape from the necessity of choosing; you choose direction and have no choice but go on to the next choice, the only comfort being that what is let go of often follows and lingers with a 'scent' of that forever unseen way.

69

Once again the bike was pushed into the evening, seventeen kilometres from the town of Kermah. The only reason I wished to get to Kermah was because of Akasha, the young teacher whose father I had helped. He would be there that evening and had scribbled an address. Seventeen kilometres is nothing on a tarred surface but on soft sand…at night…I wasn't going to make it. Then, like a bat out of hell, a 'box' came roaring towards me. This time I stood my ground and, no surprise, the afro-haired driver and his skin-headed mate skidded to a halt. With minimal fuss they threw me and the bike in the back and tore off.

In the two years of travel, that seventeen-kilometre ride ranks as the wildest, craziest buck-and-bronco ride of all. There was nothing to hold onto but the sides of the 'box', and I held on for dear life. With one leg I tried to keep the bike from rattling to bits and cursed myself for getting on board, but there was nothing I could do. Shout out? Their music was so loud I imagined it could be heard in Chad. At one point, going over a pothole-infested stretch, I honestly thought they had forgotten that anyone was in the rear. They stopped at some village *chai* house, the curly headed driver telling me to 'wait five minutes, Mister', and I telling him I was getting out, that all I wanted was to meet a guy named Akasha in Kermah and I'd prefer to walk than be rattled to bits. 'Ah, Akasha, Akasha, he is our friend. Yes, Mister, to his house we go. Stay please. We will take you.' Crazy but true, so I stayed, and Maher, for that was the driver's name, brought out a *chai* to calm me down.

After his tea break, he shot off again as if being chased by an invisible police car or being pulled by some powerful thought of imminent ecstasy. He drove through the village Argo like a madman, winding in and out between donkeys, telegraph poles, even people. Things went by my field of vision at an alarming rate until Kermah came and almost went, but on its outskirts we finally stopped only to be told that Akasha had gone to Maher's own home. Thankfully that was just round a corner.

On seeing me wobbling through his door, Maher asked if I was okay. 'Hey,' I replied, 'have *you* ever sat in the back of your own "box" with a crazy driver driving?'

'Oh no, no, but I would love to do that,' he laughed.

I suggested he try it sometime.

'…but we arrive safe, yes,' he said and put his long arm on my shoulder to lead me in. Akasha was there, along with a Khalid, a Faté, three Muhammads, a Tarig, and a Baageri. The door was bolted behind me, and for a moment I was concerned about my safety. Then Akasha asked, 'Ah, Mister John, it is so good to meet you again. Do you wish a drink?' The instant thought that came was, 'Oh God, not more tea, spare me please, not more bloody tea.' But it wasn't, and I should have known.

The *aragi* was as good as the best poteen. A single glass was passed around so everyone got exactly the same. A *shisha* pipe was already on the go but not fast enough, so someone 'rolled'. Smoking was not my thing and by the time Camal, the local doctor, arrived, I was certain I could understand all the Arabic jokes being thrown around. I was laughing at nothing but the laughter of others, until the good doctor translated a joke for my benefit.

'A Sultan,' he said, 'was deeply depressed. His vizier enquired as to the reason. "Ah," replied the Sultan, "I am in love with another harem."' Already on the edge, that sent me over and I lay on the floor in fits.

Dr Camal took the lid off a bowl of camel liver in a spicy sauce. Someone pulled me up and we sat with our backs to the wall, chewing the tough, greyish, stringy delicacy. Chewing and chewing as more *aragi* was poured and a third fat one rolled. I was on course for stardom, singing whatever came to mind.

It's a long, long way from Clare to here …
I sometimes hear the fiddles play, maybe it's just a notion,
I dream I see white horses dance on that other ocean,
It's a long, long way from Clare to here
It's a long, long way from Clare to here
Oh, it's a long, long way, it gets further day by day,
It's a long, long way from Clare to here.

From 'A Long Way to Clare' to 'The Rocky Road to Dublin', I sang bits of ballads from the back of my head and felt absolutely certain it sounded just great and my fans applauded without understanding a single slurred word.

Khalid pulled a red plastic wash-hand basin from under the bed and placed it in the centre. It was full to the brim with a salad of lettuce, beans, onions and hot peppered tomatoes. Rounds of flat bread were tossed in, then everyone's eating hands cut loose. Hot meant *hot*, and wishing to cool my tongue I stupidly

71

drank more *aragi* from a bottle, thinking it was water. It was like putting out a fire with methylated spirit. My fans rolled with laughter.

I never saw food disappear as fast, and in an instant my ten friends went from sitting eating to standing dancing. Nubian music played and they flowed in a graceful easy rhythm, full of suggestive shoulder and hip movements, with gentle turns of wrist and hand. Dr Camal tried in vain to teach me but I was a drunken elephant among peacocks, more used to Gaelic football and karate than the subtleties of Nubian dance. As high as I was, it felt strange to be part of this all-male erotic display.

Did I fall, faint or collapse? Did I sing too many Irish ballads, driving them away? It was all a blur with no recollection of the ending. When one eye opened, I was face down in a room full of light, floating on the softest mattress in all Sudan. It was midday, and Maher, chirpy as ever, burst in to the room to suggest we go meet his friends at the *chai* house. If he'd been some long-standing friend, I would have thrown something across the room in his direction, but when you are the guest and your host invites you to tea, you have no choice but pull your trousers on and follow bleary-eyed along. In his uncle's courtyard he pumped up cold water for a jug and bucket shower. I shivered with the shock of it and revived slowly. The only definite reminder of the night before were the stringy bits of camel liver between my teeth.

Four other 'box' drivers awaited us in the *chai* house. The topic of discussion was…well, me! Or more precisely, my route south. The pros and cons of my next travelling step became quite animated among the five drivers. Not understanding a word, I leaned back on the tubular metal chair, sipped a *chai* and watched desert sparrows pick crumbs on the nearby table. I may not have understood but strangely I felt a pleasure in letting the locals decide 'my way'. Like the signpost in the desert south of Delgo, a directional coin had to be flipped to continue. Did it really matter who flipped it, me or someone else? In the grand scheme of things, probably not, for the thin tenuous slice of life I followed would intersect with whomsoever or whatsoever, whichever way I went, and it all seemed to make perfect sense in the end.

But, oh, to have understood what was being said. Here and there Maher interpreted the apparently rich debate on my options. It centred, Maher explained, on whether or not I should take 'this side or that side of the river'. Occasionally he had to remind his colleagues that it was 'a guy on a bicycle' they were advising, not a bloke on a powerful motorbike or driving a well-stocked jeep. Finally there was consensus. I was to cross the Nile right there, near Kermah.

Feluccas are crafts of great timeless beauty, steeped in the Nile's DNA. The one anchored before me was all of that and more, no frills or fibreglass here, no starched white sails to catch the tourist eye. It was a humble single-sailed vessel with a large sand-brown canvas and ancient timbers that creaked and squeaked in the gentlest of motion. Its wizen old skipper had no doubt seen it all, yet my guess was, going by his stare, that it had been a while since he'd last seen a 'visitor' standing knee-deep in the river and shouldering a laden bike out to his craft. Maher's young brother helped, holding up the heavier rear end.

The ferryman, with a nod and a smile that spoke decades of chewing sugar-cane, welcomed me aboard. He pointed to where he wished the bike to go and I dropped his fee of twenty-five piastres into his calloused hand. With his four passengers settled, he eased his craft into deeper water. Maher waved a final salute and then, as crazy as the night he first picked me up, he revved his 'box' and tore off in a cloud of fine dust. It hung like a stage curtain, ending what I symbolically took to be another episode in the drama of Sudan.

Half-way, the ferryman dipped a bowl in the river and kindly offered everyone a drink. Apart from it being river water, the image of the dead diseased goat which Maher's father had flung into the river that very morning refused to float out of my mind. I declined! Then, from behind, my arm was gently tapped. A fellow passenger, an old man with a gappy grin, pointed downstream. Several crocodiles were entering, but his finger wagged from side to side, assuring me there was no danger. There must be thousands of islands in the Nile, and we silently drew close to one of them. It was the smallest of the two islands which separated us from the far side. Ten metres from shore, the elderly passenger hopped over the side into waist-deep water like a young lad. His arms shot up in my direction; if English was his mother tongue he would surely have said 'Come on, come on, pass me your gear and lets get on with it!' The tiny island was just a hundred paces across, and the old man escorted me in silence every step of the way, his hand resting on the rear pannier to let me know he was there to help. It was a small but dignified gesture which, for some odd reason, I've never forgotten. He helped carry the gear out and onto the second boat to the second island. This was a steel engined craft and what a change from the creaking old wind-catching magic of the *felucca*.

The second mid-river island was much larger, and I could see neither its northern nor southern ends. It had at least one village and many small fields of onion, water-melon and, of course, sugar-cane. When my gappy-toothed helper was satisfied that I would be okay, he shook my hand and strolled on. I may have been, but the bike was definitely not. The sound of grinding coming from the freewheel bore into my brain. Sand was deep inside, and as I listened to every turn I could almost feel those bearings being irreparably etched. Like a parent with a sick child, the grating sound was upsetting, and I wondered how long before it would seize altogether, and then what? I knew that friends were shipping a new freewheel and various parts to Nairobi but that was 2,500 kilometres distant. There was nothing to do but find a good workshop, strip the freewheel, check the balls and grease the hell out of them!

The *ooup-ooup-ooup* sound of hoopoes playing hide and seek took my mind off bike problems for a while. Indeed, hoopoes and every kind of bird were everywhere, darting here and darting there. Little did I know then, that on this island in Sudan—an island in the Nile—I was walking into and across two kilometres of a birder's paradise. A lone male desert wheatear, with his black face and pale brown cap, stood boldly on the trunk of a fallen tree watching me pass, and then—then came the *pièce de résistance*, the jewel of the afternoon, making me stop dead in my tracks. Five seconds was all he gave before darting off but it was enough…a vivid green body, lilac-blue throat with a jet-black line across the eyes from beak to ear, giving the little fellow a masked look like Robin in *Batman*. I dug the *Mitchell Beazley* out and flipped it open. Though it was nothing like its European cousin, it simply had to be a bee-eater. What a wonderful treat. Once again I made a mental note to thank Jim Wilson, a proper birder, who had given the gift of that pocket book. Thumbed, stained, creased and marked but, oh, how many hours of delight it had given.

The sand was warm under foot, and with shoes swinging from the handlebar I ambled on slowly. The path cut through a wide open area surrounded by palm trees, acacias and scrub grasses and my quiet arrival sent a cluster of turtle doves bursting from the ground into the highest branches, fifteen, maybe twenty metres up into the bluest of skies. The reflected heat rising from the sand brought drowsiness. I fought it, until a fallen palm ahead beckoned like a pit-stop. It was the perfect place to take a break and so, with my back against the trunk and my butt feeling the warmth from the ground, I stretched out a pair of deeply freckled legs and pulled the shrunk blue hat over my eyes.

Like Alice in a desert wonderland I slipped down easy into a tunnel of flashbacks, the unconscious doing its best to knit a thousand disparate cameos together—old Mr Olsen, north of Tromso, bending over his foot-powered sharpener to skilfully edge my knife, that look of disdain on the Check Point Charlie border guard, my father's hand in farewell salute, my hand rubbing the worn seat of Ted Simon's motorbike in a Coventry museum, ex-Turkish Flight Commander Ali Bozdag in Kaymakli telling his son to get pizzas for Eamon and me, and on and on until a squeak like a caught mouse snapped me out of it. The squeak was followed by a babbling chatter. I opened my eyes to a pair of blackbirds. 'Hang on,' I thought, 'There are no blackbirds in Sudan.' With their long legs, they hopped and probed the ground. The obvious male wagged his tail which he kept perpetually erect but he had no blackbird orange beak. They were not the blackbirds of home but something else. I took note and later discovered who they were, a Mr and Mrs Desert Scrub Robin, he flirting by fanning his tail like a peacock. They flew off and I looked around. The sun had noticeably shifted. It was late afternoon and I was taken aback that over two hours had passed. There was no sign of habitation, and the idea of making camp didn't seem an odd one, until the thought of 'crocs' coming from the river forced a momentary rethink. That primal ancestral fear, buried in my genetic code, caused a quick, unconscious calculation. 'If a croc came, could I get to and shimmy up that nearest tree?' In the end I took a gamble and hardly moved, just made camp where I was while watching harmless ants weave up and down along the hairy bark of the fallen palm.

The stove threw out its bluish petrol light as ants marched indifferently through my 'kitchen'. Night had swept all before it. Beyond the ring of trees, dogs barked-out their territory while, above, the night sky swung its arc. As if in tandem with that existential fear of crocodile teeth there came a desire for fire; with each layer of fronds and super-dry twigs the flames leapt higher and higher until sparks replaced stars, and I felt as good as I could possibly have, sensing it was one of those nights you travel far for. I pinched my mind to look where I was, camping in the middle of the Nile. The only annoyances were those few mosquitoes that braved my eventual smoky defence.

By mid-morning I stood waiting on a mud-sand river beach. A flock of some kind of snipe or wader perused the shore while further along a white stork stood to attention, waiting just like me. Two fishermen rowed upstream in a dugout. They waved, one calling out in Arabic and pointing back the way they had come. Sure enough a *felucca* approached, its off-white sails catching a breeze. Sacks of dates were piled up near the loading spot but no one was around. Then, just like locals arriving to a village bus stop at home, knowing exactly the departure time, people appeared. The sacks were carried out into the water and placed on the bow, where I too was once again instructed to place the bike.

A woman dressed in a red head-scarf and a blue-coral-green batik-like *thoub* took her place, using a sack as her seat. For the entire crossing she gazed at the bike. I wondered what was going through her mind; '*What is that doing there? Who is he? Why does he push that across the sand?*' Maybe she took this trip every day and looked at that same spot, except that on this particular day there happened to be a bicycle there. A yearning arose to talk with her, to ask some ordinary questions. Feigning disinterest, I looked the other way, then clicked my tiny Rollei camera. Something about that moment, something about how she looked…that was it, click.

On reaching the final shore and paying my due, the boatman put a huge tomato in my hand. Our hands shook firmly. I had thought mine tough but it was nothing like his, roughened by years of rope and sail. His smile and gift gave me an unexpected boost, and his wizened look said he knew all about comings and goings. I imagined his life of ferrying, over and back, over and back. He whipped a rope, the sail flipped and his craft eased out into the river once more, and I moved on toward Mushu with a deeper respect for ferrymen.

Of the seven or so kilometres to that town, I cycled four, pushed three, not bad. On reaching the outskirts I was led around by a growing band of helpers when all that was asked for was a tent space. No one quite knew what to do with me, and in the end I was taken like a hot potato to the hospital and to a bemused Dr Essam. 'Tent, tent?' He would not hear of it. I was to sleep like a proper member of the human race, in a bed with a clean sheet, a pillow and enough blankets to survive an Arctic freeze!

Dr Essam was a bearded, good-natured, good-humoured man. He spoke several languages fluently, had spent seven years in Romania studying medicine, had a Romanian wife, a Sudanese wife and three children, though he did not say whether they were half Romanian or full Sudanese. He was posted to remote

Mushu for six months but eighteen had now passed. 'Why?' I innocently asked. 'Why?' he replied, '…why indeed?' Khartoum was his (and certainly his wife's) preferred option, but the challenge of running a small hospital with no laboratory, no X-ray, no back-up services as well as coping with a malfunctioning generator, keeping tabs on stocks, encouraging his small team, and, of course, seeing his patients—all this called up inside him, as he said himself, 'my father's grit'. He would remain for a while yet and 'get the place better prepared for the one to follow me'. I liked him and his clear matter-of-fact way of accepting, honouring and marrying his deceased father's energy with his chosen endeavour to the benefit of others.

That evening it became apparent that my presence was made an event. Along with his beautiful Sudanese wife and two nurses, who I guessed were asked because they had enough basic English to chirp in, we sat to eat, talk and drink *aragi*. In reality though, it was he and I who got stuck into drinking and talking, the women retiring to another room. We spoke of all things Irish and Sudanese, from beef steaks to camel steaks, rain and no rain, ocean sounds and desert sounds, grey clouds versus blue sky, grass versus sand, but, in the end, it was religious divisions, the tragedy of war and the killing of innocents which gave a sombre edge to our sharing. Though he was Muslim, he felt the Muslim North - Christian South division would not be the problem it was if the region had not been artificially divided by the British. 'Eventually we would have done business there and they would have done business here, but that was prevented for a long time,' he said, '…as it is also, I believe, in your home. Did the British not also make a border to divide your country? Did they know what they were doing?' Whatever about 'my country', he was right, the policy of the British of the day was indeed 'no Southerners allowed North, no Northerners allowed South'.

He was the first to tell me of John Garang, leader of the SPLA (Sudan People's Liberation Army), of whom I would hear so much for the remaining time in the country. John Garang, I liked the sound of the name. Che Guevara came to mind, men fighting for a new way, a new beginning for their people or adopted ones. 'Garang and Guevara? Oh, I'm not so sure about that,' said Essam, replying to my insinuating question of some similarity between both. 'You must read about Thomas Sankara in Burkino Faso. Now *he* is much more like Guevara, but then I suppose, like Mr Garang, he too began his revolution only a few years ago [1983]. Perhaps there is some symmetry between them after all…but, you know John, they may all be revolutionaries but they will all be killed or assassinated. That's usually how these things end.'

From revolutionaries to tropical diseases, our conversation shifted to the health risks I would face as I moved further south. 'What will you do about malaria?' he asked. My only answer was popping Nivaquine and using a net. 'It is getting worse in the South, you will need to take care. I strongly suggest you begin your prophylactic tonight.' And so I did, the first of many in my anti-malarial defence, and how prophetic the good doctor was, for two months later in Uganda, in another hospital, a genus of that virus indifferent to prophylactics would bring me to death's door and all the Nivaquine in the world was of little use. Yet the big event of the night was his hilarious attempt at translating my rendering of 'The Rocky road to Dublin'. Afterwards we agreed it would be better and easier for all if I had learned it in Arabic.

I woke dehydrated, with a head throbbing from *aragi*. One after another, every water bottle I had was gulped down but the throbbing throbbed on regardless. I thought of Dr Essam's head, and hoped it wasn't as bad as mine. He was long gone and his wife, who spoke no English, guided me with gentle gestures of her arm to the breakfast table. I followed, gazing at her naked hennaed feet and her feminine shape within her multicoloured *thoub* of chiffon. Breakfast was fried goat liver with a side dish of onion, tomato and a peppery yogurt sauce, sumptuous. She went outside, leaving me mentally split at her table between the sense of being a child excited by the gifts of a home and that of a young man aroused by a woman's perfumed presence. What really surprised me, though, was not the woman or her home but rather the actual act of sitting down at a table at all. I sat with my back straight, then stood, sat down, stood, sat down again. So easy…so easy to forget. I could have counted on one hand the tables I had sat at since leaving home, such a simple act magnified by absence to the point of heightened awareness.

I wrote up my diary until Dr Essam returned to take me to the local sheet-metal workshop. The two young fabricators there informed him that they had never worked on a bicycle before but would try to fix it. 'No better continent to be on than Africa,' I thought, at least when metal-work skills were required. The freewheel was put into the 'operating-table' vice, while the good doctor looked over their shoulders with obvious admiration for their skill. He had never been to the workshop and was impressed enough to consider the two guys for some hospital project he had in mind, leaving me privately chuffed that my little bike problem had connected them.

We returned to his home for the midday meal, yet another wonder: freshly ground peanut soup made with stock from a goat head, followed by the head itself, with breads, garlic and tomatoes, followed by a sweet herb tea. Then, when we were settled in soft chairs, came Essam's unsurprising question, 'John, tell me about Northern Ireland?' The question seemed everywhere in those days, and I tried hard to tease out an honest objective answer. How odd that British travellers I'd met had never once been asked about this part of Ireland, though it was politically tied to the UK. How ironic that it was understood globally, even by most British, as an 'Irish problem', yet the Ireland I lived in then was precluded from having any input to its resolution. 'Politics is a strange game indeed,' I said to him, but he knew that only too well.

I told him also that what surprised me most was how those English fellow-travellers whom I'd met along the way had only the barest inkling about the centuries of bitter and bloodied involvement their country had with its nearest neighbour. It felt as if a veiled curtain hung on the English side of the Irish Sea, behind which 'nothing of much consequence happened'. As one bluntly put it, 'I'm sorry to say, but in our English schools Ireland's history doesn't feature much.' To which I often replied, 'We all have our blind spot.'

Doing my best to explain to Essam, I told him first that, just as in Sudan, the British had enshrined into policy the divisions that were already in situ, and thus a line had been drawn on the map to partition the country. In explaining the history to others, who often had only a tenuous and often slanted grasp of a complex issue, I was inadvertently giving myself a history lesson. The more I explained to whomsoever asked, the more my understanding felt exposed and shallow to my own ears. That night I lay in my gracious host's soft bed and mentally kicked myself.

Two months before leaving Ireland I had cycled to Dervla Murphy's home in Lismore, Co Waterford, to talk about the trip. The following day I purchased her book *A Place Apart*, a superb analysis of the matrix of 'Norn Iron' (Northern Ireland). Unfortunately, it lay unopened on the bedroom floor with a myriad other pre-departure paraphernalia, until it was boxed and sent into quarantine in my brother's attic. I kicked myself for not reading it, recalling all those who asked about that troubled place. They might have had a more insightful answer had I done so. Her book was probably born out of similar questions during her own travels and, as she said herself, you travel as much to learn about your own place as the places you travel through. I could not agree more. That hot sweaty night in Mushu, Sudan, I promised myself I'd read *it* and other books on where I called home. So for me also, it was already coming to pass: you go far away only to rediscover your own country. Irony indeed.

Dr Essam, I salute you still. You were never to know how your tenacity stayed with me. Outside the broken pillars of your hospital we wished each other well. To be told that my unheralded arrival had given a welcome lift to your spirit was your gracious parting gift. It lifted mine also. Someone took a photo and then I turned south to Dongala. I rode out into another desert-empty stretch to the next village, feeling rested, ready and refreshed.

The great river was now on my left. The irrigated plots were full of working men, one tilling the soil behind a pair of oxen, others re-directing a channel of vital water to a new plot, others again doing what I took to be maintenance work on the labyrinth of waterways, most no more than a foot in width. The shouts, waves and entreaties to come join for tea were many. I would be there yet if I responded to all, yet it made for a welcome and safe feeling to be in this vast country so full of emptiness and generosity. The time in Mushu had given time to dig out Sekida's book on Zen from where it lay since Cairo, beneath spare underwear at the bottom of the right pannier. Along with Samuel Bakers *The Albert Nyanza* and Gurdjieff's *Beelzebub's Tales to his Grandson,* it was the only other book to make it all the way. For much of a hot, enjoyable bike-pushing morning, I pondered *Mu* to keep me on the 'straight and narrow'. So much so that I became absent-minded. What a joke! Sekida, Baker or Gurdjieff would have kicked my ass…but no matter.

A grizzled old man approached on a donkey. Usually, without a thought, I'd steer clear of the animal and give it space but I was lost in the *koan* and not paying attention. The donkey bolted, throwing the man to the ground, and then cantered off. I dropped the bike and ran to where he had fallen. He lay still, his hand on his heart and the whites of his eyes showing. My instant thought was, 'heart attack, he's had a heart attack.' I moved close to hear his breathing, too close. Seeing a red-bearded white face with dark-brown sunglasses hovering above his face, the poor man let out a holler of terror. He must have thought an angel of death had come. Two teenagers came instead, and one, by pointing to his own eyes, explained how the old man was half blind. Together we helped sit him up. He was visibly shaken but more upset that he could not find his sandal. It was found and handed to me, and I gently placed it on his foot. By then men were running from a nearby field. I let them at it, there being nothing more I could do. I watched as four of them carried him to a nearby house. 'Shit,' I thought, 'I nearly killed a blind man.' So much for enlightenment, but then again perhaps it was the old man who became enlightened! More grounded than before, certainly more reflective, I quietly slipped away.

A few kilometres on, as if to reconnect with people once more, I accepted an invitation. Five builders beckoned as they tucked into a huge, hearty-looking bowl of layered bread on top of soup. There was no way to converse, just convivial gestures to the enjoyment of simple food. I dearly wished I had the Arabic to tell them what had just occurred further back the way, but reckoned sooner or later they would hear all about it. Then they would tell everyone, 'Oh yeah, we fed that fellow and he said nothing about it…huh!'

By late afternoon, at long, long last, Dongala drew close. I was tired and, as if to test what little enlightenment remained, the derailleur spring lock-nut came loose and lost itself in the sand. 'Great, just fucking great …' So went the self-talk as I sifted sand on my knees. A few men on donkeys passed. '*As-salaam alaykum*,' they called out in unison. '*Alaykum as-salaam*,' I responded from a dog-like position. They smiled, nodding politely, before gee-upping their steeds as if they couldn't get away fast enough from an odd looking *khawaja* (foreigner) guy talking to himself on all fours. I stood up and looked at them looking back at me, then looked to the sky while arching my back into a good stretch. 'Holy God,' I said, 'could this get any more ridiculous?'

Like the outskirts of many small towns throughout Africa at that time, it was easy to spot the metal workshop. I dragged the bike towards its dark, doorless doorway, wondering what else might be in store. My experience of such places told me you usually got extra to what you went there for. With some devious outside-the-box ingenuity, so typical of Africa, the problem was sorted and, as I anticipated, the extra came. 'You can stay at the house of the German nurse,' they said, the presumption being that Europeans would naturally accommodate each other regardless of which country they came from.

So I followed my chaperones to find no nurse at home, but as we turned to leave who should come along the shady alleyway but Tom, a bag of buns from the *souk* in his hand. We stood swapping a story or two, but there was a coolness between us. He had found something of what he was looking for, and it was obvious he was staying in the home of his compatriot. Once again I bade him adieu, then followed my guide to the local Christian church, the only one in that Muslim town. 'Church' is what they called it, but in reality it was a sand-filled, high mud-walled compound with a variety of shed spaces on two sides. One such space was a canteen by day and a church by night.

Every country has its underbelly, and in Dongala I met Sudan's. There, in that enclosed haven for Southern Christians, William, from far away Malakal, gave me such a gracious welcome as if he and his group had been anticipating my arrival for a long time. If Dr Essam had the tenacity to keep a hospital going, William was equally tenacious in keeping alive a place of welcome and respite for his Southern 'brothers and sisters'…and, of course, any passing stranger. They came North to work, just like John Azambi at Station 14, but more often than not found little, or found discrimination instead.

Like oil and water, the black-skinned Christians from the South did not mix well or at all with the lighter-coloured Muslims in the North. Whether Dinka or Nuer, up here they were in the same boat, though too often, to release frustration, their own intense feuding rivalry broke out to no one's benefit. During those five days in that hot rectangular open space, screened from the outside world by mud walls and tin sheeting, I got to know William's gentle, unassuming compassionate nature and his core of steel.

Uniquely, he saw beyond his tribal roots and wished for an independence for the South, but one where all its tribes could work together. William worked every hour he could, humping sacks of produce on and off trucks. I accompanied him once to collect his wages from his employer. The fat man in a laundered white *jalabiya* sat on a high stool and was more than surprised to see a European come through the door with his employee, but it changed nothing. 'Less than what it should be,' was William's assertion, opening his fist to show me his measly lot for the week. 'You ask what I can do,' he laughed in response to my naive questions about 'protest' and a 'fair wage'. 'It is part of what we face here, do you understand?'

Back in what they all called 'The Club', he would organise food and delegate jobs before focussing on the real work of the day, study and prayer. His own dream was to become a university student in Khartoum. 'I would like to become a teacher,' he proudly said. 'You're half way there William,' I answered. He had procured a blackboard and fixed it to an outside wall, where literacy and numeracy came to life with broken sticks of chalk. Throughout the day under an intense blue sky, others came and went, some adding to, some just staring at the lesson. Into the night he would teach the younger ones to read, spending hours under the oil lamp, and from my place in the shadows against the opposite wall, I looked at him, encouraging them. It was no surprise that by the second evening I was well and truly roped in to add my tuppence-worth to educational progress.

To walk with the perceived underdog was a new experience. William and his close friend Mary took me through the busy market and down a side street to their out-of-the-way eating place. As we passed, the eyes of some Muslim traders took note. I had had an almost entirely Islamic-centred cultural exchange coming down, many Muslims speaking of 'the war' and 'the tribal conflicts' beyond the vast marsh of the Sudd. Indeed, there were two worlds in one country and it felt, walking that dusty Dongala street, that I was walking along the bruised and untrusting border line between them both. I had no problem in doing so, and though there was a sense of switching sides, I was impartial.

In the eatery, dark-skinned Southerners of various tribes sat at metal tables, men and women, though women mostly went to a different room. Mary joined them. Over bowls of millet and hot milk I listened to our mutual universal story—the yearning for one's ancestral place. Each of those gathered added something new about the South, the sky, the weather, the food, the people, even the donkeys! 'Everything there is better than the North…you will see,' they said, 'you will see.'

A tall man came to our table. Beside my bowl of millet he placed a larger bowl of *marissa* beer, said something with a smile, then walked off. I asked William's brother Abraham what he had said. 'I do not know,' said Abraham, 'He is Dinka, I do not know their language.' Until that moment I was unaware that I sat at the Nuer table. Old tribal tensions, old bitter rivalry, goes on and on even here, so far away from their homes. 'One week ago a Dinka man was killed outside here and I am very sad for this,' said William.

Watching me as I slurped my *marissa*, William let it be known, more I thought for his young brother's ears than mine, that *it* was too often to blame for the inter-tribal brawls or worse. He did not drink it anymore. 'Alcohol is alcohol,' he said and warned me not to be deceived by the innocent-looking light-coloured cocoa-tasting brew, akin to an alcoholic porridge. Would that they could all share their same sense of loss and longing for their mutual home-land over a few bowls of *marissa* beer—to talk and sing and smooth historical hatreds. So I innocently mused, spooning milky millet from one bowl and slurping marissa from the other. With guys like William, maybe it would be possible. Abraham though, light hearted as ever, lightened the subject. 'It is the women who make the beer,' he said. 'to earn money.' He spoke of 'the women's well-guarded secrets...to make it well', and how their menfolk would ask them to make beer for 'a party', at which no woman could attend. I imagined what would be said at home if friends turned to their girlfriends or wives to ask for a fresh brew 'for the lads' and the football game at the weekend. 'Take a jump' would probably be the reply.

Back in the compound, school space became church space. Three benches were positioned on the earth floor in an area the size of a semi-detached front room. Psalms were sung in Nuer to the rhythm of two drums. I felt an out-sider, an onlooker-guest until William turned to ask if I would 'honour them' by reading Paul's Letter to Titus from his own English language version. 'Can you please explain it to us' he asked. Knowing nothing at all about Titus I stood behind the homemade lectern and gave it my best shot. Afterwards when we all sat around the flames leaping from a split fifty-gallon drum, I suggested priest-hood rather than teaching to William. 'You'd make a good priest, William, just like Titus.' 'The Lord will decide,' he said. Mary brought *chai* and I sipped it slowly, half listening half reflecting, while the four of them spoke in Nuer, its syllables and sounds rising and falling with the flames.

Suddenly Abraham turned and led the others in regaling me with all the possible 'nasties' in the South, as if they had decided to balance the picture of paradise that they had earlier painted of their country. Stories of bad bats, dangerous spiders, poisonous snakes, biting ants, malaria, hidden land-mines and maverick young soldiers. 'Ah, but do not worry, Mr John, you will have no problems with this,' said the older, wiser smiling William. I wasn't sure whether they were just taking the piss or genuinely forewarning me. One never knows in another culture. Whatever about ants or bad bats, it was land-mines and boy soldiers that filled my head as I lay on a sheet of cardboard for the night. Yet these unlikely dangers eventually dissolved away, and I imagined the 'green' they also spoke of. Green, green, green—oh how I missed that colour. My eyes closed and I floated over emerald fields of long wavy grass, '... tomorrow... tomorrow I leave here,' were the final words that floated me into sleep.

How should you act when someone, who cannot really afford to, puts money in your hand, looks at you straight and says, 'Take this'? I bucked, refused, insisted and tried to push it back. I gave all and every reason how I did not need it and could not take it. 'We are all brothers in Christ. You must take this,' said William. 'Christ indeed,' I thought, 'what would *he* do?' But it was Mary who nailed me. In the five days there, I had never heard her speak, not once, not a single word. I knew she was no relation to William, wasn't his wife or girlfriend, just a young women who came there to convalesce from some 'brutality' as he had put it. She uttered one word, 'Please'. I took the money. William smiled and we embraced. She knew what it meant to him.

★★★

A journey is a mental game. The easy part is dealing with the physical way in front of one's nose. Whether you can see it clearly or not, it's there waiting, dead ahead or a day ahead or a week ahead. It breaks down into varying sized bits, and one bit just follows the next. Daily bits might be pushing the bike to 'that telegraph pole' a hundred metres away or to 'those trees' a kilometre away or getting to a village forty kilometres away, before taking a break. It's easier when you can see the goal in real-time or within a few hours, but when the route is challenging and over a few weeks, it's best to pick an obvious town as a psychological marker, a lighthouse so to speak. Dongala had been my first lighthouse on the way through Sudan. A lighthouse along the Nile, and now I was leaving it, heading out into the ocean of possibilities where the narrow line of life I drew intersected or sometimes engaged with a myriad of others. Everything and anything could happen. and I let go a little more, letting go to be vulnerable, for that's when travel really begins.

The other part, the internal part, goes on inside your head, sometimes quietly, sometimes explosively, and at times being sparked by people like William. I departed Dongala thoughtful and questioning...his values, my values, money, morals, gratitude and how to receive and why those who have little invariably give, and other such timeless questions. Many would ask later, 'And what did you think about day after day? You must have been so bored.' Bored, bored? No, not that. Every other imaginable emotion, but not boredom. Round and round a velodrome, now that would be boring. Yet I found it difficult to say what it was I thought about, like asking yourself what were you thinking about last year, or ten years ago. You ponder in the moment, thrash things out in the moment, and allow things brew in the moment after moment after moment. Cycling week upon week, you enter a paradox: there is continuous change on the outside, but inside there is a timeless state where events, conversations, heartfelt connections and inspiring happenings merge into a singular complex experience, a matrix where *you* are at the still-centre-point of your own world as you move continuously through it.

Today (2016) I read with a wry smile how mini-groups and even peletons of cyclists are almost queuing up to trundle in convoy down a smooth road to Khartoum, on a 'trek' through Africa. How much more any one of them would experience if they left the group, the road, the security, the cultural bubble and trusted themselves to find their own way, alone and by a different route. I read the blogs, the constant updates, the websites, and feel sad at the almost desperate need to spew out as quickly as possible and tell the whole world 'the what and the where'. Better to chill out, cut the cord or cable and just be there, wherever it is. To get under the skin of one's journey takes time, and time alone. So many now go in groups, even those who go separate to the organised tours seem to go with a friend or friends. Kitted out in sponsored gear (even lycra!), helmets, speedometers, heart monitors, GPS, even satellite dishes, for God's sake…and some even with a back-up truck to carry the kitchen sink! I ask what is it all about, but remind myself how the travel world has changed utterly, or indeed the World has changed utterly. I recall what Ted Simon and Dervla Murphy said, though in different ways, 'to be grateful, eternally grateful to have travelled in that pre-tech World'. It was often physically more demanding, but so much simpler on both sides of the travel divide, that of the one passing through and the ones in situ.

I wonder about travel today, for those who wish for something different. There is the commercial, the slick, the smooth and costly, the dumbed-down and safe, the symbiotic liaisons between sponsor and traveller. It's all there, and in any format you want, it would seem. For those who ventured out before the advent of the communication revolution, before the minefield of sponsorship and the plethora of business interactions—for those, travel was very different and it raises a question. Is it difficult to travel today, difficult to cut the technological umbilicus, difficult to allow oneself to go solo, to be vulnerable and trusting? Who would want to do that? But that is what you have to do if you want a great and even a possibly seminal life experience for all the effort you are going to invest. For those who want that, the bottom line is to do it alone, quietly, on the back roads, and yes, without technology. Bury the phone so deep in your pannier you won't want the hassle of digging it out. Pretty soon you may even forget it's there as the real journey takes over.

★★★

So, it was farewell to the guys in the workshop who, on that first day in town, had solved the derailleur nut problem. Farewell to the old man who patched my shorts. Farewell to Abraham, Mary and William. Farewell to five days of rest. The track out of town was joyously firm, and I honestly rode it with a feeling of having just arrived in Sudan. It takes time to 'enter' a country, to relax enough to notice and enjoy the small things. It was 22 February 1986. Khartoum was the next lighthouse in my mind-map, more than 700 kilometres away. It would take fifteen days of on-and-off slog, a two-day river trip from Al-Dabba to Merowe and an eventful crossing of the Bayuda desert to that last leg from Shendi to Omdurman and finally Khartoum. I would arrive there as sick as a dog, but for now I was departing Dongala feeling strong, fit and ready once again.

Chapter 4
Shukran to the women

The firm track ended a few kilometres out, then the on-off stretches began. Nothing for it but get off and drag. It wasn't a problem, and I noticed how those fine four-letter expletives of those first dragging days had melted away. I was chuffed with myself. There seemed less mental resistance to doing what had to be done, but then the *nimta* came like a slap in the face from a Dojo master. Just when I thought I had everything sussed, a cloud of black midges swept all over me and I yelled obscenities worse than before. 'Ye bloody black bastards.' They drove me utterly, utterly crazy. At noon I stopped in the shade of a wizened old acacia, but the buggers were too much so I kept on going. Lapland again came to mind, riding into the light of night to avoid them. I calmed down. 'A midge is a midge,' I thought. Arctic or desert, they're all the bleedin' same.'

In some village I shared the shade of a *sabel* (water vessel) with an elderly man, and in wonderful pidgin English we chatted about scorpions, the big guys and the small guys. He strolled off and returned with a big guy, then sent a young lad off to get some small ones. I'd seen those everywhere but didn't know what they were. Thankfully they wouldn't hurt a fly, but as for the big guys…'*Mish kuwayis, mish kuwayis* (not good, not good)', said the man with a grin. With a wipe across the back of my neck, I gathered sweat and dead midges in my hand. Taking one between my fingers I held it up for him to see. He laughed, pointing to the date palms. 'Ah, of course,' I blurted. They were the dreaded date palm midge and they came with the date season. So just like me they also loved the *balah*. From then on, I cursed at them less, and bit by bit, like a bull with flies round his nose, I practiced the deep meditative art of letting them be as they hovered incessantly and tormentingly before me.

By evening, at the far end of Teiti village, a mosque minaret stood like a beacon. I drew closer and closer until two men in white walked out to pay greeting, then a group gathered and then as suddenly they all excused themselves for prayer. In fading light I sat against the mosque wall watching children play. A teenage boy brought tea on a platter and I was guided to a place in the courtyard to sleep, the same boy pumping up water from a well so I could wash sweat and flies from head and shoulders. He handed me the bucket, then scampered up a free-standing brick stairway leading nowhere. From the top he called out in his soprano voice to all who wished to come and pray for the final time that day. He seemed too young to be a *muezzin,* but I guessed that things, as everywhere in the world, were more flexible in the so called 'sticks'.

Ten men came to stand in line, the elder leading, they answering. Afterwards, some sat to eat. Trays appeared from the darkness. More tired than hungry, I ate modestly. Then tea with sugar came, the *de facto* conclusion of every meal, and the talk began. It takes energy and focus to converse without a shared language. It is hard work. To those who offer their food, their shelter and their humanity, they at least need to know who you are and why you are there. That you may have done so ten times already that very day is no excuse. I answered those same usual questions until the older man saw the tiredness in my eyes and called a halt to proceedings. He motioned me to rest then turned and said something to the young boy. Moments later the boy returned with a tiny radio in his hand and two words in English, 'Your country, your country.'

'Wow, what…a coup d'etat in Ireland?' I thought, but no, nothing that exotic. I accepted the pocket radio with a gracious *shukran*, knowing there was no point in explaining that 'my country' was simply too far away to listen to its radio stations.

Yet that palm-sized black wireless did tell a story. It woke me to what so often goes on behind the scenes. I thought of those unsuspecting, unprepared hosts who worked equally hard to make such a brief stay as homely as possible. All the women who I'd never seen and who, out of the blue, were asked to prepare food for some *khawaja* passing through. It was ironic that often a more 'welcoming' welcome was given by those for whom I was but 'that passing stranger' than by friends of friends who half expected me. The little radio reminded me of what people do for a traveller, especially in Muslim countries, but that night even my most welcoming hosts had no control over the frogs! Near the river a thousand of them made love-noises through the night, and I lay twisting and turning, exhausted and full of tea, while nearby loud snoring from a window rubbed salt into my sleepless wound.

I could not be certain when slumber came but am certain when it broke. At 5am an eye opened to see an old man shuffle from the shadows. He had not been part of the group the evening before but with steady care he mounted the steep holy stairway. From step to step his right hand led the way, his left lifting his greyish *jalabiya*. He stood erect on top with both arms raised, and I heard him clear his throat to suck at the chill dawn air. His voice called out to wake the faithful, an old lone voice falling across those few homes by the river, and I was transfixed by the beauty of it and riveted by his truth. In the timeless state I was already in, nothing separated the boy and old man, as if their lives were as one. The boy from the evening before had become the old man of the morning. A whole lifetime passed before me, boy to man to old man, one timeless voice calling out the *adhan*. Four men waited in line as the old timer slowly descended, step by step, there being nothing to hold onto, one of the younger men guiding him off the last step. Then, as they all turned to face Mecca, I turned to face the wall and one last-ditch attempt at sleep.

Breaking fast is not a big event in this land. People begin with a humble *chai-leban,* a milky tea to you or me. Breakfast proper comes later, at 9.30 or 10am. Not to embarrass anyone, I surreptitiously ate the other half of my pot of rice from the day before, which tasted okay. By 8am the day was already warm, and a blistering blaze of blue sky stretched from horizon to horizon. Half way between two villages I passed a large area without obvious boundaries where small mounds of stone and dry dirt covered the dead. Some were adorned at the head with a larger stone about a foot high and some had smaller round stones painted in colours around the edges. I saw this go by with the joy of being able, for once, to sit on the saddle and cycle. The way was firm. I felt good, and even waving to the goats did not feel crazy. They poured out of their wooden pens after the night, a few chasing each other across my path. On my left, children ambled to school, as they do everywhere. Sandwiched between their randomly spaced homes and the river was a hundred-metre strip of fertile land. It was already busy, men working here and there on various plots of beans, corn, and what looked like a legume crop for the animals. Sudan is no Egypt; the growing of things is even more tightly focussed, with the sight and sense of the vast Sahara everywhere.

By 10am it was hot, and my headband, pretty much useless, could absorb no more. Sweat dripped like a leaking tap, falling from my forehead onto the sunglass lenses. The right lens had a diagonal crack running from top right to bottom left. Drops would run down along the crack line onto my nose, then drip off its tip onto the cross-bar, then down to the crank-shaft and finally fall off the bike into the ocean of sand below. For fun I would count them to see how far I'd get before the next drop hit the deck. Crazy, but at times sanity had to be protected at all costs, even at the risk of going nuts!

The track played its on-and-off games, soft then firm then soft again, 50 metres on, 150 off, 20 on, 200 off. That's how the morning went. Moving became trudging, minutes became hours, time timeless—5, 15, 20 kilometres, it made no difference. I passed a dead donkey half buried in sand and recalled three living ones I'd seen that morning near El Khandaq. One had its hind leg deliberately tied to a wooden peg, and was unable to move to nearby shade. Another, in the worst scene I had witnessed, was purposely tied out of reach of a bucket of water in heat that was around 37 Celsius. I saw its lips move, its eyes plead, while fifty metres away its 'friend' munched on all the fodder it could in glorious shade. What to do? To to cut the rope, push the bucket closer? The homes were but a stone's throw distant. and there was neither sight nor sound of anyone. 'Who is going to see me?' I thought. 'No one.' But I just stood there, looking from the dying donkey to the homes, listening to a raging debate in my head. 'Do something, ya bollox, do something…no, this is not my business…don't know what's going on here, gotta pass on…for Christ's sake, move the bucket…it's not my business…bloody coward.' Torn up, I moved on, but the scent of shame followed me all day, and each time I reached for the bottle of lukewarm water, the donkey was there in my mind's eye, it's lips cracked just like mine.

I reached Al Goled Bairi by 6pm, stopping by a sandy soccer pitch. Barefoot boys kicked ball in the twilight but the game ended abruptly when they saw me. We talked as best we could, then moved close to the light of a tiny stall-cum-shop where I began to prepare food. '*Laa, laa, laa,*' (No, no, no), they chimed in unison, one lad waving his hand to stop me. Apparently someone somewhere was cooking up something…for me. Minutes later a round silver tray with its *tabaag* cover like a Chinese hat made from palm leaves was placed on the ground. I wondered how food could have been prepared so fast. One of those boys must have left the soccer pitch when I arrived over an hour before and run to his mother to ask her to prepare a meal for a *khawaja* on a bike. I found that generosity extraordinary; it was simply off my hospitality scale. I hadn't asked for anything, just wanted a safe space to set up the stove. Only then I understood what others meant by the hospitality of this country.

In the full-on light from the shop, the *tabaag* cover was lifted to reveal a splendorous display of nourishment. Steam rose from a dish of okra stew beside a small bowl of parsley-sesame paste, a bowl of mashed fava beans, a giant tomato and some flat breads (…*and again my older self says to all those women who may by now have passed away or who are still here in this life, who prepared such wonderful food, women who I never set eyes upon or who* never *saw me…shukran, shukran, thank you, thank you. These words are to honour you too.*) Inevitably, I ended up in a back room behind the shop. Not long after I turned off a gas lamp, the door opened quietly. Two of the soccer boys entered. One lit a match to see if I was asleep, then pointed out the *ageela* (the bike) to his friend. They spoke in a whisper pointing to this and that. I kept quiet, not wishing to startle them and shatter their special moment.

★★★

Allahu Akbar
Ashhadu an la ilaha illa Allah
Ashadu anna Muhammadan rasul Allah
Hayya 'as-salah
Hayya 'al-falah

As-salatu khayrun min an-nawm.
Allahu Akbar.

God is the greatest. I acknowledge that there is no god but God. I acknowledge that Muhammad is the Messenger of God. Hasten to prayer. Hasten to salvation. Prayer is better than sleep. God is the greatest.

The a*dhan*, the call to prayer, entered my brain at 5am. For months I'd been woken by its deep rhythmical *aah* sounds (*la ilaha illa Allah*) . There is no escaping it. As the bell tolls in the lands of the Christian or the *shofar* horn is blown in Jewish ceremonies, the *Adhan* seeps into one's psyche in the lands of the Mussulmen. Unconsciously expecting it, I allowed it wash over me, even at that early hour. The sixth line says how prayer is better than sleep. Maybe, maybe, but I never could break free of my warm cocoon of rest. By 6am I had returned to the depths.

I heard no one enter, but tea and a jug of water were on the floor when I woke. Rubbing sleep from my eyes, as I squatted over a long-drop, I pondered the day ahead. One thing was certain, it would be hot and *hot* it was. I followed the truck-tracks, as more often than not they cut straight lines rather than following the curves of the river. By 10am the heat intensified and the cloud of midges round my head must have looked like a black quivering helmet. They did not seem to bite, just hung about tracking every sweaty step. Why were they so removed from the river, I wondered? Midges in Ireland preferred moist, boggy places out of direct sun, the polar opposite of these guys. I flailed at them with my sweat rag, shouting like a mad man—'Bugger off, will ye, and suck ye'er effin dates'—but after each flail they merely regrouped and seemed to grow in number with every outburst.

'You're a bloody masochist…no I'm not, this is adventure…oh, come on, you wouldn't be doing this unless you…ah, shut up this is the best thing I've ever done.' Strangely, despite the internal monologue and the annoyance of midges, I honestly felt pleasure in where I was. It was everything I could never have known I wanted, and never could I have anticipated the absurdity of it and the challenge.

Out toward the horizon the sky looked as if it was being sucked downward into the ground, where a liquid mirage shimmered. The sky above and the desert below melted into each other as a pool of heavenly blue penetrated the hazy yellowness of a trillion-trillion grains of sand. By mid-day it was too hot to scratch, but by afternoon, in a teacher's room, I took a siesta. They had seen my human shape a half mile out and sent two students on donkeys to 'fetch the crackpot from the oven'. When they reached me I was under a small prickly bush offering enough shade for a child, with my legs stuck out in the sun, each one covered by a tapestry of odd garments. The youngsters waved their arms for me to follow, rattling on in Arabic, imagining I understood everything. 'Wherever the hell they want to take me,' I thought, 'it's surely better than staying under this bush.' So off we went, my donkeyed chaperones galloping ahead as I slowly pushed behind.

Two teachers stood at the school gate, watching our approach. Once they saw my state, I was ushered to their rest room with great fuss, the 'chaperone' boys being sent off for something or other. The room was spartan: two cot beds, two hand-made wooden chairs beside a simple square table, a bookshelf of planks, a picture of a former class on the wall, but the teachers' aliveness more than made up for the lack of fancy furnishings, and I had barely finished the welcoming cup of milky tea when they opened up their dream of revolution against the Nimeiry government.

Stretched on the rough home-made beds, and happy that I was no tell-tale spy, they spoke of anger and revolt. I became their sounding board, and they wasted no time in venting at Nimeiry, his government's direction and its salary priorities. In less than a minute I got their drift.

'Nimeiry,' said one, 'he wants to keep the people in their place. With education they might get ideas. He pays the army and police far more than us teachers.'

'I get 30 dollars per month and I need to grow my own food to survive,' said the other. As he spoke I noticed two mice under his bed but said nothing. One of the 'chaperones' entered, bringing a lit cigarette for one of them.

What they said was true. Nimeiry was a military man and had taken control of Sudan in 1969 by the well-trodden, blood-stained path of the African coup. In 1981 he allied himself to the Muslim Brotherhood and two years later he imposed Sharia Law on all Sudan. From Christians like William in Dongala to liberal Muslims like Dr Hassan and Maher, I knew this was causing serious problems. Imposing a strictly Islamic law on non-Muslims was asking for trouble. Flogging, stoning and other gruesome ways of righting apparent wrongs are valid under Sharia, but John Garang and his SPLA down South were having none of it.

Why was it any concern of mine? Because it was another strand in re-igniting the war between the Christian/animist South and the Muslim North, and this instability would scupper my plan to travel overland to Juba. In fact, four weeks after I left Ireland, Nimeiry had declared a state of emergency in Sudan, so I knew going overland was a very long shot, but there could be no final decision until I reached Khartoum. Thus I listened carefully to anything these teachers had to say on the bigger political picture. Little did any of us know, as we languished on those rough beds, that not two months later Nimeiry would go as he came, by the path of the coup. He was ousted while in the US getting cash from the IMF to 'save Sudan'. Still watching mice under the bed, I tried to make light of their intensity, telling them I had received more dates and cups of tea from teachers than the military and I would thus support any insurrection! 'When do we march on Government Buildings?' I asked.

By 4pm it was cool enough to move, so out the gate I sallied forth, pushing of course and accompanied by a teacher on the school donkey, '... to show you the best way,' he said. There really was only one way but it was his 100 square metre plot of vegetables that he really wanted to show. Down in a two-metre deep pit where a pump sucked water from forty more metres below, his vegetables looked happy. It was an oasis of cooler air below ground level, and he was rightly proud of his crops: corn, onions, tomatoes, aubergine, radish, hot peppers, okra and others I had no name for. I never asked who dug out the enormous pit, but what a neat idea.

For much of that late afternoon my right arm ached, dragging at the saddle. I would shake out the tingling pins-and-needles then change to the left and drag on. In the distance a woman stood alone. She pulled at something, her black *thoub* swishing with the effort. As I drew closer I saw what she was doing: hauling water from a deep well. She motioned me to drink, and drink I did. Oh so cool and pure compared to the awful stale stuff in my bottles. She was as aware as I of the approaching darkness. *Chai* was the only word she uttered, pointing toward her home, but I declined her offer, shaking my head with lots of *shukrans*. What must she have thought as I pushed on into the dark is anyone's guess. How utterly surreal it must have been for her to even contemplate inviting a foreign white man to her home and at night, but then weird and wonderful situations often break taboos.

In the far distance a green light on top of a minaret guided like a lighthouse, indeed it encouraged every step. The minaret was in the village of Kankalab and Kankalab, so I had been informed, translated as either 'There are dogs' or 'There were dogs'. I never found out which but hoped it was the latter. Way behind me and way ahead lay the faint lights of habitation. To my left, a whole section of river was in darkness but for a scattering of individual lights, telling me that few people lived along here. To my right was the deep dark of the desert while arching above was a star-studded night. Along the western horizon the Plough lay flat like a saucepan, and the North Star was lower than I'd ever seen it. The air was now cool and my skin relished the change. Somewhere in front of the front wheel there was a stoney piste track. I rode slowly, keeping sight of it by averting my vision. It held firm for two, three, four hundred metres. I could hardly believe it. That sacred green beacon atop the minaret was now perhaps two kilometres away and all I wanted was to get to it and rest…but then, as if some god or Allah-almighty decided to piss on my progress, a sound came…a sound that every cyclist hates but knows so well. It came hissing like a snake in the desert grass. The rear tube had had enough.

Torch batteries were too feeble to fumble around in a pitch-black repair-mode, and my candle was no match for the light breeze. What to do came quick. A few hundred metres of dragging beats a few thousand any day, so I let my green-beacon go and took off, perpendicular to the track, straight for those nearest homestead lights, and prayed the Kankalab dogs, if there were any, were sound asleep.

What goes through the mind as you push a bike across the sand at night towards an unsuspecting home? Not much really, bar thoughts of what kind of reception might be in store. Trudging toward the light, I recalled one night coming off a mountain in the wrong place, going to the farmhouse to ask permission to pass through their yard, then being asked in for tea, and several hours later being driven to where I needed to be, on a full stomach! That was Ireland, but people are people everywhere; even if you *do* knock on their door after dark, lost or in need, whoever opens will see in an instant *who* and *what* you are, if you are true or threat.

In that mile-long stretch of river there were just three homes looming before me and they had no idea someone was closing in on one of their rear doors. Which would I go for? An opening to an enclosed courtyard showed itself, and as I pushed the bike through, a crouching toddler stood up in shock. He ran screaming through an inner gate. It clattered closed. 'Bollox,' I blurted, 'just what I didn't want to happen.' At the second home, a boy of about nine squatted by a *kanoon* (stove), stoking the charcoal. I made sure I did not shock him also, so I coughed my presence and in my best Arabic uttered *masaa al kheir* (good evening). Surprise could hardly do justice to his reaction, but at least he didn't run or scream. I wanted to say something like, 'Would you go in home like a good boy and tell your daddy I'd like to talk with him please, thanks. Off you go now, good lad!' Then in my perfectly ordered imagination I would politely wait for dad to come and explain my simple needs. Naturally he'd completely understand and say, 'Yes, of course, mister, make your camp over there and I'll bring you water, hot milk and a fresh boiled egg.' Real life and daydreams forever askew.

Instead of dad, two women came, grandmother and mother, with children peering from behind their *thoubs* while following hotly though feebly behind came granddad with his walking stick. 'Oh God,' I thought, 'I've shaken up a whole family here. Should have stayed out in the desert.' Yet within the hour and within the confines of their sandy yard I had made camp where directed, had a hot bowl of *ful* beans on my lap and made no more fuss than a stray dog with a bone and, like any stray given a bit of kindness, I slept a sound sleep on a full belly.

The gentle memory of granddad preparing his mat for his morning prayer stays with me to this day. A backdrop of red dawn defined his frail frame and that of an old palm tree behind him. The scene would have drawn reverence from a stone. He stood to one side out of my view and called all who wished to come. No one came, and I wondered had anyone ever joined him. Then he came himself, as it were, and stood before his mat, raising one hand to his ear as he mumbled his prayer. The other hand held his walking stick to keep balance, for he could no longer do the complete set of movements. Such devotion I had never witnessed, and had he spontaneously combusted into a blaze of pure white light, it would surely have passed as nothing but the ordinary. As to the source of a tingling in my skin, perhaps it came from a feeling of privilege or honour or wonder or all three…at being present in the shadows as a silent witness to the simplicity of an old man's devotion.

★★★

'Al Badja, Al Badja, Al Badja'—for two days that's all anyone said, pointing to the bike and wagging their fingers. One man, to make his point, took a fist-full of sand, letting the grains run through his fingers while laughing the words, 'Ibil, ibil, ha-ha-ha, ibil.' I presumed *ibil* meant sand. Later I learned it meant camel. He was either telling me to get a camel or that El Badja was for camels. Regardless, by the time I reached the southern end of Kankalab I'd had enough. There's no doubt that being able to mime is a handy tool to have while on the road, but I was never a great mimer. My effort at miming 'a truck' humoured a bunch of old-timers to no end. They sat in the shade of a gable wall, swinging their legs from a raised bench, smiling and nodding at me, not having a clue in the wide world as to what my gesticulations might mean…that is, until I picked up a fist of sand and pointed in the direction of Al Badja. Then they became intrigued and their heads locked together in collective discussion. Out of their debate came two infamous Arabic words, *bukra, bukra* (tomorrow, tomorrow), but with some further discussion it was democratically deemed that *ba'd bukra* (day after tomorrow) was a more likely ETA for any truck attempting to cross Al Badja. I'd been warned that *bukra* did not necessarily translate into a strict sense of 'tomorrow', but could just as well mean some point in the future. Where that left *ba'd bukra*, I was afraid to guess…in the lap of Allah no doubt.

I settled in the shade beside them and got on with miming other things while waiting for *bukra* or *ba'd bukra* or whatever else came along. At that time waiting for a truck was a bit like waiting for an unofficial bus with no expectations either of being picked up or when it might arrive, and that was *absolutely* fine. Patience was no longer an issue. It *would* come, whenever; that's all I needed to know.

From an adjacent house a guy my own age appeared. He was the grandson of one of the men and in flawless English he greeted me. After learning my nationality the conversation went quickly down the path of literature. He was an economics graduate with an interest in, of all things, Yeats. I was as thrown by the seeming incongruity of that as much as he was baffled by the fact that not all Irishmen were fans of the famous bard. Kavanagh, my own favourite, meant nothing to him, so we chatted about their polarities, though he kept me well focussed on his own Irish hero. Between the talk of Irish poets he confirmed everything about the notorious Al Badja. It was a wide strip of, as he described it, 'terrible softy, softy sand' and was the bane of a trucker's day. From Kankalab they had to cross it to get to Al-Dabbah and the river ferry to Merowe. So, though Yeats was never my favourite Irish poet, chatting for a few hours about his life and work at the edge of 'softy, softy' has forever linked him in my mind to a place which is definitely not Sligo.

A truck came before sundown…so much for *bukra*! Bike and I were hoisted up, and with a few other passengers and a kid goat, we set off. Within the length of a football field El Badja struck the first goal and we were well dug in. The *turn boys* jumped down to dig us out and we were off again but not for long. Five times on the way to Al-Dabbah we stalled; each time those tough guys leapt down into 'softy softy' to dig out the wheels while the engine whined like an old mule. The fifth and final time was across the river from Old Dongala, the driver calling us all down to push. The kid goat was left on top to devour whatever it could, as we heaved in laughter and all our might. The truck took off and we ran, grabbing anything we could to clamber back on, for once a truck is moving it's moving.

Up ahead, fifty or sixty camels closed in on our path but the driver, with his boot to the floor, was not going to stop and risk a sixth stall. The herders called out. They rode their own camels and tried to push the herd faster but the beasts seemed indifferent to any danger. The trajectories of truck and herd bore down on each other. I got my camera ready but our truck powered by, as indifferent to camels as they to us. No blood was spilt, and as the last oblivious beast got out of the way with barely a metre to spare, one herder waved an angry whip.

J came to mind. I pictured her sitting on the sacks of beans, relishing every jolt, laughing at the craziness. Once she got into my head I didn't want to let her out, and for the remainder of that bone-crunching journey to Al-Dabbah, her smile, her laugh, her way, floated effortlessly above it all. The three and a half months to our rendezvous in Nairobi would not seem too long for her, or so I imagined, but for me, bouncing across the El Badja, the sheer scale of Sudan alone, quite apart from Zaire and the rest, pushed Nairobi into eternity. In the onrushing air, my old Palestinian head shawl flapped loose and snapped me back to reality.

In Al-Dabbah I asked the driver *bekam* (how much?). The question was met with his shaking head…no charge. He was going all the way to Omdurman, nine night hours of hard driving across the Bayuda Desert. If I wished, I could have been in Khartoum the following afternoon but I let the offer go. The Bayuda, well, I just had to taste it for myself. Leaning out his cab window he called to a shop merchant and pointed at me. The only words I caught were Wadi and *ageela*, the rest I guessed. Before the dust of his departure had settled, the shop owner had brought tea and had sent for someone to get someone to bring me somewhere. Pretty soon half the youngsters in the town had gathered round the bike while I, sipping *chai*, kept a watchful eye on things. The 'somewhere' was the humble place of residence of four young novice teachers from England and within their small compound I once again took a corner, glad to have a space to flop for a while.

Only one of the students could I relax and converse with, as it seemed my accent ruffled the others' cultural feathers. I had been too long out of Ireland and hadn't an inkling as to what was happening back home, north or south. Barely ten weeks previous the Anglo-Irish Agreement on Northern Ireland had been signed off by Irish and British leaders, Garret FitzGerald and Margaret Thatcher, causing a furore among Unionism. On that first evening with the students, in a rather pointed conversation, the 'war in Northern Ireland' arose briefly and there was nothing much I could say to deepen or broaden the context. Except for that one student, the minds of the others were as fixed and as blind as Thatcher's was about the complex cause of the so called 'war'. They spoke of the British army's 'duty' in Belfast and of 'terrorists'. That was enough. Thereafter I knew exactly where we all stood and decided to avoid the subtle animosity of the space and spend the days wandering about the town or reading in the Pink Cafe. It was a pity, but such were the times.

When I recall those Al-Dabbah days while waiting for the ferry, three things come to mind—Pepsi, prolonged solitude and 'The House of Obedience'. They have fused into a single, tangled memory. It was Friday, about noon, thirty-six degrees; in or out of shade didn't seem to make any difference, I sweated regardless. Ambling to the bank of the river I had to remind myself that *this* was still the Nile. It felt as if we'd been together for so long. The steamer pulled away, heading down river to Dongala. It would return to Al-Dabbah on Monday when I would board it to head up-river to Merowe. Watching it depart, leaving a dirty brown churned-up froth in its wake, I felt a familiar sense of solitude turn to loneliness. Home, family, close ones…their faces floated-by in the brackish water. That this feeling should come in a place where I could easily converse with native English speakers was ironic, but I knew it had nothing to do with that.

You don't travel solo unless you at least get on with yourself, yet the intensity of days, feeling like weeks or months, brings a new dimension to being alone. Sooner or later the *joie de vivre* turns inward and opposite. The journey's yin and yang I used to call it. Setting off on such a trip, solitude is the main 'ingredient', not loneliness, but loneliness will come for sure somewhere along the road, and in Al-Dabbah, 700 kilometres from Khartoum and nine months and ten days after setting out from home, it hit hard for the first time.

Al-Dabbah was then a town of about 15,000, an easy and pleasant place to walk around, and I walked around! It was hot and busy with traders trading, school kids coming or going, trucks and river craft bringing commerce and fumes. Today, like so many other towns in Africa, its population has spiralled to 52,000. Then there were few if any tourists, but of course there was the 'Pink Cafe', dubbed that by the English teachers because of its awful gaudy shade of pink. As I returned from the river to the teachers' compound, I diverted to present passport and papers to the police. Whatever else, at least it would be known where I'd got to in case anything should happen. At the far end of the main thoroughfare the cafe's pinkness leapt out and I realized the genius of the colour choice. As bright as a yellow daffodil in winter, it drew me down the street. Under its awning of pink-painted corrugated sheets I chilled out with a god-sent Pepsi and Juliette Minces' book *The House of Obedience*. Borrowed from one of the teachers, it was a mood-shifting book if ever there was one.

After all I'd experienced since entering the Islamic world in Turkey three and a half months before, her book opened a whole new vista to the lives of all those women who had catered for my needs behind the scenes. For my western-tutored mind, it was anathema to read of the veil, incarceration in the home, circumcision, forced marriage and, of course, the *pièce de résistance*...the *Bayt al-taa'*, 'the house of obedience'. If a wife left her husband even for some valid reason, he had the right to bring her back and, with the blessing of authority, place her in a house, room, apartment or whatever until 'she came to her senses' and returned to him.

Not all Muslim countries are the same in this regard, but those families who had welcomed me, where the women looked out from the shadows, having done their duty, those families I recalled. Rightly or wrongly, I felt they and

102

their menfolk were caught in the twin vice of Islam and tradition. I had always presumed that their hospitality came not from a sense of external imposition but a normal human desire to care for a passing traveller. Yet beyond a personal angle came the bigger questions—Islamic values versus western, and modernity or post-modernity versus tradition.

I knew well I was living the so-called modern life of the individual, completely responsible for myself and thus had to accept the quid pro quo of that deal—the sometimes solitude, isolation and separation from those one holds dear. That's the deal in the western model: do what you want, be what you want, act how you want (within reason), once you remember that the unhinging of family and tradition can bring that existential gut feeling of separation and even terrible loneliness to right the scales of balance. As Minces wrote, '…what room is there for modernity in societies where the very notion of an individual remains vague and where traditional structures are still so powerful.' Entwined with and built on a religious bedrock, as I witnessed in the Muslim world, those very traditional structures can be unshakable. A second Pepsi got me almost halfway, but as evening came I closed the book and walked. I walked with a feeling of having stepped behind a veil, to re-imagine the reality of a hidden world.

The following day was market day in Al-Dabbah and trader numbers quadrupled. Hand-crafted jewellery, fabrics and *thoubs* for the women, spices, foods, water urns, cookware, tools of all sorts, goats, camels and donkeys of course, to name but some items on display. I was back at the Pink Cafe, book and Pepsi in hand, wondering why Pepsi had the town to itself. The 'cola wars' between it and its obvious nemesis were always covert or overt, blatant or silly, and no one knew the half of it, but here in this part of Sudan, Coca-Cola was pawn to Pepsi's king. The former, though, would go on to dominate the African space. Yet my guess is that even today the top brass of both pray for a tidy resolution to the 'Sudan crisis'.

Gum arabic from the thorny Acacia tree is one of the secret ingredients of those sweet brown liquids. As an emulsifier, an edible glue if you like, it binds to sugar and keeps it in suspension, otherwise you would buy a can only to find all that sugar sitting at the bottom. And where do you find the best gum arabic? Sudan. As in the cotton industry days of Egypt one hundred years before, countries and corporations will always find ways to secure the passage of key raw ingredients, despite even war.

103

Unbeknownst to me, that day, 10 February, was special to Al-Dabbah for another reason. Sudan's presidential elections were in full swing and Dr Al Turabi was coming to town. Throughout the morning Toyota pick-ups full of young white-*jalabiya*-clad men roared up and down, blaring out their message, their bull dust settling on book, Pepsi and me. I was fed up with them, and so too some of the traders, yet no one said anything. Out of fear, as I was to discover.

Dr Al Turabi was the real brain behind the blanket Sharia law imposed by the Nimeiry government, the 'September laws' as they were named, and here was I reading about the impact of such laws on Muslim women. He was an out and out radical Islamist with an apparent slogan, 'Islamize modernity'. In the noughties I read with great interest how he would invite other jihadists to Sudan to strategize their agenda. Osama Bin Laden and Ayman Zawahiri were top of his guest list. They were also top of the FBI's list, No.1 and No.2 respectively, Zawahiri being the presumed brain behind the 9/11 atrocity. Turabi said later how Bin Laden was merely a businessman buying land in Sudan. Perhaps he was. Buying land for the training of al-Qaida operatives was probably business as usual for him. So Turabi was coming to town and even the minaret speakers were requisitioned to blare out his imminent arrival.

The boat to Merowe was due to depart at 6pm. The English teachers were off supporting their schoolgirls' basketball team in some local derby and I, in the shade of the Pink Cafe, turned the last chapter and sipped a last Pepsi. As if on cue, four black Range Rovers came thundering up from the far end of the street. The dust rose as they shot past, hooting and honking—*beep, beeeep, beeeep, beep*. Al Turabi had arrived. I watched them speed out beyond the town to a prepared marquee near the river. I had had enough of dust, so I popped a Nivaquine, washed it down with a final gulp and went back to pack.

At six there was no sign of the ferry. 'It will come,' said the green-uniformed soldier sitting beside me. We sat on a low wall looking eighty metres towards a white marquee in which cheered the whiter-than-white clothed dignitaries, enraptured by their hero. The boat came, and the last thing I heard as I wheeled the bike up the plank were the screams of delight from the basketball girls vying with the shouts of support for Al Turabi…young girls full of life having fun with a ball versus older fanatical men envisioning a radical Islam for all. It was time to go.

The ship was a twenty-metre double-decker with barges lashed aft and starboard. She manoeuvred her bulk out into the river, into the evening light. It felt good to be moving again and I knew a good chunk of the heaviness I had felt was stagnation. Motion, ah motion, I had got to know it well, but its opposite, stagnation, was new-found. Motion was my new tonic. I had underestimated how much I needed it and wondered how it would be at journey's end.

In the lower third-class deck beside the livestock, floor space was shared with two guys from Karima. A lattice work of palm planks separated us from the animals and to this I tied the bike. We would be two nights on board, plenty of time to settle and get to know each other. A goat put its nostrils to a crack, sniffing peanuts in my handlebar bag while one of the Karima boys felt the side of the pannier. 'Engine?' he said. '*Laa*,' I replied, '*laa* engine.' After that introduction we ate together, neither them nor I wishing to spend money on ship grub. Their bread of crushed dates, oil and wheat flour was delicious, but eating hard-boiled eggs shell and all was a first for me.

Near Abu Dom we pulled into the bank for the night. No navigation equipment, no night sailing. Sometime after 3am I fought a full bladder but lost and was glad. Half-naked on the deck I let go in relief, yet wishing to silence the splash as it hit the river below. The night was still, so beautifully still that breaking its tranquil peace seemed just not right. A meteorite streaked across Orion, cutting its belt in two, then another. I stood for a while hoping for more, but it was too chilly in boxers and vest, so I returned to the warmth of the sleeping bag and the earthy smell of animals, their cud-chewing, belching and explosive farting, along with the Karima boys in their full-throttle, synchronous snore. Surprisingly, it all blended like a lullaby, settling me back to sleep.

Abu Dom sits at the lower end of the Great Bend where the Nile swings northwards again, having coursed its way over the fourth cataract, past Karima and Merowe. Along with those infamous granite cataracts, the Bend is an unexpected feature of the river. For several thousand kilometres, out of Lakes Tana and Victoria, the Blue and the White flow north, right into the middle of a desert. Here the Bend begins. The great river turns south-west, inland and away from the sea. Then between Korti, Abu Dom and Al-Dabbah , as if it realises it's going nowhere fast, and to avert disaster, it turns north for the final 2,000-kilometre run to Cairo, the Delta at Alexandria and the Mediterranean Sea. Looking at my scuffed, creased Michelin map, I pondered what the outcome might have been for western civilisation had that Nubian tectonic plate shunted the Nile in a different direction and forced it westwards to empty itself into the Red Sea: no Egypt, no Egyptian culture, with the knock-on consequence for the Greeks and the rest of us. Hypothetical ponderings, but what *was* certain was that in between this enormous meander lay the Bayuda desert, 300 kilometres from one side to the other. Today a tarred road takes a car across in a few hours or three 100-kilometre bite-sized bicycle rides. In the mid-eighties, it was a glorious yet unforgiving week of drag and trudge for much of it, though beyond midway there were some stupendously beautiful ride-able sections through boulder-strewn scrubland and acacia-splattered savannah.

This tiny bit of the African trip had put fire in my belly two years before, when a new, spotlessly clean map was fingered for the first time across a cleared kitchen table. As the months of actual travel rolled on, 'Bayuda-imaginings' would occasionally come at night and in an odd way acted as another magnet pulling the journey onward. Now on a river boat heading up-Nile to Merowe, crossing it was no longer imaginary; it was so under my nose I could smell it.

All day we made headway against the current, the old engine chug-chugging while the Nile passed timelessly by. If ever there was a relaxed place to read and, if ever there was an appropriate book with which to do so, it was right there on that deck with that very book in my lap. With my backside to the rail and a pair of suspect Polaroids on, I turned a page of Alan Moorehead's *The White Nile*. It had been a parting gift from one of the English teachers, and like many such recommended books, my own copy (at home) had little chance of being read before leaving. Nothing is as three-dimensional, or even four-dimensional, as reading about a remote place when you are actually there, in it. At the turning of each page, I would look up, hardly believing where I was, half expecting a soldier-filled gunboat or a fleet of silent *feluccas* to appear out of history.

Moorehead had chiselled out that bit of history well. His words made it easy to picture Wolseley pushing hard past us, knowing the clock was ticking down for General Gordon. I flicked sweat from my brow to the river and considered that the barren bank yonder would have looked just the same in 1884, the sun just as hot and the murky waters just as steady flowing. Along those very banks, long, long before Wolseley, Kitchener, Baker, Livingston and their like came down here with so much 'agenda', the camel trains and *feluccas* went to and fro, and turbaned captains in full rig waved greetings to the camel men. They were

106

all brothers in transport and, oh, the silence…the silence that must have been when sail and camel passed each other in the dead of night.

To travel is to step into history, layer upon layer, buried beneath the surface of our seeing. Even to 'see' and attempt to comprehend the everyday routine in a strange country is challenge enough for the traveller, but to add some layers of what went before enriches that everyday present…from the humble cup of *chai* to the spaces where a people live, to what the generations gone by had to contend with. For me, of the many and extremely varied landscapes I travelled through, it was the empty desert ones which gave my imagination more license to roam back and forth through the histories, and yet I often struggled to comprehend what was right in front of my nose, knowing how nothing is as it seems.

There's nothing like a sticky mess to shove reality up your nose! That last day in Al-Dabbah , heat had liquefied a small jar of Vaseline and the contents flowed into *The White Nile*. It had oozed onto the book's binding and into its pages; what a mess. 'If it ever rains it'll be well protected,' I thought. Thankfully it was not to be returned, rather to be passed on to *any* other interested traveller. The book itself had a unique story and deserves a special mention. The teacher who proffered it into my hand, like a relay baton, suggested I might well have been the fifth or sixth traveller to be holding it. Some north-bound German had passed it on to him in Wadi Halfa, saying it had been given to him in Nairobi by some other traveller who had journeyed south. Indeed, inside the cover were the names of three other previous 'couriers' with well wishes to future 'Nile trekkers' to enjoy the read on a possible 6,000-kilometre journey.

I promised to continue the tradition and pass the book on to someone else heading north with an unwritten code that it would be read, looked after, then handed on to the next person who would do likewise. How chuffed Moorehead would be to know how his famous book about the Nile spent its days being read over and over by various travellers as they went up and down that very river. Maybe that book is out there still, battered and worn, being passed from soul to travelling soul, preserved by all that Vaseline from long ago!

★★★

Bouncing along the deck came a man's belly laughter. He was the ship's short, rotund postmaster, and his genuine smile cheered up all before him. He lingered to practice his German with a Polish-German archaeological team, on a break from digging in Old Dongala, but eventually he moved on and stopped where

107

I sat. His round shape put me in the shade. He had a decent grasp of English but first asked me, '*Sind Sie Deutsch?*' When I said Irish his eyes lit up and his smile stretched further. Apparently I represented a rare enough species in those parts.

His name was Abbas and he was in charge of the TPO, the travelling post office. On its wall he pointed to the inscribed name of 'another cycling-man from Europe'. I could hardly believe my eyes when I read, 'Arie Baas was here.' Wow, so Arie, last seen in Aswan, had taken the ferry too, fifteen days before. He certainly wasn't wasting any time. I added my own name, telling Abbas that soon dozens of other cyclists would contribute more graffiti to his wall. He seemed to relish the idea of a truly international and inspirational TPO. 'Come, eat,' he offered. His two melodious words were music to my ears, and in the galley we joined the crew for the afternoon meal.

To refuse sugar in Sudan is akin to refusing water. Sugared tea is *de rigueur*. Even Abbas pulled at his ear in wonder, but I insisted I had had enough. I pleaded how Sudanese sugar was the best in the world, 'Even better than that Egyptian stuff.' They liked that I played the national card. My back-up assertion that many in Ireland were giving it up was received with incredulous shaking heads. 'Eat, eat,' they said, but still being a novice at one-handed eating I didn't stand a chance. The speed of consumption was scary, five fast hands scooping all in sight. 'In my country we eat more slowly,' was my excuse for the slow pace. Abbas mumbled to the others, then pushed the remaining bits of meat to my side of the communal dish and laughter followed.

Back on deck the river banks went slowly by, as if it were they, not we, that were moving. On the western bank a lone man, silhouetted by the evening sun, stood near his pump. The pump belched black smoke into clear sky, its hose snaking down the bank into the river, sucking it up to somewhere. We watched each other pass and I raised my twenty-five piastres glass of *chai-leban* in his direction. He raised a limp hand in response, then turned to his pump. Some hours later, as light and life left the deck, the ship pulled close to the bank again and anchored for the night. The lights came on, and I descended the steel steps to sleep with my friends—four goats, a pair of donkeys, one camel and two egg-loving snoring bucks from Karima. For half an almost sleepless night, the snorting, munching sounds from this little menagerie became an acoustic backdrop to my Bayuda imaginings.

Chapter 5
Ali and Kabashi

The human chatter above became animated. Merowe was drawing close. Through a crack in the palm partition I slipped my last few peanuts to my favoured goat, shook the hands of the Karima boys, grabbed the bike and hit the main deck. Abbas was there, laden down with water jars. He needed help to carry them up the steep bank to his waiting Toyota box, so I did. 'Come to my house please, come, come,' he insisted, 'it is on your way.' By late afternoon, having trudged the five or six sandy kilometres, I arrived at his beautifully painted ornate front door. The door was recessed deep into a metre-thick, smooth-plastered mud-brick wall. In the cool within there was a warm welcome, when his wife and children were formally introduced, followed, of course, by the obligatory tea. His wife smiled as her husband explained how I took it without sugar!

Over tea his story came…a fall from a palm tree years before, a serious back injury, prayers to Allah and what I took to be his dark night of the soul…'Then after I became postmaster on the ferry I was the happiest man,' he said. He may have been the postman officially but deep down he was a date farmer. His bouncy, affable nature became sharply focussed as he described the intricacies of propagation and pollination. As with all fruits, it was all about males and females. Two male trees were enough to pollinate one hundred females, the male pollen sac being carried up and placed in close contact with the female parts. I jokingly asked was it from this the caliphs and sultans got their idea for harems? 'Maybe, maybe,' he chuckled, 'we have learned a lot from this tree.'

He called his son, told him to climb up to show how it was done. The teenager shimmied the fifteen-metre female as if out for an evening stroll. Abbas watched him and rubbed his rounded tummy, saying how once he could climb, 'but now I sit in a floating post-office sorting my letters, not my dates.' I asked if he was not afraid for his son. 'No, no,' he answered, 'My son knows the danger, he has seen my scar.' From up above the boy called out to his father, asking would I like some, but they were not ready, and anyway I wished to eat nothing.

Stomach rumblings all day had moved to a crescendo point, and later in Abbas's long-drop, and just in time, it felt as if my entire insides fell away. With both hands resting on a deflated delicate abdomen I lay listening to the same few dogs barking at each other, wondering how anyone could sleep. At precisely 3.17am, a second round of the runs beckoned and I shuffled to the long drop, feeling my way along the wall in total darkness while squeezing my anus tight. At 6.30 I made my way again to avert another rush. This time the long drop was occupied. Away from the house I squatted behind one of Abbas's old palms. Feeling there was nothing left to come, I looked between my bare feet to see two white wriggling worms. In mild shock I held the tree for support. It was the kind of shock you might have when you turn the key in your front door to find you've been burgled, that awful sinking feeling of intrusion, of intruders breaking through your defences.

At 7am, Abbas's fifteen year old son brought a glass of sweet *chai-leban* with bread and tahini. I didn't have the heart to explain how I could not eat it. 'Shukran,' I said, and when the boy departed I poured the sweet tea out a window and put the rest in the pannier. I scrubbed my hands vigorously and, to be blunt, I felt like shit. All I wanted was to lie down but did not wish to stretch the hospitality of my host and his wife, so I bid them farewell. He was a kind man, even insisting I pass greetings to Arie if I saw him. It was impossible to ride, so I pushed, turning once to wave. Abbas, his wife, son and two daughters stood together. He called out something in Arabic which I didn't understand. That was it.

I pushed my little world out onto the sand trail, away from the last of the homes, out into the Bayuda. 'Why didn't you stay, just tell 'em you needed rest…why go on…of course they'd let you, Christ you're a fucking eejit.' Fool or not, I felt weak, yet my concern was not for my well-being but rather how to cross the Bayuda feeling so shattered. I decided to starve the white buggers out, but in doing so would I have enough energy for the physical demands of the crossing?

A truck stopped. I declined the driver's offer of a lift, but he was equally adamant that it was sand all the way to Dengazzi where the road branched off to Atbara. My decisiveness was squashed, so up went the bike. We hadn't gone 500 metres when the truck broke down, the driver nonchalantly strolling off with a jerry-can, leaving me stranded on top. To escape the heat I climbed down to write the diary in the truck's shadier west side. He was gone for an age. Finally, tired of waiting, I decided to push on but then remembered where the bike was, three meters above the ground and I was too weak to lift it down. Nothing to do but stick my torso and my frustration under the chassis to escape the sun. Three men came riding and I hailed them. With their help, bike and gear were lifted down, then doffing my shrunken hat I pushed off, leaving them… wondering. Though weak, I needed to move, and if the driver returned to see me gone I didn't think he'd be too put out. He had probably forgotten he had picked me up at all.

A few more hours of dragging saw me enter the intense heat of early afternoon. Where was I? Perhaps 500 kilometres north of Khartoum, perhaps twenty-five out from Karima and Merowe, in a vast hot sand pit! The track was…well, there was no track, just a typical hundred-metre-wide truck-scudded way. One could take one's pick and push along any of those truck trails, as they all went in the same direction, but direction wasn't the issue, it was water. I had six litres from Abbas's well but was down to the last two. The diarrhoea had me drinking twice as much as normal and eating nothing, not even a date. I spoke to my friends on the inside, 'I know ye're in there and ye're finished…

going to starve ye out.' I told them to surrender, to come out with their hands up or tails up or whatever the hell they had. I talked to myself and to them, but at times the nauseous image of white worms slithering up and down my insides was too much and I'd sing some bawdy song to distract myself.

There were cycle-able sections but each time I mounted the saddle my bowels moved. The last time they had moved as much was on that long smooth road from Homs to Damascus, where trucks full of soldiers cheered at my roadside squatting and where diarrhoea had me wrecked and dehydrated. At least then there was company and water was easier to come by. Here, there was only the silent company of my shadow, and as for water . . . I looked ahead and behind, trusting some other truck would come.

(Recently a friend told me to check out a blog for, as he put it, 'an amazing crossing of the Bayuda'. I did—two cyclists on a straight, smooth, tarred road all the way to Atbara. All I could do was smile at the beautiful picture. 'Amazing' is such a relative term but to those cyclists who take that new smooth road I say again, spare a thought for those who crossed here before the road was even dreamed of, or better still, ride or try, for a few hours, on the sand parallel to that new road. There will be no faster way to appreciate its smoothness.)

Within the hour a truck did come and I gratefully accepted water and a lift. Eight kilometres out from Dengazzi, it halted at a usual pole and palm-frond *chai* stop no bigger than a rural bus shelter. The driver was going in a different direction, to Atbara, but his mute, simple-minded 20-year-old helper became upset and quite agitated by my un-wellness. In his own demonstrative way he pleaded with his boss to take me. With their tea and rest taken, the driver had to physically bundle the upset boy into the cab. I presumed he was telling him that I would not go. They drove off, the eyes of that sensitive soul fixed on me until I disappeared to him.

The *chai* boy who manned the station prepared another tea. '*Laa leban, laa sokar*,' I insisted. For him the request for no milk and no sugar was almost inconceivable so I repeated, with gesticulations. He tore a page from his pornographic magazine to restart the fire. Other pages full of bleached boobs and whiter than white asses from a parallel universe far, far way were strewn on the sand behind his *kanoon*. I imagined how his boss or passing drivers kept him well-stocked for his lonely vigils out here. He handed me the glass with a grime-ingrained hand, and instantly a thought flashed about hygiene and where his hands had been, but I snuffed it out. What was I going to do about it? Ask him had he washed his hands in hot soapy water or had the health inspector visited recently? He looked on fascinated as the drop of iodine darkened and diffused in my glass.

I sat in half shade, sipping the hot sweet-less liquid tasting of salt and iodine, a vile concoction which I believed would do me good. From this oasis of tea and pornography I thought I could see the hazy line of palm trees across a dead flat sand plain. Was that the river over there? Surely not, but apart from that there was nothing to catch the eye. For one helluva-hot hour we shared silence, not a word exchanged. I wondered how much he earned, if anything? Did he harbour a dream, to go to Khartoum, become a driver, a fisherman? For a short while he looked from bike to me, but as exotic as I must have been I was no match for a fresh glossy magazine. Off he went into fantasy, his eyes glazing over.

On my hairless knee a pair of black flies found each other and began to mate. I dipped a finger into the tea and lifting a drop, let it fall near them. They were too consumed or entwined to notice the splash and continued oblivious, and I, out of exhaustion or indifference or just letting things be, let them finish. They flew off into the heat, and I closed my eyes to images of white worms and *chai*-station masturbations before slipping into a soporific but thankfully restful siesta.

By 3.40 it was still hot but not as intense. It was time to move on. I gave the boy his due, and more, then got on with it, trying to ignore the state I was in. A half hour of dragging was tiring, to say the least. A thousand plus metres to the east, a pair of dust devils whirled over the sand plain like dervishes, and mirages were two a penny wherever I looked. Two trucks approached from opposite directions but again, let's be clear, this was no road. Each driver chose his own route across the sand, with at times quite a distance between them. I waved one on, and as the second came closer, the driver called out '*Tamaam?*' (Okay?) '*Tamaam, tamaam,*' I answered, for just at that point I hit a solid section and began riding. His co-driver looked on in disbelief. A third lorry passed and I accepted water from their large metal storage container suspended below the chassis. The driver pointed upwards to where his passengers gazed down, suggesting that I was welcome to join them. '*Tamaam,*' I repeated, and off they went. A fourth truck came, going in my direction and again the same offer, the same response. '*Tamaam, kuwayis,*' I would say. '*Mish kuwayis, mish kuwayis* (not good, not good),' came the driver's reply. I waved them on but they were right, it was '*mish kuwayis*', but not in the way they had meant. The desert was not the problem. I felt weak and really should have accepted the offer but there was something else. I had a sense of what it was but fought it away, at least for a while, until it rebounded and hit me in the back of the head like a boomerang.

The desert, so old it has seen it all. There are few places to hide, and my pride was exposed. Pride, that was it. I would not accept the offers for pride. I wanted to cross this place on my own, 300 kilometres, that's all…on my own. Though weak with a pinworm parasite and aching with fatigue, still I would not accept a lift. It was difficult to swallow. I felt raw, exposed to myself. Why? 'What's the fucking point?' I roared, 'For who? Who's ever going to know what I do out here…no one!' The questions came and in my self-defence a familiar reasoned voice took over, 'But you've come all this way, you've one shot at crossing this on your own bat. It's what you wanted…isn't it?' The debate went on until it went dead, and a step-step-step-step rhythm took over. I trudged on in the shadow of a 'new' silence; it was…freedom, it was release, it was a hint of forgiveness.

★★★

It is a peculiar thing, a lone acacia, a freak of nature with not another bush for miles, but it drew me on. Huge from a distance, it slowly shrank to its real size the closer I got. Perspectives were corrupted here. At times things did not seem what they were, shape-shifters changing with the light. Nearby, boulders rose up like beasts out of the sand, revealing their true nature. Earlier, the heat had melted these granite sentinels into a fuzzy softness. Now it felt like they were watching me pass. Across this vast landscape the harshness of day was waning, softening into another glorious evening, and the cool air was as good as a cold shower, but the light…ah the light, like some transforming blanket, it fell across everything.

Near my lone acacia bush beside a monster boulder I would make my camp, but it was not to be. With just one pannier unclipped, I saw the headlights. The sound grew until the truck stopped before me. I had shone my torch, but the captain and his men had me spied and without a thought I accepted their offer. Like a marooned sailor or a drowning man being pulled from the sea, I and my belongings were hoisted to the safety of the top deck and the ship ploughed on into the night.

Onward a few hours to another oasis-like station where two teenage boys stood waiting. One began to collect money, so I dug for my pouch but the driver stayed my hand; the *chai* would be on him. I noted he paid nothing. Perhaps he had a standing order here or was being 'taken care of' for bringing business. The boys placed a tray of samosa-like nibbles near the fire. They were as swift as any McDonald's crew, ensuring their clients were content. If a real road was ever to cross the Bayuda, so I thought, these guys should be given first refusal to open a truckers' *chai*-house.

In the shadows behind the huddle of men around the fire, I lay to rest. I must have slept deep, for when I came to, there was no one about. For a few moments I wasn't sure where I was. Fatigue and dehydration had me disorientated. The silence had returned, but had my truck departed? I wasn't sure. A crescent moon hung like a crown in the east and directly beneath it the two boys approached, one bearing a bowl of basil-onion soup with a scattering of wind-blown sand on top. They squatted to watch me eat. Bit by bit, I learned how 'a driver' had instructed them to let me sleep and had paid them to bring me soup when I woke. How's that for hospitality? How many times had I heard, 'You are a guest in our country'?…so this is what they meant.

The boys disappeared again but left an oil lamp burning. In its light bats came swooping in and out, barely two feet above my resting head. I could not have been closer, yet all was a blur of speed. One swept upwards to the roof and stalled for a fraction and I noticed a mouse-like tail. I lay mesmerized seeing, or rather not-seeing, insects disappear in a feeding frenzy. A scratching noise made me turn on the torch. There, under the karimat, a whooping great beetle was trying to crawl out. I flicked it away, wondering what else would explore me in the night.

One might presume that 160 kilometres out in the Bayuda, all would be quiet in the small hours. How wrong one can be. The trucks came and went, shattering some naive belief that I was in a remote place, in some far flung region to which I'd laboured to get to. The labouring may have been correct but as for the reality? Effectively I was taking my midnight rest at a busy truckers' pit-stop along an equally busy thoroughfare. It just happened to be in a desert! In fact, I thought it busier at that hour than some national routes back home and of course it made sense. The nights being cool, much transport is done after sundown and on throughout the night.

The boys were kept busy coming and going, making their small fortune. At three or four there came a different sound—Jeeps and Germans. One of their group shone a light onto the heap that was me in the corner. I heard the word *fahrrad* so knew that they had spotted the bike and were obviously discussing its relationship to the heap. It was strange after weeks immersed in Arabic to suddenly hear those short crisp Germanic sounds. They tried to restart the fire but failed, and then came the sound of their loud engines revving and they were gone. 'Bloody hell,' I mumbled, 'I should have stayed out there under that bush.' But sleep swiftly returned and I went to the depths.

J was just ahead, running towards the waves, excited. She wore that swimsuit…a happy mood. I ran to catch up then began to sink into sand. I called out but she could not hear. My eyes bulged. A voice, a doctor's…'Look, his eyes, he is dehydrated.' Fearful, scared…I was bound to the ground. Suddenly a hand came from nowhere. It gripped my shoulder tight and shook hard…

I was confused when Ali called me, though I did not know his name at the time. His hand gripped my shoulder and in pidgin English I heard him say how I should go with him and that he would leave soon. I rubbed sand from my eyes. They were not bulging. I had been dreaming. I sat up to see Ali's helper Kabashi tending the fire. Ali came over again to explain that a sand storm had covered some of the hard track and it was best if I went with him to his father's house north of Shendi. He pointed to the bike, then to the track, saying with a smile full of beautiful white teeth, '*Ageela, mish kuwayis, mish kuwayis.*' His face reminded me of some actor, I couldn't recall who, but it was he who had paid for the basil soup before climbing into his open cab to sleep. I thanked him for that. He nodded, then got up from his squat beside me to attend a pot of boiling water on the fire. We had our hot *chais,* then drove off.

Three things got me into his doorless cab: his calm assertiveness, my depleted energy and, last but not least, my visa. The date was 14 February, and it would expire three days later. I had run out of time. No choice but make haste to Khartoum to renew it. We left that forlorn *chai*-station at 6.10am, and fourteen hours later we were still driving; by fifteen I was once again conked to the world after an exhilarating strenuous day, relieved that I would make the capital in time and sated by a massive bowl of his father's sweet rice—but that is getting well ahead of the story.

It felt colder than an Irish winter when we departed the *chai*-station. I rummaged for a pair of trousers, pulled them on, then climbed in between my two companions. Ali, before he turned the key, rearranged my Palestinian head *shaal* '... in the arab fashion,' he said, 'to keep the sand and cold out', but my concern was for the bike. It lay on the metal floor of the empty truck, tied to both sides with rope and cushioned by every item I could find, including panniers, a tarpaulin and a two old tyre tubes. This care for a bike bemused Ali, and for a good hour I tried to explain how 'it and I' had become a team and as a team we had to care for each other, so to speak. We had a long way to go.

I had never been sentimental enough to give the bike a name. It was an inanimate object, after all, and I often felt bemused at those who christened their bikes names like Rick or Roger or whatever, yet the more I sat on that Brooks B17 saddle, the more I oiled, greased, tended and repaired, the more I tightened nuts, straightened spokes, coaxed or even kicked it in frustration... yes, the more I lived, trudged, battled and soared with this machine, the more a bond was formed and respect grew. The bike became *me*; that's how it felt, like I was caring for myself. If I was to give it any name it would be my own.

Attempting to explain this in English with bits of French and the odd word of Arabic while Ali drove hard across the sand was not quite futile, but close. In the end I resorted to that ancient and wise technique of the Irish—wit and humour. Without mentioning Flann O'Brien's classic work *The Third Policeman,* where molecules 'transfer' and a man becomes his bicycle and vice-versa, I steered Ali to considering the molecular theory of becoming what we use most or held onto most. 'So', I told him, 'I am slowly becoming 100% bicycle and you Ali, after fifteen years driving, you are already 100% truck.' To my delight he got it and we laughed and laughed, though Kabashi was totally confused until Ali translated. Then all three of us howled above the engine as the wind blew in one door and out the other.

Thus we went, skimming over a wide open plain to reach our first *chai*-station at 9.30. There, firewood was available but no 'Arabs'. 'Arabs', Ali explained, were those who lived 'out here in the desert.' They were not Nubian; they were 'different', he said, many making their living providing sustenance to truckers and travellers passing by. We made our brew and drove on. The day progressed and the desert changed again and again, along with my mood, from rolling fine sand to sand plains with stubs of wire grass, to rugged rocky moonscapes of browns and blacks. In places the track was firm and I bit my lip. I wanted to be out there, but gradually I let go of that piece of the dream.

117

Ali was a good man and no fool. He knew that by picking me up, though it helped, I would feel a sense of disappointment. Maybe to compensate, he began pointing to things, a chocolate-coloured clump of rocks, types of scrub vegetation, a Bedouin settlement on the horizon, but I was barely grasping his explanations above the revving and thrusting of the truck. 'Oh for some Arabic,' I thought to myself. Then he began singing in a light hearted way, Kabashi joining in.

La-ilaha-illa-Allah.
Muhammad rasul Allah.
Khawaja kuwayis,
Ana Sudani, ana Irlandi,
Sudani kuwayis, Irlandi kuwayis.

There is no God but Allah
Muhammad is his messenger.
Foreigner good,
I am Sudanese, I am Irish,
Sudanese good, Irish good.

We twisted and shook through a blistering noon while singing our Arabic ditty like a mantra. Kabashi climbed on the cab roof, and I moved close to the open door, holding the hand grip overhead. The morning chill was now a distant memory. Warm air rushed by, blowing dust into and out of my tangled mass of bleached curls. We arrived at another station, Kabashi lifting the bonnet to let the engine cool before starting to prepare a pot of macaroni. Ali pulled out his prayer mat and I, feeling somewhat better, did some stretching and karate *kata*. His focus was on his prayer, reciting in a low voice, and I felt respect for him, adhering to his faith no matter where he was. How he knew the *qibla* (the direction to Mecca) I couldn't say; perhaps he had a compass, or just knew. As for my own routine, it turned into an unintentional coaching session for both of them and two others who arrived. I thought of my karate Sensei, Tim Harte, and what he would think seeing this, me leading a band of Nubians through their first lesson. I could almost hear him: 'Keep your heel on the floor. Twist your hip!' Watching their awkward movements across the sand, it occurred to

118

me that the only calisthenics most Muslim men do is at prayer, but then perhaps it's enough, and at least it's done regularly.

By late afternoon the terrain changed to a flat plain with acacia trees scattered about. An 'Arab' (Bedouin) settlement was off to the left. Suddenly Ali swung round; he had spotted a group of men and girls gathered about a well. He needed to fill his tank. From the cab I watched the elaborate greeting between him and a beaming leather-skinned elder. Greetings are drawn out here but partings are short and sweet, the direct opposite to home.

There were lots of ropes attached to lots of goatskin sacks, lots of nibbling goats, lots of mangy dogs, lots of banter and good cheer and lots and lots of children who seemed to appear as soon we did. Another truck arrived carrying several tonnes of oranges. A kid came over and gave me a bag full. I don't think I've ever tasted a better one. Ali jumped back in the cab. We were ready to go.

'Now I have water but not fuel,' he said. I wasn't sure what he meant. He pointed to a thorn bush as we drove off. 'Fuel, fuel,' he said, 'for the cooking of my wives.'

'You mean fuel for your wife's cooking.' I replied.

'Yes, yes, my wives' cooking.'

'Oh,' I said, '…how many wives do you have?'

'Two wives, two wives…lots of fuel I need,' he replied with a wide grin.

'Wow, two wives that must be great,' I said.

'Great? Great? No great, very hard work. I not see them for six days. Tell me, Mr John, which do I go to this night?' He looked at me for my reply. I took a coin from the dash and flipped it. He banged the steering wheel with a loud laugh. 'Yes, very good, very good. I do this.'

… and now as I write I laugh again, remembering that time with Ali…flipping a coin to help him with his wifely dilemma. Perhaps a child came of it. He was certainly eager and happy! Flipping a coin…as good a way as any to come into this life. Naturally enough, I never was to know which wife he went to that night but I hope she was happy too.

He drove off track to a place where the thorn bushes were plentiful. For an hour the three of us walked in different directions out into the scrubland, uprooting and dragging dozens of hard-thorned *Acacia nilotica* bushes, then loading them into the back of the truck. My hands and arms were scratched to bits though strangely no blood came. 'That's odd,' I thought at the time; the suffering came later. Dragging thorn bushes across the desert floor, the job was surreal enough to make me stop and take a long look around, to *really see* where I was, to *check in*, as it were, with what the hell I was doing. 'This,' I told myself, 'is what a cycling adventure is all about', but it's not really about cycling at all, but about riding far enough to get stuck into such hard-to-forget situations. Ali and Kabashi were a hundred metres apart, each pulling hard towards the truck, their huge thorny piles making long scratch trails across the dirt. A perfect golden disc of sun sat square on the desert horizon, and bit-by-bit-by-bit, like the second-hand of a tick-tock clock, it slipped away, bit-by-bit-by…gone! My two dragging friends hardly noticed, they'd seen so many sunsets, but for someone like me from the cloudy north, every such sunset was rare enough to be longingly gazed at and stored for the winter. It was a moment that anyone at all might surely have felt the Earth itself turn.

By the time we were done the bike was buried under a ton of thorn, with a few old tyre tubes preventing certain damage. It had been in peculiar situations, and this for sure was another for the list. Loaded to the gunnels we left that place to head back to the main drag and the final leg to his father's house. It was dark. The temperature had dropped and Kabashi was now on the roof. How he stuck it up there in the wind chill I could hardly imagine, though in the cab Ali and I could not have been much warmer. We were wrapped up well, as the wind drove sand in his door and out mine. Three times we became dug in, Kabashi and I shovelling sand from the rear tyres to position the metal boards in the dug-out trench. Ali would drive forward up onto the boards, sending sand flying. The boards would pop out behind the wheels where we would grab them and sprint to reposition them again in front of the same wheel…again and again until we were through the soft section. It was hard work.

Keeping up with a moving truck while holding a six-foot metal plank was difficult enough, but in soft sand, in the dark! Once, thankfully only once, I lost my shoe. There was no point shouting out…a split second decision, 'Get it now…now, *now*.' I dropped the board and ran back to look. In the reddish glow of the tail lights I spotted the black toe protruding like a shark fin, but the truck had gone on regardless. Ali was unaware he was now progressing on only Kabashi's board. I shoved the shoe inside my trouser and raced one-shoed to throw my board in position. No one was the wiser. We reached solid ground and climbed aboard to hunker down for the last few hours. The Bayuda was behind me, and the dream of a solo crossing seemed innocent. I had been given the best of both worlds, half of it alone, half with locals; how could I possibly complain?

I woke in the Nile-side village of Keli, Ali's village, 240 kilometres north of Khartoum, and looked at my hands. They were puffed with inflammation and tingled with pain. It felt as if I had dipped them in a bed of nettles. 'The thorn bushes, of course, they must have caused some reaction.' Ali entered the room. He had returned from a night with one of his wives and grinned, mimicking a flick of a coin, but the grin faded when he saw the red sore-looking scratch marks. 'Do not worry, not poison,' he said. For once, I had my doubts about his opinion.

Perhaps to make amends for my discomfort, he offered a trip to the pyramids of Meroe. (Today tourists pay thousands to travel to this UNESCO heritage site. Today I'd jump at the offer, but then I shrugged unknowing shoulders and declined, preferring instead to read, rest and attempt writing the diary.) I think he was secretly pleased. He went off to see wife number two, and thus today, the pyramids of Meroe and wife number two are joined at the hip in my memory. Oh, he'd laugh at that! That evening he promised to return for a farewell meal, but she must have strapped him to the bed, for he never made it back.

Ali had lifted my spirits when they were low. We'd had some good times, and he'd given me a mini-adventure into the bargain. How different he was from the first Ali I'd met on the Aswan ferry. One a serious student of agriculture in a Cairo university, the other a fun-loving, compassionate desert truck driver. I stole out of his father's house at 4.30am with bandaged, throbbing hands and a tinge of regret at being unable to say farewell. His teenage brother escorted me out of the village. I needed to get a good start, and the boy had been given the job. He shot ahead like a phantom, along narrow sandy side alleys between the buildings, darting around corners, and but for his cream coloured *jalabiya* I'd have lost him. I pushed the bike in the semi-dark as fast as I could, trying my damndest to keep up and feeling certain in that maze of homes that if he had lost me or I him, he'd not come back to look. I stuck with him until we popped out on the outskirts, whereupon he stopped dead and pointed into the dark, as if to say 'that way'. He had no English, and my attempts to express a 'thank you' to his older brother were useless. All I could do was shake his limp hand. He turned quick and sped away to his warm bed, as any sensible teenager would. I turned too, in good faith, to where I hoped the way to Shendi lay.

121

From the village of Keli to the town of Shendi was a push of five or six kilo-metres, but they were on opposite sides of the river. To continue to Khartoum the river had best be crossed at the town.

As before, the way was 'softy softy', and the Nile, though parallel and close, was out of sight. I pushed past thankfully sleeping dogs and tethered camels with their heads held proud and, here and there, Toyota 'boxes' looking always out of place; past homes still in darkness and homes with lights and lanterns on; past homes with sleepy women's voices coming from the far side of high-walled courtyards; past men already in the field and men on their way with hoes and tools on their shoulders. I stopped to find that scrap of paper where someone had scribbled the appropriate greetings of the day. '*Sabah al-khayr*,' I'd say, paying attention to the intonation of any reply. '*Sabah an-noor…As-salaam alaykum*,' came the soft responses from faces still shrouded in the pre-dawn shadows. At least I'm understood, I thought, so I said it again and again to anyone at all who passed, even trying out my Arabic on a tied-up donkey chewing the cud of its breakfast. With new-found confidence, I added '*Wa alaykum as-salaam, shukran*', feeling absolutely at home here as if going about my day's work like any of them, and then it dawned on me, how more richly rewarding it was to see and listen and move through a place on the cusp of its own waking-up.

I reached the crossing just in time, joining a hundred others on a packed single-platform ferry. These days a modern bridge straddles the Nile to Shendi, but then there was no bridge and crossing took its time. To wheel a laden bike into a dense crowd always grabs attention—but on a crowded ferry with no protective side barriers. People pushed back to let the bike on board, and I could only surmise that the calls from the outer edges said 'Hey, *hey*, stop pushing or we'll fall over.' I was taking the volume of five passengers, but the ferryman asked only double the fee. Decent of him, I thought.

After devouring a heaped plate of pan-fried tilapia in Shendi I walked out of town looking for the smooth road to Khartoum. There was no smooth road. For some odd reason I presumed there would be a tarred surface all the way south and I'd coast into the capital, cutting through a red tape like a Tour de France rider. Stupid really. Why I imagined the worst would be over in getting to Shendi, I just don't know. 'Khartoum, Khartoum?' I must have asked, and someone must have answered, pointing to the wide sand-track leaving town. I looked in that general direction and my spirit sank, yet rose again when a not-so-crazy idea occurred.

Except for a perfectly straight line of conspicuous telephone poles, I would never have noticed the train track. 'The track, of course, the track!' Suddenly the way to Khartoum became clear, dead straight clear, and for the bones of that day I made my way between the rails. Once you avoid being hit by a train, cycling on a railway line is not so bad. The sleepers were buried under a ballast of grit and stone, and layers of wind-blown sand covered intermittent sections, in places almost to the rail itself. Riding would have been a dawdle but for the corrugations—those dastardly little rolling mounds shuddering bike and body to bits.

Corrugations, every trail-blazing, dirt-road driver's agony, but for a cyclist it's a whole other bumpy story. Why were they up here between the rail lines? I had only ever experienced them on dirt trails where the wheels of vehicles were frequent, but here? Did passing trains or wind eddies stir-up these bumps into their corrugated shape? As I shuddered over them I cursed them, then got to know them, then forgave them, recalling Amsterdam's cobbled streets and those ancient pavements in Kracow. How easy it was there, when spokes went twang, with bike shops everywhere—but here, Jesus!

I stopped to drink, to wipe sweat, to give my arms a rest, to look around into a yellow glare of space, and I was transported back to my old flat with Brian laughing loudly and Paul advising sombrely, 'You'll need heavier gauge spokes.' Gee, guys, if you could see where the wheels are now, and then in that very moment I sorely wished they could have been transported, like Scotty transporting Kirk and Spock, to materialise before my eyes and we could ride a little way, and we'd all see the glare together and they'd know...yes they'd know what this ride was really like, but they left me and the glare returned and the spokes held, but you never knew until you felt the wobble or heard the twang.

The constant jarring vibration was tiresome and was probably damaging to the bike, but there was another painful issue. Pus oozed through the thin bandage around my hands. They had festered. Each tremor, each jolt seemed to stop at the wrist, as if every nerve-ending had migrated down my arms. Unable to curl them into a grip, I could barely touch the handlebar, and thus with arms straight and wrists pressed against the outer edges of the dropped handlebar, I guided the bike with my fingertips.

Every fifty-metre section was hard fought, and I knew precisely the passing of every one. Parallel to the track, electricity poles ran off into a shimmering distance and fifty metres separated each one. I began counting these blocks of fifty…one, two, three, four…a minute or so of wobbly pedalling dividing each count. At first it was a game, then a mental yardstick, then a motivation and then, in the end, a meditation, each pole luring me on to the next and the next and the next. Eventually I lost count of the number of fifties counted; 227 was the last, after which I can't recall anything. I let it go, and anyway it didn't seem to matter; my brain was fried, and any attention remaining was sucked down into the throbbing across the back of my hands and a big lump under my armpit.

Thoughts wandered like nomads in a hot head—to John Azambi 800 plus kilometres back along the track at Station 14, lonely with his jam-jar of *aragi,* to General Gordon, lonely too, waiting for his rescue, to my reaching Khartoum, to J, to my pus-filled hands, but mostly I thought nothing at all, just unconscious stuff passing in and out as clouds across a clear sky. The pedals turned slowly and I watched the stones ahead of the front wheel, avoiding the bigger ones with a little twist to right or left.

An overstretched and long-past useless sweat-band hung off the handlebar. I kept it for some sentimental reason and to mop my brow occasionally when it was dry enough, but the salt irritated, so I left it hanging there along with two T-shirts like Tibetan prayer flags. Being headband-less I'd flick sweat with the back of a thumb, my forehead becoming red raw with hundreds of swipes. And so it went. I made a pact with myself to stop at every fiftieth fifty (about 2.5 kilometres). There I'd eat dates and tuna fish and sip lukewarm water with lemon juice and iodine from a metal Sigg bottle stuffed in the cool of a pannier.

Once I had to get off the track to give way to a northbound train, but not before laying the bike down and taking a photo. As it passed, with passengers looking aghast then quickly waving, I scolded myself for clicking too soon. The chance for some dramatic shot had gone. I got back between the rails and rode on. If it felt strange being led by a sleepy teenage phantom through Keli's sandy back alleys, riding mile after mile along the main Khartoum rail line was positively surreal. The electricity poles were a short walk to my left. To my right, a few kilometres away, the thin line of palms looked like battalions of infantry standing to attention. Beyond them was the river and habitation; at least that much was certain.

Could I have gone all the way to Khartoum Central? No doubt it was possible and I had fun with imagining—the look on a station master's face seeing a bike pull in to Platform 1 ahead of the Wadi train! Yet, before the evening had turned crimson I had abandoned the track, and the decision was an easy one. With throbbing hands, no water and an underarm lymph lump the size a cherry tomato, it was a no-brainer really. So I struck out across the flats towards that presumed string of habitation.

Where I would rest that night was the absolute least of my concerns. There comes a point on a long-haul trip when you *know* there *is* a bed out there waiting, that there *is* someone who right at that moment, though they have no clue that a *khawaja* is approaching, will no doubt embrace the impending engagement as fully as I, and together bits of our mutual stories will be shared. As I drew closer, I veered to the only house with a Toyota pick-up outside, for a pick-up in these parts was symbol of something more than just transport. Two young men spotted me and, to cut to the chase, to one of their homes I was taken without question. After a *chai* I was shown a small room with a bed, whereupon I threw myself fully clothed and did not wake until morning.

In the local medical clinic I was given Ampicillin and told in no uncertain terms by the kind staff to take a bus to Khartoum. It was then my young host, who had brought me there, added that the tarred road was only fifty kilometres further. It may as well have been five or 500, I would take the bus! In 1986 the tar from the capital only came north only as far as Al-Gaili, that was it. Once again the decision was easy. With the bike strapped to the roof of the bus-cum-truck, I gave thanks to all and set out on the last leg. I'd left Cairo on the 1 January, having bid my buddy Eamon farewell with a glass of guava juice. I arrived in Khartoum on 17 February, and the first thing I did was buy a double mango juice at the bus station. It had been one helluva trip down.

Chapter 6
Of trucks and trains

Over the Blue Nile I rode, leaving Khartoum North behind. From the bridge's vantage point the Al-Mogran was clearly visible, the famous confluence of the two great rivers, the silt-brown Blue merging with the clay-grey White; 'the marriage', as the Sudanese call it. How apt: the pulsing male and the easy flowing female joined at last for their joint journey into Bayuda-Nubian deserts and beyond. I could see why they put a sexual twist to this merging, and for quite a while I watched the endless co-mingling of dark and light waters as they diffused outwards and onwards. Here was one of those historic places, and having come the way I came, I savoured the moment. You might not be so fortunate these days, but on 17 February 1986 no one came to push me on or confiscate my camera.

Two hundred and sixteen years before, a Scotsman arrived here. He had trekked over 1,500 kilometres from the source of the Blue Nile in the Ethiopian highlands and may well have been disappointed to see 'his' Nile joined by another mighty flow from the south. Was he the first European to see the Al-Mogran, who knows? If I had felt my own travel arduous at times then a second's reflection on that walk by James Bruce in 1770 from beyond Lake Tana put things sharply in perspective. To my surprise no sign or notice or explanatory-cum-historic plaque was to be seen, but on reflection I thought the locals right not to pander to this most European of sentiments—as if Europeans were the first to discover these timeless places. 'The bragging rights of far away nations,' as Dr Essam had put it. Bruce may well have agreed to leave his name out of it and to let this confluence stand for itself as it always had.

Stanley, Livingstone, Speke, Baker…a whole slew of explorers could be rattled off by a certain generation, yet until now I had not even heard of James Bruce. Nearly one hundred years before any of them set their feet into the fever of African exploration and Nile-source-hunting, Bruce had located the source of the Blue Nile. Its annual swelling, bulking out the river and contributing most of its sediment, infused it with the power to create those incredible Nubian/Egyptian cultures further down-stream 5,000 years before. Yet the Nile has been flowing for five million. Who knows how many civilizations it has given birth to? So here's to Bruce; regardless of plaques, I felt his name deserved to be rattled off equally with those other luminaries of African exploration.

Where two great rivers meet and continue as one, there will be three corners for a city to construct itself. Khartoum is really a tripartite city, Omdurman, Khartoum North and Khartoum. I rode into Khartoum on the southern corner, on a brand new road with the heavy smell of fresh asphalt hanging in the air. It was hot and workmen moved equipment further down the street to pour the next section. Pouring roads in Europe is one thing, to do it here in this heat! Yet the men looked happy, and as I pulled over to a police station one of them gave a friendly looking wave. I shouldered the bike up three steps into a fan-cooled office, thinking to myself, 'Let's get it over with'.

This formal check-in and registration of papers was an innocuous affair, but picture the scene: some guy enters with a dusty, bushy beard, matted curly red hair, unwashed clothes, hands wrapped in a dirty bandage pushing an even more filthy looking bike laden with a pile of bags like junk. To his eternal credit, that Sudanese policeman took it all in his stride. His response said more than any travel book could say, about the strange mix of oddballs, roughnecks, birders, backpackers, dreamers, adventurers, archaeologists, terrorists, that have come to this amazing though sadly un-harmonious country down through the years. Basically, I wasn't the first bum to push through his door. If you had asked him where next I would most likely go, he would have told you straight—the Central PO, for its Poste Restante was where every traveller went in hope or expectation. It might not mean much these days, but before securing a roof over my head I simply had to seek it out, to quench curiosity and retrieve any mail. To lie in my bag wondering if someone had posted even a card, well, there would scarcely be sleep.

Communication, too much of it and I'd drown, too little and I'd pine. I didn't wish to admit it, but on reaching Khartoum I pined, pined for any card or letter from anyone, especially from home. Ever since that river bank loneliness in Al-Dabba, there had waxed and waned a wish to read someone's news, anyone's news, or some reply to the cards I'd let fly at everyone in my address book. It didn't matter who, but of course there were those whose mail always excited.

I'd grown up in a world of wild west movies, and when I dismounted outside the Central PO, the parallel was immediate—a trusty steed tied up outside on a dusty street, a stepping through the door with a 'passport-gun' in right hand ready to draw from its holster and shove in the face of the teller! I imagined slapping the passport on the counter…'Gimme my mail, buddy, or I'll shoot ya down!' The letters came over the counter, one, two, three, and wow, four and a postcard too. I was in Poste Restante heaven.

Oh to the joy of receiving envelopes with one's name handwritten there, under a bunch of fancy stamps, the pleasure to gaze at the variety of hand-scrawls and to instantly know who or guess who, or burst with curiosity if it's writing you don't recognize. You look at the line of colourful stamps chosen to give a lift of culture and a sense of home. Some you'd never seen before, bringing to life some fresh insight to where it was you said you came from and like a dog with a bone you go off to find a quiet spot to chew over each word, each meaning, every image formed; if a photo was included, well, it was treasured. There was nothing instant here, nothing could be rushed; all was steady and deliberate, allowing the slow infusion of time, space and perspective.

No traveller or 'expeditionist' who trekked the long road in the bygone days of cards and letters did not, from time to time, yearn deeply for one. A real letter into the hand and, if it came from the pen of a loved one, the heart of even the toughest most single-minded soloist would lift and soften in the solitude of tent or park bench.

I rode down to the river bank and in a corner of a bench-less park, my back to a tree, I flipped the letters and considered the hierarchy of openings. Paul Brennan's letter was first. His words were full of the comings and goings in my old flat, the 'well wishes' of others, the slide shows he'd organised with slides I'd posted home and the money thus gathered to send spare parts out to Nairobi. Paul was a stalwart, a selfless friend and flatmate, and for a few moments I looked back into the dusty heat of Khartoum, remembering our ride through the cool clear snow peaked air of Norway. In the second letter my brothers painted a more intimate picture of home and of Dad's health. 'He wishes you well and so do we'—so it ended. Last, but never least, the intimacy of J's letter was kept like a sweet dessert, and after I had sated myself with the musings between her lines, I weaved a way back to the student hostel, brimming with romantic dreams of Kenyan beaches and the snows of Kilimanjaro.

Khartoum today, which has trebled in population, has changed a lot and has some eye-catching architecture. Yet no matter how much shimmering concrete and fancy glass, this sprawling tri-partite city, though enlivened by the Great River, is still and will be forever surrounded by desert. It was hit by a sandstorm the week before my arrival, and everywhere, along streets, walls, on carts and cars and all over the vast expanse of low two, three and four-storey buildings the storm's finest dust had settled. As I made my way to the hostel the wheels left a narrow imprint as they would on a dusting of snow along the edge of the recently tarred road.

Through the hostel's gate and, no surprise, there they were: familiar Caucasian faces from the Aswan ferry, Tony and Ben looking browner and more weathered, their heads last seen protruding from that train window as it departed Wadi Halfa. I scanned round, and there too was Arie rising from his squat by his tent, a broad grin in my direction. As the only other cyclist he gave a firmer handshake, I guess out of some mutually understood unwritten code of knowing. Familiar faces, and at times I thought as good as letters to boost morale.

Arie told me of Tom. He had reached Khartoum but in a bad way. Malaria and fatigue had taken their toll. I met Tom a day later, gaunt but with eyes that seemed calmer and steelier than I remembered, and in a stereotypical Germanic way he resolved to stick steadfast to his purpose. He would continue, 'sans bike', to achieve his dream and make it all the way to Lake Tanganyika to see the source of those fancy aquarium fish. I'd heard of lots of individual reasons to travel in Africa, but not that one. As we parted he placed a roll of film into my hand. 'Take it,' he said, 'in the name of friendship.'

★★★

Ben put enough pasta in the pot for ten. We were four but tucked in regardless. Our talk of where next for each of us was the main relish to the mountain of food. They brought me up to speed with travel and political conundrums. Khartoum, it appeared, would be a terminus of sorts. One thing for sure, there would be no overland adventure to Juba. The ongoing war down South, between John Garang's SPLA and government forces dragged on. Even gung-ho American Ben, aspiring to be a journalist and wishing to get ' into the thick of it', as he put it, concluded it was best to 'go round it or fly over it'—the 'it' being both the war and the almost impenetrable quagmire called the Sudd, that infamous swamp in the middle of Sudan, bigger than Ireland, full of hippos, crocodiles, malarial mosquitoes, desolation, depression, despair and tribes who might or might not be supportive of one's personal venture.

Tony outlined the options, either east to Ethiopia, then Kenya, or west to Darfur, Chad, the Central African Republic (CAR), Zaire, Rwanda, Uganda... then Kenya. Otherwise fly straight south over the 'it' to Juba and into the jungles of Zaire. All this twentieth century realism coincided nicely with my reading of Samuel Baker's nineteenth century torturous ordeal— his incredible traversing of the Sudd in two boats with a sick German, a bunch of mercenary helpers, a few donkeys, goats and a camel. (Anyone wishing to read a real travel adventure, put this down and read Baker's own words in The Albert Nyanza, a truly eye-opening, hair-raising escapade.) Baker sought the source of the Nile, I merely sought the best of myself, with of course some personal adventure thrown in. My venture, however, was just child's play to what went on in Baker's day. I could simply buy an airline ticket, fly over the dreaded Sudd and look down on all that hardship. What might he have said to that?

★★★

The boys were unanimous: Kassala to the east, on the border with Eritrea, was where the 'safest' action was: this, despite stories of wild, bearded men from the mountains walking tall through market streets, their swords and daggers showing. Such probably exaggerated or concocted rumours only served to salivate the imagination, and for a day I seriously considered joining them, but then on that third night in Khartoum something strange happened, scuppering all such plans.

I recall the afternoon as one with a head full of travel stuff: renewing the visa, visiting a clinic for a jab of immuno-globulin while showing them my infected hands, and later in the evening, painfully stitching shorts and tent and finishing letters fast, so a departing Piotr from Poland could post them to Ireland from Moscow. Finally, lying in the repaired tent, I weighed up the pros and cons of the Kassala trip.

The night wore on but something was not right. A pressure across the upper chest made it feel tight but it eased with abdominal breathing. 'What is going on?' I thought. Wiggling toes, moving fingers…all seemed okay but my arm was becoming numb as if blood was retreating from extremities to the core. When pain became definite I knew it was serious and I began to sweat and began to think.

Was it a reaction to the gamma-globulin jab? Indeed, I wondered had I been given the correct vial in the first place? Or was it somehow connected to the infection in both hands, some kind of acacia toxin causing cardiac 'poisoning'. All this conjecture was backdropped by the clear fact that I knew I had a congenital heart murmur. After months of exertion, had it come home to roost? 'Dad's heart isn't great, is it?' I thought. 'And his brother had a pacemaker. Maybe… maybe.' I tried to sit up, tried to stay calm and focus, but imagination took hold and there followed an imagined melodramatic scenario: heart attack, Khartoum hospital, flight home, me in wheelchair, me dead. Simple.

The chest pain deepened and my breathing went shallow. 'Goddammit, is it here it is to end? Well, fuck me!' I imagined not being afraid to die but, bloody hell, did it have to be in a tent in a student hostel in the dead of a Khartoum night and not on some high mountain pass with the wind in my hair and a last glorious view? Arie's tent was alongside. I was just about to call him to fetch a doctor when all hell broke loose in the compound. The security lights came on, fellow travellers were shouting, a girl was crying. From within my tent I heard calling, running, then guys sprinting outside the perimeter wall, Australian voices receding into the distance.

Arie was up. I heard him ask the time. A German voice said, 'Ten minutes past four'. I lay there, half listening to an erratic heart, half to the bedlam out-side. I tried to remember an old prayer, tried to accept whatever was going on in my chest. Then, becoming aware how my hands were tightly joined, I slowly released them, finger by finger, and as I did, a snapshot history bubbled up like champagne overflowing, all the way from childhood to where I lay. I cannot deny that there was no fear, but it ebbed away, leaving me in a strange state. I felt ready for any eventuality, hands on abdomen, with that piece of Finnish mosquito net draped over my face to keep the bastard mosquitoes out. In the end all became quiet outside and I must have drifted off.

In the morning Arie told how there had been a break-in; some guy had jumped the wall, cut the straps of a tied-up rucksack and ran out the front gate past a sleeping security man. 'He stole the wrong sack,' said Arie.

'What do you mean?' I asked.

'It belonged to the girlfriend of that Ozzie kick-boxer, remember!'

'Oh wow! Did they catch the guy?'

'They did!' said Arie with unashamed glee.

Over a breakfast of mangoes we surmised on the probable bloody outcome. 'He wont do it again for sure' I said.

'*He* won't, but others will,' replied Arie. 'That wall there isn't going to stop them.'

For two days I hung around the compound, Arie doing the needful by way of food and water. Then he followed the others for Kassala. What had happened that night? I had no idea, but gradually I felt better, though wary of signs of fluttering, faltering or palpitations. It would be two months later, in the Irish Embassy in Nairobi, before a possible, though far-out, reason dawned. In the meantime I learned it would be ten days to the next Juba flight. Ten days in hot Khartoum, God no, and then...Geoff! 'The Jebel-Mara mountains, mate, the best place in the whole country to convalesce.' His Kentish accent was a new tonic for my ears. 'Forget Kassala, Darfur is where you'll see the real Sudan.' We got on right from the start. He was just what the doctor might have ordered, a witty black-bearded, no-bullshit, give-it-a-go kind of bloke and a good laugh to boot. Yes, that's what I needed, so off we went, although in hindsight neither of us had a clue, but that didn't matter in the slightest, as we made it up as we went along.

We celebrated our pre-departure to Darfur with two double mango-juices and strolled down to the Nile confluence, that magical spot overlooking the Al-Mogran. Then, the space was left to its own devices, a wilderness of low trees and grasses. Today, so I have been told, there's a communal park for families and children to relax at weekends. I wonder is there a plaque to James Bruce?

Out on the river two rowing boats held their positions against the current. Two men in each, the sitting one pulling on oars to keep the tiny craft in the same spot, the standing one either throwing or feeling a line. Their easy chatter from boat to boat added to the peace of late afternoon. Then Geoff roared out across the river, 'Hoy, well caught, mate!' The man held aloft his little catch and we saluted him, raising our plastic cups. 'Bloody hell,' Geoff blurted, 'we're in bloody Khartoum and it's great.' I couldn't but agree. Watching the Nile become one river and fishermen do their thing, it did feel pretty cool, but it was the juice that stole the show, and rightly so. Mango juice might be at every airport and farmer's market these days, but for us then it was an exotic symbol of all that was sweet about our adventures, and as we fingered the dregs we concurred that these were once in a lifetime special moments.

★★★

Wad Madani, Sennar, Kosti, Tendeiti, Umm Ruwaba, Ar-Rahad, An-Nahud, Babanusa…and, at the end of the line, Nyala. Those were the places, big and small, on this, the first major tangent to my oh-so-planned route. Looking back, I wonder why I brought the bike at all. Did I imagine some slim chance of going on through Chad and CAR, or was it that I did not wish to let it out of my sight after the hostel break-in, I can't now recall. What I do remember is losing Geoff in the friendly mayhem of Khartoum station while helping a train porter put the bike in the goods carriage. That didn't seem a big deal at the time, but over the next few days I regretted us both not sticking together for sanity's sake, if nothing else.

The train was a monster, twenty-five carriages rolling out of Khartoum chock-full of humanity. Somewhere midway I was sandwiched between the smell of a wealthy camel buyer and the aftershave of a doctor, in a six-berth compartment where the miasma of ten males would, after four and half days, coalesce into its own unique blend. I'd no idea where Geoff was and there was no point looking. He was the type of guy that once we cleared Khartoum he would most likely be found on the roof among the ticketless in glorious fresh air.

So south for 300 kilometres to Sennar on the Blue, then west for a thousand more, past Kosti, on the White, out into savannah plains, John O'Groats to Land's End more or less, but that's where similarities ended. 'Sheer hell,' I wrote in my diary, though time has eroded the harshness, leaving just surreal melon-sweet memories of sights and sounds, smells and stories which seemed to roll in rhythm with the train from day through night to day again.

Stories, it was a journey of stories: stories of camel treks, oasis to oasis along 'the forty-day route' from Darfur to the Cairo markets; stories of the timeless tensions over water between nomadic herdsmen and the sedentary farmer; stories of bright Sudanese students in Eastern Europe being bedded by wily gay professors out of innocence or an attempt to ensure a good grade; stories of the 'million' nomad-drifter boys who poured out of that fractious region to the capital to beg or find their way in the toughness of Sudan. Some would remain in Darfur or Kordofan and some, in time, would learn to kill with Kalashnikovs. Of the wives, mothers, sisters, daughters there was no mention. I got on that train a mere traveller on his trip; I got off with a lot more edges rounded and a world-view sandblasted by other kinds of reality.

Half way to Wad Madani, Dr Hassan rubbed the dusty window, pointing to a flat and vast tract of 'food production'. 'There,' he said, 'is the Gezira Scheme.' My blank look told him I was ignorant of such wonders. 'It is one of the great irrigation schemes in the world, possibly the largest,' he said. The scheme apparently began in earnest in 1925, and the story had a familiar ring: Britain's need for cotton and, I suppose, food for the empire or at least part of it. Today, water from the Blue is still channelled into those ideal clay soils for a host of crops to grow. Twice the size of Kent, larger than County Cork, it stretches from one Nile to the other, and the sight of it gave the lie to the notion of Sudan being all desert and unable to grow crops. Yet, it wasn't cotton I saw through the window, rather a sea of foot-high peanut plants, hectare upon hectare. 'They are not nuts,' Dr Hassan said, 'they are in the bean family. They push their flowers into the earth where the "nut" will grow so we call them ground nuts, yes an extraordinary little plant.'

Peanuts? My interest was piqued. While on the road I had consumed more jars of peanut butter than was good for me. 'Ah but when we get to Nyala I will get you real peanut paste, how it should be, not what you buy in the West. You will see it prepared before your eyes.' I kept my mouth shut, embarrassed to tell him how I had always presumed peanuts grew on bushes.

By Wad Madani everyone knew *my* story. Dr Hassan had gleaned it from me then re-told it, or his version of it, to the wide-open faces. The faces gazed at his in open-mouthed silence, and I'd no idea what he was saying. Then came the barrage of questions (in Arabic) from all corners, including the floor where two young men sat back to back all the way to Babanusa. The good doctor seemed to come to life as he engaged with his compatriots, fielding every query and turning to me to check a detail or two, not that it mattered much. He was having fun, and his captured audience would believe anything.

'They want to know why you brought a bike to Sudan and why you take it to Nyala?' 'Why indeed' I thought to myself and then replied, 'Well, I might go on to Chad or I might go back to Khartoum and fly to Juba. Its about options.' The listening was more intent because it was a *doctor* who was doing the translating and what followed was once again one of those times when the joy of one's travel was, as it were, to sit back and watch it happen *to you*, as if watching a documentary on your very own journey.

I listened uncomprehendingly as the options of how I should proceed were tossed about the compartment. The only Chadian wanted me to see his country but admitted a camel would be better than a bike to do so. The camel trader beside me suggested I join his men to herd a few hundred across the desert to Dongala, and if I wanted go all the way back to Cairo, where he would sell them for meat and then pay me for my service. I could strap my bike to one, he said. 'He means it,' Dr Hassan assured me, as he too listened with interest to tales of beasts plodding their way to the meat stalls of Egypt's capital along some ancient desert route to avoid border controls.

To return to Cairo in such a fashion, then begin the same journey south again, what an idea! It appealed to a zany bit of my psyche but…no…pushing on was now too embedded in that same psyche to go back. (*Back? Now an older man looks back to that rare but real offer. What a trip that might have been!*) The students on the floor suggested I teach English in Al-Fashir, where they were from. Yet the option which got most heads nodding and voiced by Dr Hassan himself was to get to Al-Fashir, take a four-day truck-ride across Kordofan back to Khartoum, then jump on a flight to Juba. He made it sound like a stroll in the park, but I knew it would be the way, it had to be, if a wish to see the mountain gorillas in Virunga was to be realised.

After the stop at Sennar on the Blue Nile came and went, we heard the clamour of feet by the hundred on the roof. In the distance the great meanders showed themselves with denser tree-scapes and more abundant vegetation. Then the great train turned west to Kosti on the White, and in between those two the doctor told his story, knowing no one else could understand. 'I was younger than you,' he said, '... my country was tied to the Soviet block. Many of us went to Eastern Europe to study. I remember Belgrade in the winter. It was the coldest place for me but the *snow* for us (Sudanese) was like magic, like desert for you Europeans.'

He said 'snow' like it meant more than white mush on the ground. It was a symbol of who he was before he went there, before some gay professor bedded him and wrenched him from innocence after which he began a long crawl out of a mental hell back home in the heat of Western Sudan. The memory of snow, its whiteness, pureness, remained with him, as did the scar of being buggered for much of his student days. '...like carrying a knife in my back,' he said. He laid it out until it went beyond my own comprehension. I could say nothing, had nothing to say, but wondered why he told me...and again it came, how much a bit-player I was in this journey-drama which at times I had the innocent forgetfulness to call 'my own', but he too was bit-player for me as our respective journeys interweaved. Bit-players perhaps, but by God what a hit we sometimes had.

Two days out of Khartoum we crossed the White at Kosti where the smell of us men had built up nicely to the point of explosion. It was the last straw and I looked to escape. Confinement, heat, zero sleep and a head screaming with Arabic chatter from dawn to well beyond dusk gnawed away at any residual stamina. I liked the language, but the non-stop intensity nearly broke me. Dr Hassan, thankfully knowing how it felt to understand nothing, let me in on bits of relevant debate, notably the situation in Darfur. From him I also learned the preparatory tricks of the locals. 'We sleep for as long as we can before taking the train.' That was too late for me; I wanted out and had spied a possible escape.

A flat car, transporting two white Toyota 'boxes' lay between our carriage and the next. Sitting along its edge and dangling their legs over the side were three cheery khaki-clad soldiers, while tied to a Toyota exhaust pipe was a beast of a cockerel. 'Try it,' Hassan said, 'You must try it.' He called to a soldier, explaining my need for air and possible sleep and thus, for the remaining two and half days, my legs dangled with theirs while the ground moved slow but steady beneath our feet. Their mission, as I was to uncover, was to deliver cock and 'boxes' without a scratch or a feather missing to some high-ranking colonel. No wonder they were cheery; they were being handsomely rewarded. The cheeriest said something but I did not understand. His colleague butted in and inscribed letters in Arabic on the Toyota's dusty door, but I was still at a loss. Then the third man, older and more senior looking, wrote '42' beside the Arabic squiggle. Gesturing a wipe of his practically dry forehead, he pointed to the beads of sweat on mine—eureka! It was forty-two degrees Celsius.

As if on cue, a machete and a whopper of a melon were lifted from a back seat. With obvious skill the senior man sliced it up and his scarred arm stretched over a massive chunk. The juice ran down my chin, oh sweet heaven. They cheered me on, as fascinated by my pleasure as my sweaty nature. Another chunk of juice came with a friendly nod, and as I was about to fling the rind into the moving scrub the scarred arm shot out pointing to the their feathered friend. Thereafter I followed suit, tossing bits of rind under the chassis to be instantly devoured.

We sat sated, and for a while I listened to their animated conversation wondering what they were talking about, but gradually, as the train gently rocked us to her rhythm, I drifted into my own private world, my gaze beginning to wander out over the vast stretching-off-to-nowhere plain of sand and dust and savannah vegetation.

Travel, what does it mean? A movement like a train, past to future and always, always *now*…a spinning boomerang, knowing only where you've come from, knowing nothing really about anything, even when you think you do, just going on and on…and in the end only going home… we're all boomerangs. Home? Where was that…where is that? I left it long ago. I have no home…yet.

Evening crept in, bringing its welcome cool and then, like lights out in a dormitory, night came down sharp. My khaki friends retired to mattresses in the back of the 'boxes' and I spent the night underneath the chassis in glorious horizontal. With a Toyota pick-up as cover, my head rested on the pillow of my sweat-filled cycling shorts, right at the edge of motion. The cock slumbered too, though he would peck my shoe if it drifted too close. How dare I lie in his patch.

Bid-dum-tum, bid-dum-tum, bid-dum-tum; the heartbeat tempo of the huge train settled everyone. The bulk of me lay under the chassis of the brand new 'box' while my head jutted out from under the driver's door. Looking heavenward, I floated, as if being carried on a night-stretcher over a sandy ocean. The talking faded from the carriages, a soldier snored, and my every fibre felt the train.

I tried hard to detach, to picture where I was, on an open flat-car under a Toyota, being carried through the night across a wasteland like a wounded soldier, accompanied by a tough looking tied-up cock and three melon-filled comrades sleeping above me. I tried to glimpse it, playfully, from the distant European world I'd come from, but I couldn't. Nothing came, there was nothing whatsoever odd here. It was always like this, wasn't it? Life was always like this…wasn't it?…only the gentle rocking of the train, and like a trusting child I let the motion in, settling me, settling…*travel what does it mean anyway?*… sleep…go to sleep.

He stood proud, he did, and did what cocks do, his beady little eyes sensing those first crimson-dappled germs of light. His *cock-a-doodle-do* could be heard across the ocean. The cheeriest soldier tried to shut him up with the butt of his rifle, but the cock was having none of that and gave a burst of louder *doodles*. He was officer property so could shout as loud as he pleased. It seemed our red-feathered friend had army protection at the highest level.

That was how the day began, and to avoid the intense sun and being witness to a possible fowl assassination, I returned to my friends in the carriage. I was welcomed back as if I'd been to a foreign country. The wealthy camel trader had mysteriously procured morning tea for all and sharply instructed a student off the floor with what I presumed was an order to 'go get the *khawaja* a cup!' The tea was hot and sweet, and every man sipped slowly like it was his first ever, and, like sharing tea with people anywhere, I felt part of this motley crew and for them too, I, the *khawaja,* was no longer the central focus…*he* had melted into the scenery, sipping tea like everyone else.

Through the grubby window, a herd of camels undulated east, in that quintessential way that only camels can. Three donkeys followed carrying the herdsmen, behind a cloud of hoofed-up dust which drifted away like a mist. 'This is Sudan,' I thought, 'this is *the* Soudaan', and my thoughts rambled on, '…should have stayed out on the flat car with the soldiers…would have seen those camels better. Go back out? Not sure, maybe they'll cut another melon. Maybe, but maybe not.'

The camel trader was in full flight now, holding forth to the entire carriage.

By the time his story waned the light off the desert floor had changed to an orange hue. We had snaked 400 kilometres past Tendeiti, past Um Ruwaba, past Al-Obeid into the deserts of Kordofan and into the land of gum arabic. From the floor the students threw me an odd smiling eye, but their talk was directed to Dr Hassan. 'They ask me do you drink Coca-cola?' I shook my head, 'No, no Coca-cola.' 'Pepsi, Pepsi?' came the reply. 'No,' I replied, 'tell them I don't drink Pepsi either.' Hassan chuckled aloud at seeing how stumped the students were with someone who drank neither one nor the other. 'They wish to tell you of the secret ingredient in these drinks,' he added, and so they did.

The train stopped in An-Nahud where tired bodies poured out in relief. I, though, was led away at pace by the two students with Dr Hassan in tow for translation. Days later at his home in Al-Fashir, he told me how he enjoyed being part of their youthful brash desire to share with a foreigner something of Sudan. 'I would not have done it,' he said, 'but they made me feel proud of my own country.'

The cluster of acacias (which we now approached), stood higgledy-piggledy across the brown dirt. I had pictured straight line regiments like an orchard, but these scattered, twiggy, leafless, camel-high trees did not seem at all like the source of the seeping sap which held the interest of so many for so long. 'These are wild trees,' explained Hassan. 'In a few months, after the rains, the resin will be cut off the bark…and what they say is true, the world would be a poorer place if not for this tree, and we Sudanese know all about it and what it offers.' I still wasn't fully clear what that meant, but slowly a bigger picture emerged and then I understood why they wished me to see for myself. Those trees may have looked desolate but, of the hundreds of varieties, the ones before us were jewels in the crown of the acacia family.

Acacia senegal grows across the swath of sub-Saharan lands from Senegal to the Red Sea, and from what I was told its gum has been a prized article of trade for 3,000 years or more. Like the date palm further north, the entire tree offers a cornucopia of goodies for those in the know but its *pièce de résistance* is its oozing sap, now referenced as E number 414. Once its unique properties were understood, civilisations throughout the ages wished to get hold of as much it as they could. The Egyptians used it in the embalming of their dead or to add to sweet foods or to bind and hold hieroglyphic colours onto tomb walls—just as a thousand years later those Irish monks who painstakingly scripted the Book of Kells mixed it with their dyes to give the colours life and bind them to the page.

From postage stamp adhesive to mascara to medicines, from pesticides to print, from glues to ceramic glazes, from M&Ms and jelly bean coatings to... yes you guessed...keeping all that sugar in bubbly suspension in Coke, Pepsi and a host of other fizzies (otherwise a fine sugar sediment would sit at the bottom of your can), gum arabic, the ace emulsifier, is in there somewhere. Everyone still wants it, and Sudan is still the lead producer. No wonder Osama Bin Laden invested in tracts of acacia to fund his 'projects', some suggesting that behind his assured Mona Lisa smile was the simple knowledge that every can of Coke drunk, especially in America, was helping him along. No wonder the US government was seriously lobbied to exempt the gum from its 1997 economic sanctions on Sudan, and by none other than the soft drinks lobby.

It takes years to see a story, years putting jig-saw bits together until one day you stand back to see it all—the journey of gum arabic—and to recall where it personally began, in late afternoon sun in An-Nahud, 500 metres from the train with a lump of hard resin put into your hand as a gift and you saying 'thanks' in ignorance and wondering where to put it. A beautiful hard lump of golden gum, and somewhere months later in Malawi that lump would be gone, lost, stolen, who knows? I hope it's decorating someone's window sill, but unlikely.

The train sounded and 2,000-plus bodies poured back in or scrambled on. We left An-Nahud, turning south into night, reaching Babanusa by 4am. I can't say if there's much to Babanusa; I didn't see it, but some places stick. The extraordinary sight of lanterns one after another, longer than the train, left their mark. Women sat or squatted, shrouded in the dark, ready to make their money, the small lanterns giving just enough light to show what they had to sell and a little left over to reveal their eager faces. The lucky ones squatted on the short platform, the others strung out in both directions along the sandy track.

Through the windows and along the ground hands of cash met hands of food. The banter and exchange resounded against the train. The dialect and even the language was different here; even with my rudimentary Arabic the attempt at purchasing flat bread, mangoes, *chai* and a few oranges was too full of pointing and money fumbling to allow my own 'lady of the night' to make more business. Hassan must have being watching, for he came to rescue us both. I slipped the women a fistful of piastres for her trouble and clambered back to

141

my spot by the cock. I spotted Geoff way off down the platform, his arms laden with all sorts, and then he too disappeared into the train. All was well. I would catch-up with him that afternoon in Nyala.

A whistle blew followed by a sudden shunt, and the platform crept slowly backwards and woman after woman stood and stretched, gathering what was unsold and I leaned out to look, to watch them walk away, while tearing at an orange, letting the peels fall to the moving ground, and the east was on fire and we pulled a little faster into cold air and I pulled on my red wind-cheater, making it four layers…and in a few hours I'd be stripping it off again, and the damn cock crowed to wake the train and then…then, 'Fuck, ah fuck, fuck!' My cherished cycling shorts were nowhere to be seen. In an instant I knew. Somewhere along the way they had slipped over the edge. 'Damn it, *damn* it!'

I thought of those cycling shorts many times. Over the side they went, an unintentional message in a bottle in a semi-desert night near Babanusa. I don't remember what was in the pockets. Were they ever again worn? Did some drifter boy find them on his way to Khartoum, try them on to be disappointed, or did they shrivel where they fell, covered by sand forever. I'd left my back-up shorts and my only long pants in a tailors shop back in Khartoum. Brilliant! That afternoon, in loose boxers and wondering what I'd wear, I watched as the grass-roofed mud and wattle homes grew more numerous, heralding a denser metropolis ahead. There were more animals about too— goats, cattle, camels and scrawny dogs here and there among bulging baobabs and scrub bushes barely hanging on.

The buzz of talk and movement spread along the roof as if, like sailors in a crow's nest, those up there had spied civilisation on the horizon. Soon it seemed the entire train smelt the town and everyone, even the soldiers, began to gather their possessions. Passengers from above climbed down to fill up 'our' Toyota flat car. The cock was shoved unceremoniously into his basket, and I too gathered my bits, but nothing happened. An hour passed, then another and then at last…at last the great train curved into Nyala.

On such a train for such a time across such terrain, it was easy to forget, well, almost forget, that two wheels awaited me in the goods wagon, that I was actually on a bike journey. As the big wagon door slid open, I stood back, looking as local as I possibly could in a spare white *jalabiya* donated by Dr Hassan. What greeted me was painful to look at and but for the good doctor and his friend standing beside me ('to see the machine', they had said) I would have exploded in a torrent of obscenities.

The 'machine' was there, for sure but barely recognisable. The handlebar looked deformed and the front wheel was twisted upward beneath a ton of galvanized sheeting and a mountain of grain sacks. The sight of one's one-and-only steed so flattened and battered was distressing, to put it mildly. Geoff arrived to cheer me up but even he, a well-trodden backpacker, could barely grasp 'the cyclist's agony'. Only a cyclist would understand.

We walked slowly in procession, towards the town centre, a band of willing hands carrying the bike like a corpse. The spectacle must surely have looked odd to the onlookers: there was Dr Hassan, his elderly dignified friend, two young students from our carriage, Geoff, looking like a genuine bum, and a bunch of excited kids all grabbing a bit of the bike...while I walked behind, as a pasha would, wearing Hassan's *jalabiya*, compassionately donated to cover my butt.

Mustafa, the genial manager of the nearby Darfur Hotel, stroked the saddle as he ushered us from the heat. 'Put it in the grain store,' he instructed one of his staff. We followed and laid it gently there on the concrete floor as one would do for a dead general about to lie in state. And there it remained for a deserved rest, proudly wearing its mangled handlebar and wheels like battle scars. It would eventually travel over 2,000 kilometres, out from and back to, Khartoum, without a single metre being peddled. Don't ask.

Dr Hassan led Geoff and me away and, true to his word, he treated us to a bag each of 'real' peanut paste. He spoke to the burly woman who squatted beneath her colourful *shaal*. Whatever he said made her quiver like jelly with the giggles, as she pestled her nuts to pulp. Oil was added, then some herbs which the good doctor recommended. Five fistfuls of nuts, five dollops of oil, two pinches of herb and a shake or two of salt. I watched her smooth, pounding movements, swearing I'd never buy a commercial jar again. The taste was divine and no jar of eco, organic, fair-trade, sustainable whatever...has ever come close since.

Dr Hassan slipped Geoff a bit of paper with his address in Al-Fashir. 'I am known there, you will find me,' he said, then shook our hands and wished us well. We hitched out of town, like a pair of devil-may-care clowns—Geoff black bearded with patched-up bleached blue jeans, I with red beard and borrowed starched white frock. The bike was battered but safe and my ripped sleeping bag was under a Nyala tailor's machine for multiple stitching. Over my shoulder a borrowed knapsack, full of the bare essentials, a kilo of ground-nut paste and other goodies, while stuffed in Geoff's arse pocket was Mustafa's pencil-drawn map which had the vital village *souk* days circled. I felt light and free, ready for anything, and onward we marched to our real destination, a humble waterfall on the far side of the tiny hamlet of Golo.

Birds, good banter and bulldust enlivened our walk until another hot blast billowed over us. Two Save the Children jeeps shot past, causing Geoff to hold out his arms in exasperation. 'Christ, they'd nearly run you over…just when we need a lift. You know, mate, back home I gave money to those guys…hey, *hey*, ya just lost a sponsor!'

'Bet if you'd bought the T-shirt they'd have picked us up,' I joked.

'What? At five quid, I'd sooner walk. You know they're going to need a lot more than jeeps to save these kids…you don't need to go far here to find a kid to save. I wonder where they're they going in such a rush?'

By the time the jeeps became a wispy smudge in the distance, a group of ragged teens flip-flopped passed us to Nyala, their clothes ripped and torn. Some, apparently, would deliberately rip donated clothes to better look the part for begging or just to feel part of the group, a peculiar world indeed. Yet we did get lifts, two or three of them, all the way to Thur, and there we got drunk. In the heat, our will-power had evaporated. A few smiling heads outside a shady shack was all we needed to veer down the short path to a proper shebeen. In we went and everyone who was anyone followed in our wake. Two hours later we stepped out again, back into the heat, to find the Golo track more blurry and twisty than it should have been and the last five kilometres more a sweaty marathon. Drunk or not, we swooned along, not caring very much where we'd end up. Geoff began to sing and I joined with abandon as if we were destined for the heavenly choirs.

> *In tropical climes there are certain times of day*
> *When all the citizens retire to tear their clothes off…*
> *It's one of the rules that the greatest fools obey,*
> *Because the sun is much too sultry*
> *And one must avoid its ultra-violet ray.*
>
> *And the Sudanese grieve when the white men leave their pub,*

Because they must definitely be pea-nuts, pea-nuts!
But mad Irish and Englishmen go out and drink in the midday sun,
Mad Irish and Englishmen go out and drink in the midday sun …
The Japanese don't care, the Chinese wouldn't dare,
Hindus and Argentines sleep from twelve to one.
But Paddy and Pommy detest a siesta.
At twelve noon the natives swoon and no further work is done,
But mad Irish and Englishmen go out and drink in the midday sun.
Mad Irish and Englishmen go out and drink in the midday sun.

As an Irishman I had replaced the word 'dogs' in 'Mad dogs and Englishmen', at least in our mutual variation of Coward's song. Regardless, we were almost sober when we reached Golo, which was off the beaten track—well off. Its cluster of round huts with their conical thatched roofs were strategically positioned to catch the shade of trees. Each had its private compound fenced with tall fronds, and as we strolled by I peeped through the gaps to see cameos of normal life: a bare-bottomed toddler holding the tail of a dog, two women chopping food, clothes drying on a line, a teenage girl stooping and stirring over a *kanoon*. On seeing us through the fence, older children ran with glee to tell others of our coming; it was a pure and joyful delight to our tired, inebriated squinting eyes.

We walked straight through the village, down a steep bank to the stream, where the coolest water bathed our feet. The women's easy chatter seemed to up a tempo when they saw us, their giggles making us feel at home. Some were wrapped in colourful *shaals*, some bare-breasted, but all were engaged in washing or pounding clothes or filling urns to carry back up the slope to home. How playful and easy it seemed for them, compared to their female compatriots who queued to pull goatskin sacks from deep wells in the Bayuda. Yet now, in hard hindsight, would they not have swapped that ease for their sisters' desert hardship if they knew what would befall their region a few years later? They looked at us and smiled, knowing what we had come for and knowing too that their youngsters would, without asking, quickly and giddily lead the way.

Beyond was the waterfall, not as big or as splendid as I had imagined but in the context of where we were and where we'd been it was perfect beyond words. It was this that lured us for five days across the savannah. A simple tale told in faraway Khartoum of a 'cool cascade near a wonderful fruit-filled village', with its colourful birds flying through the clear air of the Jebel Mara mountains. Naked, we stepped in to waist depth, and I raised my arms like Andy Dufresne standing tall and free after years in Shawshank.

Evening, and the little band of kids who had gathered waved goodbye reluctantly. Geoff pushed back a tide of ants and we laid out our meal of Tunisian cheese, oranges, dates flat breads and peanut paste. The twigs I gathered fired easily, the flames reflecting in the pond and up the column of plunging water, out across the whole magical space. We ate in an absorbed silence against the background of an endless cascading and burbling, added to occasionally by the shrieks of an unknown bird or bat, which would momentarily halt our spooning and finger-licking. Later, after a few more short swims in absolute darkness, we slept soundly head to head.

The Jebel Marra mountains, the 'bad mountains' in Arabic, are at 1,000 to 3,000 metres high. Anciently bad, perhaps? The last time they exploded into the sky was in 1500 BCE. The volcanic caldera was up there in a hazy skyline, and no matter where we walked along the foothill paths from one village to another, the 'Bad Peak' looked down on us. The earth was parched dry, the air cool, and soon, so we were told, the rains would turn those scatteredtrees green. Our walk was more a pleasant amble than exploration; climbing the mountain never even entered our minds.

The African grey hornbill may not be your full-on coloured bird, but to see it perched on a thick branch hardly ten metres away was enough to animate even Geoff, a most indifferent non-birder. 'Must be the male,' I said, but I was wrong. I had presumed the bird's long curved red-tipped bill had male written all over it, but later discovered it belonged to the female. She was not alone; her husband was close and we watched as he arched his neck up, throwing out a high-pitched call like the squeak from an old wheelbarrow. He would soon have to feed her through a tiny hole in her self-made sealed-up nest in the cavity of a tree. In there, having shut the door with mud, she'd remain safe with her eggs until the time came to peck her way out again.

Back at the pond a line of black-billed wood hoopoes reminded me of starlings on a telephone wire. Pied crows were everywhere just like the crows of home, except they wore little white waistcoats, and who would not grin to see a parrot? As we stood for a morning dip, a cluster of Meyer's parrots flew across the pool and my day was made before it even began. Geoff didn't quite share my interest, but he too was blown away by these flashes of 'real parrot'. For him though, it was the high-flying majesty of vultures which took his attention skyward. My pocket *Mitchell-Beazley* was useless here but later we learned from Hassan that they were Rüppell's griffon. Without them and others like them, the plains of Africa would be littered with the waste of carrion. Rüppell's griffon, what a bird! All I saw of it was a revolving speck high in the hazy blue, but that was enough to bring privilege again. With a wingspan of two and a half metres these guys hold the world record for serious high flying even, by all accounts, above Everest.

In the cool of our tea-lady's fenced-off corral we waited with the patience of enlightened gurus for our last *chai*. It was time to leave. Two mammas were ahead of us, one with a toddler on her lap. Nothing at all was rushed. Water boiled, then poured through a sieve of leaves into a first glass. This was then poured through the sieve again into a second. Double strength! I didn't open my mouth as she put her hand into the large tin of sugar lumps but Geoff, guessing I was about to decline, said, 'Mate you've your whole life ahead to do without sugar.' Indeed he was right, and it felt right not to intervene with personal preferences. Every culture has its 'way of tea' and as in Japan there was such dignity and poise here. So after the sweetest tea ever we paid our due, bowed to the tea-lady and the mammas, walked out into the 'oven' and struck off back down the trail to the shebeen for a mug of potent local brew before hitching to Nyala.

If there were to be cherries atop of my two-year odyssey cake, Golo village and its nearby cascade in the Jebel Marra Mountains would surely be one, but sadly when I remember that place it's not tea, tranquillity or exotic birdlife which come first to mind, rather butchery and chaos. It is difficult to write about this now, about that brief time, knowing what happened some years later. Tears are close to the surface. To know that Golo was one of the first villages where the rape and killing began makes its memory in me a memorial. It's impossible not to hold in the mind's eye the young women who happily pounded clothes, the children who led us, the older woman who poured for us, the teacher who chaperoned us. Whatever happened to them amid the slaughter?

The outside world may have come to know of the Darfurian genocide in 2003, but what did happen and is happening there has been bubbling under complex social-cultural surfaces for generations. It's the old worn story of inequality and hegemony, between governing elites and those on the periphery. A hegemony of power and greed, now aided and abetted by the growing environmental crises of desertification, overpopulation, access to water and resources. Throw in the militarization of rural villages, the probable power play for oil and gold in the Jebel hills, the gum arabic in Kordofan, the mistrust, even the question of 'identity'...all and more feed the fire of savagery.

According to the UN, in 2014 alone over 3,000 villages were destroyed, some for a second or third time. It has been officially called 'the world's greatest humanitarian crisis' compared to what happened in Rwanda. Sudan's three-time elected president Omar Al-Bashir is the first sitting president to be indicted by the International Criminal Court (ICC) for genocide, rape and pillage against Darfurians, but I'm sure he will never see The Hague. There is evidence he has armed the *janjaweed* militia (pastoral northern tribes, who have much to gain from ethnic cleansing) and loosed them to fall on innocent villagers.

Perhaps China, which buys oil here has, more than anyone else, access to al-Bashir's leaning ear. Perhaps they might say or do...but...then again perhaps wishful thinking. Pools like the one we swam in would literally become blood-baths in later years, and today sadly, not far from where the train curved into Nyala carrying Geoff, me and a thousand happy home-bound people, lie tens of thousands of homeless, shattered refugees and IDPs (Internally Displaced Persons). They are spread across several enormous tented camps. Enough said... but not enough, never enough.

★★★

Just before noon, on top of a truck, we left Nyala. The bike was strapped to two fifty-gallon drums, in turn strapped to the truck's rear end. I could barely look at the deformed front wheel. For those first few hours, leaning over the cab with my head wrapped in the trusty Palestinian *keffiyah,* I went over what had to be done: stitch a ripped front pannier, straighten both wheels, replace four spokes, re-grease bearings in bottom bracket, clean sand from chain and freewheel, re-grease gear cables, replace snapped left brake cable, fix punctures, find a welder or machinist, to weld or brace cracks in both carriers...and all that for starters.

My little 'break' was over, and it was time to return to work. I almost envied Geoff his light rucksack and two feet, well almost.

Through the night the powerful headlights led the way and at 8.20am the following day our convoy of two pulled in to Al-Fashir truck station. It had taken a bumpy, sleepless, twenty and a half hours to cover the 190 kilometres from Nyala, with a few *chai* stops thrown in (today you'd drive it bump-free in less than five). The word 'knackered' has a harsh bluntness to it, but that's how we felt. The journey to Al-Fashir, though, was but a warm-up for the more arduous four and half day ride across northern Kordofan back to Khartoum. Thankfully, courtesy of Hassan, there would be a few days of rest before that.

Al-Fashir, capital of North Darfur, was home to 20,000 inhabitants in 1985. Roll on thirty years, it's now 270,000 and rising. The African sub-Saharan baby boom is no joke. I showed Hassan's slip of paper to a young guy. He read the Arabic script and immediately beckoned us to follow. Not ten minutes later we were standing in our boxers in the seclusion of his courtyard, bucketing our heads with glorious cold water.

Three huge clay *dabangas* stood against the opposite wall, shaded by an old mango tree. They looked just like urns in a Beckett play, and if three encrusted heads had popped up spouting gibberish we'd hardly have considered the scene anymore surreal than it was. *Dabangas*, life affirming *dabangas*—I'd seen a few, but not this close. Their rounded sides of cob felt rough to touch. In threadbare boxers which stuck to white wet skin above suntan demarcation lines of deep brown, we dried our fast drying bodies with tiny towels. Geoff wondered if Beckett had ever been to Darfur, but as unlikely as that was, we laughed that we could easily have passed for a pair of half-naked bums in one of the master's plays.

Hassan came and told what was within the *dabangas*. 'One is for animal fodder, the other two food for my family.' Like the ubiquitous water urns along the Nile, the thick cob walls kept foods safe and dry, at times keeping famine at bay. For centuries they were central to survival, some people even using them like the proverbial mattress, stashing their money in among the corn cobs. '*Ed duniya dabanga, dardago beshweish*'—so a Darfurian proverb goes ('Life is like a *dabanga*, roll it carefully'). When the attacks and destruction of villages began (from 2003 on), *dabangas* were always looted…then smashed. Life indeed is like a *dabanga*, fragile, so, so fragile. Today Darfur has its own radio station attempting to broadcast to the world what's going on there. No surprise it's called Radio Dabanga.

Chai and biscuits awaited us post ablutions and a cool room prepared for a few hours' welcome rest. Hassan's hospitality took us to the edge of feeling awkward and, privately, as I put it to Geoff, 'We like to think in Ireland how we're friendly to visitors. Compared to Sudanese we're not at the races.'

'Bloody hell, mate ,where does that leave us Brits?' he said. 'We're not even in the race.'

If Hassan could not guide us personally he had his brother do so: to the *chai* house, the souk, the camel market, the welder's shop, the tailor, the police station (to register) and the truck station (to book a space to Khartoum). In the *chai*-house, the owner had been instructed to give us *chai* 'on the house', or more likely on Hassan's tab, and there one afternoon we were introduced to his friend, the Treasurer for the Darfur region. It was another world in the Treasurer's office: solid oak furnishings, plush leather chair, cool air, low light with heavy green velvet curtains keeping out the intense glare. We drank Johnnie Walker from Waterford cut glass, I making light that it should be Irish whiskey in an Irish glass! 'Ah, you are Irish…good,' he said, 'I have Irish whiskey at my home. Please, you must all come this evening.'

We washed and dressed in our very best, which was a joke, but what could we do? Then on time, a whiter than white 'box' arrived to take us and Hassan to the Treasurer's residence. We two bounced in the back, Geoff wondering was the 'box' the one I had slept under?

'Maybe,' I answered. 'If it has cock shit on the exhaust pipe, definitely.'

★★★

The Treasurer and one other greeted us in a richly furnished, well proportioned reception room. A silver tray with five sparkling cut-crystal glasses was the first thing we noticed. 'Welcome, my friends,' he said. He could not have been more courteous if he tried. Then, swiftly and proudly, he pulled his rare Irish whiskey from its box, emblazoned with a picture of what to my eyes looked like the Rock of Cashel. The label had a colourful map of Ireland, the four provinces, Leinster in yellow, Munster in blue, Connacht in red and Ulster in green, but it was the box and the bottle's label, more than the whiskey within, which got the Treasurer talking about anything at all Irish. 'I know much about your neighbour,' he said, 'but it is your country which interests me more.' He led the conversation down a familiar historical route: as he put it, 'a country's desire for independence against the aggressor'. I'd heard this expressed elsewhere en route and was always intrigued how certain people in lands far from Ireland were tuned into its effort for self-determination. That seemed to mean something to them. His friend poured, but he led the toast to 'the right of a people to decide their destiny'. I bit my lip at that, knowing what I did about the Christians of South Sudan and the strife of farmers in the Marra Mountains.

More whiskey allowed us be more brazen. Geoff pushed the boundaries with awkward questions about reported tensions between Arab nomad and African farmer in Darfur; then, remembering William and Mary in Dongola, I followed by asking of John Garang and the rights of Christians in the South. Dr Hassan showed no sign of being embarrassed, but he must have been, yet the Treasurer was skilful and shifted the conversation back to Ireland, or Northern Ireland, to be specific. We would have preferred to talk of Sudan but he was a government official and we were just two passing-through, off-the-street guests, lucky enough to be shepherded by his friend.

What shouldn't have, but did surprise me was not the interest in far-off politics by our Sudanese host but Geoff's complete lack of knowledge of *his* country's connection with Irish history. However, he was blunt and honest enough to tell them that. 'In England we don't learn much about Irish affairs or about what we did over there. Before this war in the North most Brits knew little about Ireland and still don't if you ask me.' It was perhaps a bit unfair to many of his countrymen, but then again, in the mid-1980s not far off the mark. His fuzzy grasp of his neighbouring country's history begged a bigger question of his nation, but the Treasurer was far more intrigued that we would travel together at all, given, as he put it, 'this war between your countries'.

'Oh no, there's no war,' said Geoff, 'just bloody-minded indifference on our side of the Irish Sea…but with him (pointing to me), I have to watch my back constantly.' We both laughed.

'Yeah,' I added, 'and I'm just waiting to push him off a truck.'

A rare Paddy and one regular Johnnie divided between five men made for a heady morning-after and, along with food way too rich, we paid for it the following day, blowing wind from both ends. From the humble offerings of remote Golo village to the over-indulgence at the Treasurer's residence…it was a dietary bridge too far! Whatever else, it was no way to prepare for part two of our desert crossing. Thankfully, on seeing our state, Dr Hassan suggested we rest the whole of the afternoon. The truck would depart that evening carrying two tonnes of tobacco, the same of sesame, two barrels of something or other, thirteen passengers, two helpers, a driver, a goat (as usual it seemed!) and one battered bicycle. All going well, it would take us four plus days to reach the capital, four days along a straight line of sand from Al-Fashir, capital of Darfur, to Khartoum, capital of a divided country.

★★★

'No, mister, no! No, camel is not ship of desert, it is truck, truck…my truck.' So said our proud Nissan driver. He had no regard it seemed for ' those smelly beasts'. Perhaps he had a point. Trucks in Sudan did all the hard graft, ferrying merchandise, animals, people, soldiers and guns. Trucks were everywhere, going everywhere, and the truck station was a more animated place than the camel market. He took our money and ushered us to climb.

We were last up the timber siding and the scene on top was chock-a-block with bodies and baggage. Thirteen fellow passengers were already hunkered down but they kindly guided us as we manoeuvred about searching for a good 'seat'. All the best spots were taken and we weighed the options. Geoff went starboard to a half-decent depression between two sacks of tobacco. I had no choice but go aft to an awkward place between the truck's spare tyre and my own crooked front wheel, but at least there I could keep an eye on my jumble of bags. That was it, we had chosen our positions for the duration of the journey, the equivalent, distance-wise, of a roof-top ride from Le Havre to Marseilles. Sudan is a big country.

My legs hung over the side to cool, but the heat was waning. For an hour or more we waited, not that it mattered. This was no scheduled official route. Effectively we were stowaways, there at the discretion of the driver, allowing him earn some easy extra cash. We would depart *only* when he was ready, not a minute before. The camel market was drawing to a close, but he still had obvious talking to do. Camels were being led away, and the camel buyer from the train was holding court in the midst of a white turbaned group, gesticulating like an Italian. I waved but he didn't see, and for a second the thought came of jumping down to take-up his offer and join his north-bound caravan, but the dice had been thrown. The engine revved soon after, and we set off into Kordofan.

Chapter 7
Knowing nothing about anything

If the train trip out had been claustrophobic, the truck ride back was as open to the elements as one could imagine. We powered into a cold night hunting meteorites, Geoff pointing and calling from one end, I from the other. The locals thought we were crazy but it was all good fun. For me though, the fun was sorely tempered by my rear end. Five hours sitting on a vibrating sack of sesame had chafed away on my precious buttocks. The soreness had snuck up on me, and I winced at the thought of having to let my ass down, sooner or later, on the hardened leather of a Brooks B-17. Not for the first time the black and white *keffiyeh* came to the rescue; folded carefully into a neat square, it was stuffed between the sack and the sorest cheek. The sleeping bag would have been a better cushion, but in darkness atop of a moving truck was no place to go rummaging.

By 1.53am, according to my Casio, we'd gobbled up desert

for the bones of seven hours. Everyone was pretty much shattered, and when the two engines stopped only the sound of tired Arabic mutterings broke the silence. Some chose to slumber above, some beneath coats and blankets on terra firma below and some watched curiously as Geoff and I pulled our thermal bags up around us before joining them on the sand for the four hours' rest. The goat was lowered too, in a sling, letting out a confused *meh-eh-eh, meh-eh-eh* as he was tied tightly to the siding. Within what seemed but seconds the Sudanese were asleep and they appeared to do so as easy as if they were in their own beds. Geoff followed soon after but perhaps my testosterone was rising for I twisted and turned, sculpting my shape in the sand until I eased at last into a wet dream of women, their dark liquid-alluring eyes beckoning and soothing.

In the morning everyone spat. The breeze caught one sticky one for a bull's eye on my arm. I wiped it off a tobacco sack and said nothing. Up front, Geoff sang to himself. I admired his seeming unbridled energy, but then he was on a high, *he* was going home. As for me, butted up to the spare tyre I felt flat and, as if to prove a private point, I raised a limp arm to let it fall like a wet rag. I wondered had ten hard-riding months depleted me. That was the question, but the truth was otherwise, and I would soon find out.

Half a day beyond Umm Badr the desert appeared more hostile, more in-tolerant of mishaps, at least to European eyes. Our partner truck was some 300 metres behind when its tyre blew. Its driver blew his horn and we about-turned. To sit with legs-a-dangling watching the matter-of-factness of repair would have given anyone confidence. The Automobile Association could hardly have been more efficient. It impressed Geoff at any rate. 'I feel safer out here than go-ing up the M1,' he said. We were about to set off when another truck closed in. Back in Umm Badr, *its* partner truck had died of a packed-in engine; knowing we were a few hours ahead, the driver had driven hard to catch us. Our convoy was now three, and the sound of that many engines revving for traction con-trasted with the notion of camels quietly plodding.

Yet the sandscape seemed to resist motion, any motion, that of truck or thought or even bowel. In three days neither of us could recall a single crap, and just as I was reminding myself of the importance of hydration, Geoff roared 'Oasis mate, oasis.' Sure enough it came, a well-worn siesta stop, looking more like a mangrove swamp with pools of shallow murky water surrounded by date palms.

We were down like a shot to commandeer the shadiest spot we could find, and with my back to the trunk of a palm, I watched Geoff stroll to the water barrel. A black-veiled woman was reaching in to jug out water for the *chai*. Geoff turned, shaking his head. 'You don't want to look in there,' he said, 'I think it's time to break out the Puritabs…hey, you feeling ok? You look shit mate.' I had to admit, I felt it. Of course, what he didn't know and what I didn't know was that I had hepatitis. Could I have done anything different had I known? Probably not. The thought of it had passed my mind but was dismissed as fast ('Hep? *Me*, no way!'). I had explained away my ever darkening urine by telling myself that it was 'just dehydration'. If I'd looked into the truck's wing mirror I might have been more honest. Eyes don't lie, especially yellow ones.

We sipped our Puritabed *chais* beside a middle-aged man whose lower face protruded like an ape. 'Geez,' said Geoff under his breath, 'we're drinking with the missing link. Gotta tell the Leakeys…just gotta.' From then on, and unfairly of course, we christened him 'the link', but a more affable, considerate man one could hardly have met. I bought him a *chai*, and several hours later when the night wind blew chill air over us all he pushed a spare blanket in my direction. Not until dawn did I see it was not spare; it was his own.

Our driver honked his horn, the signal to climb on board. He was on commission; the sooner he got his sesame and tobacco to Khartoum, the more money he would make. He pushed his 'turn boys' to the limit, shouting at them to keep the wheels rolling, to dig out the sand faster, faster, faster. And they did, even in the dark, chatting to each other under the chassis. One of them, the son of a driver, was a student in Khartoum and on a week break 'to make money'. I wondered how much and at what cost, breaking his back digging sand over and back across the desert. I imagined his equivalent Irish student, comfortable and supported in the US on a J1, earning serious cash by comparison, in cafés, bars, and construction sites…and having a whale-of-a-time to boot. What different worlds we live in.

Draw a straight line from Al-Fashir through Umm Badr to Khartoum; that was the line we took. We were all suffering. Two days out, two days without sleep. Us *khawajas* kept ourselves going with general knowledge quizzes, batting questions over the heads of our fellow passengers. No one spoke English, but it was clear they too wanted to be part of the craic, and thus I began teaching them 'My bonnie lies over the ocean, My bonnie lies over the sea'. Word by word we were making progress, or so I thought, until Geoff chimed in with his own boy-scout version. 'My daddy lies over my mammy and that's how they got little me.' 'Oh for fuck sake, Geoff,' I shouted but I was in stitches and, to cap it all, my choir, led by 'the link', preferred his version (our hunch being that the word 'ocean' had got their tongues in a twist.) Of course no one understood anything, but that was utterly beside the point.

There were no wealthy camel buyers here, no Dr Hassans, no soldiers or merchantmen. None of *them* would travel so. These were grassroots people, salt of the earth types—labourers, herders, dispossessed farmers, most with little education but with families and dreams back in Darfur and dreams ahead of making it good in the city. So went my presumptions, and statistically they may have been true, but it was still conjecture. I looked at the faces, then looked out over the vast expanse of North Kordofan, and I knew I knew nothing about anything here. I barely knew my own experience.

There was a hole in my Michelin map north-west of Umm Badr. I imagined we were passing right through it. That told me something about travelling.

Like people, the landscape is never what it seems to anyone visitor or local. I could only witness a snapshot of a snapshot, a sliver of a spectrum. Not much at all really. The locals swim in it, swim in its memory, but even they could miss a fresh take on things…familiarity making the eye sleep. Hidden to me were the subtle seasonal changes and of course the composite generational ones, but I could at least vouch that I saw sand etched with tyre trails and between the ruts a bleached coke-can, a plastic bottle, a piece of metal, a discarded cigarette pack, while beyond stood a single scrub bush, then a few more heralding a wadi dreaming of water, and the entire vista was cut in two by a dead straight horizon-line splitting the infinite from the very scratching of life. The blue above lifted a tired, fried mind to endless dreamy possibilities, while below the parched brown spoke symbolically of skulls and bones and death and…and time, endless time. I asked myself how my Sudanese fellows saw all this. How wonderfully different might they understand what I did not.

We arrived at our place for the night, four huts and an open shelter, at the edge of some village perhaps, but I could not be certain. The driver raised four fingers: four hours to sleep or do what we want. 'No people list, no people list,' he reminded us. He had his money and was unlikely to do a roll-call before his dawn departure. If we wandered off or overslept we would miss the boat—240 kilometres out from Khartoum. I watched him join the other drivers around the fire, lifting his dirt-stained white *jalabiya* as he sat. Their helpers served them well, one being instructed to bring food to us *khawajas*. It duly came, a basket of bread and a basin of goat meat in a peppery sauce. He turned, nodding upwards to us with a smile, and we acknowledged with our most gracious *shukran*. 'He's not a bad bastard after all,' Geoff said, ripping into a lump of goat.

Fires, I had grown to love them. Here there were two, creating a homely atmosphere from nothing but crackling and flying sparks. One was harnessed to heat the goat stew, the other to heat a battered black kettle for *chai*, homely indeed! I had sat by more fires in Sudan than in all other countries combined, and for some reason the country was hard to beat for its special kind of fire-sidedness. Was it the desert skies or dewey-eyed notions of parched remoteness, the bleating goats, the strange dialects, or was it the softening of a sense of time? Camp fires, they had a habit of halting time in me, mesmerising by their old magic, suspending the spark-gazer in a liquid state of Being.

After food our driver directed us away from the others to the furthest hut and, with prayerful hands beneath a tilted head, indicated how we might sleep better there. The 'others' preferred to talk around the fires, but it did not take much to see what was really going on. He wanted us out of the way for a reason. I tapped Geoff on the arm and we watched as he guided the young *chai* girl of no more than 14 or 15 into an adjacent hut. 'Christ,' said Geoff. We prepared for sleep in silence and unease. The ease of an older man whisking such a young girl away gnawed at some cultural basic. 'The link' arrived and like us he was the only other who appeared to value some shut-eye, but unlike us he didn't seem at all perturbed by the young girl's muffled gasps and giggles. Not to judge was nigh impossible. I judged. It was wrong, my moral reasoning went. I never did ask Geoff what went through his head that night, but I guess it may well have been similar to mine. 'Let it go, mate, let it go.'

Pre-dawn constipation…nothing quite like it! I walked barefoot to the edge of the wadi, sand cold underfoot, nose sharper in the dark. It caught a familiar stale odour…me! The odour had developed of late and trailed like a loyal dog. 'One day more, then a shower,' I thought and I was powerless then to stop the images of that rusty communal faucet back in the hostel with its trickle-trickle of water. I found the ideal shitting spot that I was looking for and hunkered down to wait.

The desert floor was still dark and the dome still studded with random jewels. Venus was radiant, but Mercury, a pin-prick by comparison, barely held his own, twenty-odd degrees above the horizon. To witness this rarity was another of those unsung delights of being on the road. Unsung to the point that I wondered did fellow travellers notice at all, for few if any spoke of such celestial matters. How many times back home had my attempts to catch a glimpse of its mercurial nature been dashed by damn cloud. Here above the desert plain it was so plain to see, a child would have done so, but it was dropping fast. Twenty degrees went to eighteen, to fifteen, to ten, but I squatted on, not wanting to move from what felt like a front row seat witnessing the Earth's rotation. The pin-prick of Mercury grew faint, then vanished into the rising glow, and I was left with the quirky imagining of trying to pass a stool while spinning at a thousand miles per hour.

In cloudless countries these early calls of nature rarely disappointed. Before the sun rose out of the ground, the simplest things like jet streaks, morning stars, bird calls, would give great pleasure. At times, if the light was right, they could seem otherworldly, and yet for all that, it was time itself or the *non-sense* of time which stared back at me from the vastness of sky and sand. Time, my time, no time, endless time, timeless time, all merged…and I? 'I' was the pin-prick in it all, a mere passing reference point, squatting now at the threshold of that transition, before the sun rose up to blast itself about the sandscape.

A first hard turd passed, then a second like iron, but my eyes were fixed to the lift-off spot; sun-up was coming fast, coming, coming, yes, no, not yet, yes *there*—there bursting like a boil, the tip-most-orange-top of its curve—*sunburst*! Out of a dead flat desert plain it's like nothing else on earth, with no mountains, forests, fields or cityscape to steal the impact. It had the perfect barren stage to its awesome self.

I looked back at our little group, slowly arising around the trucks, yawning, stretching. It would be our last day before immersing ourselves again in Khartoum's bosom. As for wadis, there were wadis everywhere but not a drop to drink, dried-up river beds that hadn't seen water for years, and as certain as there would be sun, it was certain there would be no rain. I stood to buckle my shorts, imagining the millions who had shat across the Sahara, and with the heel of my shoe pushed the soiled paper into the sand. If the rains ever came, the fertility was waiting.

A guy walked past toward the trucks, a jerry-can in each hand. He had climbed out of the wadi behind me. His lips were cracked. '*Laa ma'a, laa ma'a* (no water, no water),' he said. The driver's helper filled his jerry-cans and off he went again, somewhere. '*Laa ma'a*,' said 'the link', showing three fingers—three years no rain. I turned to Geoff, '...fuck me, I wont complain about Irish rain again.' 'Sure thing, mate, any rain,' he replied, 'any bloody rain.'

Everyone did what they had to do. Geoff slotted his last roll of film in his camera, the driver checked his engine, the turn-boys cleaned the windscreen, and I checked ropes holding the bike in place, manoeuvring round a snoozing teenager who had taken my pannier as his pillow. Directly below, a father stood patiently beside his little girl as she crouched for a final pee. Her little rivulet puddled round her tiny feet then vanished into the all-swallowing sand. He lifted her up to helping hands, then climbed up himself. 'The link' was already snuggled down, reading from his old Quran. I slotted in between him and the tyre, trying not to disturb. We were ready.

It may well have been the last day before we reached Omdurman, but by God what a day. (Today, some satellite would have informed us but then we had no inkling.) By noon those who had been quiet for the morning began to talk among themselves. Some spoke to the turn-boys who relayed questions to the cab. They began to fidget, to pull out blankets, and plastic covers. The girl's father tied a *hijab* tight around her head, then one around his own. I was clueless until 'the link' directed my attention to the south-west. 'Haboob, haboob,' he said. Then above the engine roar, Geoff called back, 'It's a sandstorm!'

Sandstorm, yes, but *haboob,* I had never heard the word. The dirty brown amorphous wall of cloud stretched along the horizon as far as could be seen and, like looking out to sea, it was difficult to gauge its distance. It appeared to be sitting there, four, five, or more kilometres away and except for a fuzzy puffiness it could have passed as the solid flank of a hillside. The wind, now warm, picked up, blowing over my right shoulder. If it was to hit us, it would do so on our starboard side.

The trucks could go no faster, and within the hour, dust and the first tiny grains splayed across us. It would take awhile, but for sure we would be swallowed. The wind strengthened and surprisingly grew warmer and, as if on cue, the drivers pulled over in close proximity, leaving their tail-ends to face the onrushing wall of sand. As a sort of bulwark, sacks of sesame were stacked along the rear and then we dived beneath the covers. 'The link' poured water on my *keffiyeh* and showed how to wrap it around my mouth. Moments later like a slap, the *haboob* struck for real and washed into us like an avalanche.

The engines stopped but the noise was deafening. Wind whipped sand in great splashes against the tarp. We were in it. I sunk my covered head into the zipped-up wind-cheater and pulled the hood-cords tight. Nothing to do but wait it out. Despite the layers, dust and the finest grains got everywhere, everywhere! Everyone shallow-breathed. Lips were pursed, eyes watered and my nose worked overtime, half blocked with dirt. Once, to grab a decent breath I opened my mouth and the tiniest grains got in. With what spit I had I swallowed hard, thinking sand in the stomach a better option than a grinding and grating between my teeth.

It was eerie but exhilarating, like being sandblasted in a darkened turbulent car-wash. The *habb* (wind) did it's utmost to rip the canvas off but we all held firm. Just as well we were dug-in on a truck top, for at ground level the bigger grains would have stung like hot sparks. Beneath the plastic tarp the temperature felt like fifty degrees and the claustrophobic heat sent me off in bouts of day-dreaming.

There's not much to do under a tarp in a sandstorm. You listen, you plan ahead, you drift off. You hold tight and pick the dry scabs of dirt from around the rims of your nose. I picked and flicked them out into the wind, letting my free hand be sandblasted for a split-second. Then a childhood memory came of my father telling a story about how he was on a high tower in Libya as he watched a super sandstorm come rushing to 'his oil-refinery'. The oil frenzy of the 1960s had taken him to the great Sarir field in the Libyan desert where dust made his bronchitis worse, eventually causing him to leave Libya altogether. My mother was glad. She never wished to go there and have her sons 'leave their friends and a good Irish education'. I was 12, ready to take on the world and bitterly disappointed to have such adventure and one-upmanship scuppered.

Did his story plant a seed? Was I in this *haboob* because my father had been in one too, or because my mother had called a sensible halt to the exotic dreams of her son. Was I living out an unconscious backlash? Who knew? Under the tarp it struck me then, that often we travel for reasons we don't fully know, but more often than not the reason is of no consequence. The process of travelling moves us beyond reasons. So here I am, I thought, holding tight to a tarp, listening to whipping sand. Must write to Dad. He'd enjoy reading about this, he'd understand.

By late afternoon we again shook like jellies. We were on the move with time apparently against us. The wind had gone but the dust hung-round like a smog and dusk, if it came at all, was brief. The truck lights got nowhere in the murky dark but the drivers drove even faster than before. We looked like a deadly band of Ninjas on a mission, thirteen pairs of focussed eyes peering out from head-scarves, while above our heads a hole appeared in the dust cloud. It stayed with us as we moved, a chimney to the stars, relieving the smothering claustrophobia. Then as sudden, we were out, out into crystal-clear night air, and there, way off on the north-east horizon, lay the faint but certain halo of a huge city: Omdurman-Khartoum.

The hazy glow grew and with it the thought of a wash and a sleep at journey's end but then, incomprehensibly—to Geoff and me at least—that yellow-orange arc over the metropolis drifted by to the north. More precisely, we, being at least fifty kilometres due south, were moving further east. I called to Geoff, 'Hey, what's goin' on?' 'Don't know, buddy,' he replied 'but it looks like we ain't goin' to Khartoum tonight.' He was right. We watched as the dim glow of the capital drifted away.

Sometime in the night in Jebel Aulia we pulled in to a truck park sixty or so kilometres south of our destination, and there all was revealed. A young Khartoumian going our way and seeing our confusion explained. 'But we are not official,' he said. 'You must leave this truck and wait here.' Apparently trucks carrying merchandise across the desert had to check in with police and customs and we passengers were not considered 'official merchandise'. We had to be dumped somewhere, so there we were, 3am in a truck park, our truck gone for its check-in. Raw-eyed with lids like sandpaper, I gathered myself, my bits, bags and bike and found a corner to crash… *'travel, what does it mean, anyway?'*

★★★

The man beside me quietly stood to begin his *fajr*. Darkness was fading fast. *'Allahu Akbar, Allahu Akbar,'* four times he intoned. Unwittingly I had slept on his prayer mat, oh dear! I offered to move but he instantly declined and once again I was struck by the reverence and adherence of Muslims. So I rose too, and by six I was looking at a 75-piastre fish in a chipped dish, telling myself to eat, yet at the same time feeling nauseous with fatigue and whatever else was going

161

on. But all that was academic. Geoff and I hung in there, as they say, and four hours and two different trucks later we arrived at souk Ash-Shaabi, Omdurman, shy of five days since leaving Al-Fashir. We tipped the driver and bid 'the link' goodbye (never did get his real name). Geoff took off straight to the campsite to shower but I had a bike to repair and stoically pushed through the *souk*, feeling like there was a dead pig on my back.

It was a hot March mid-morning. I dragged my two-wheeled buckled comrade down narrow busy streets, seeking a sign of a workshop. White *jalabiya*-clad men were everywhere crossing over and back, some with cups of *chai* in the hand, and the morning chatter and clatter of bustle and business was all round me. Mini ripples of 'noticing the *khawaja*' followed me but, feeling utterly bedraggled, I had barely the energy for the attention. The camaraderie of our tight little desert-crossing group was gone, and it felt strange to be anonymous again. Anonymous but certainly not un-noticed. From one side of the street to the other the bike and I were pointed at. Older men ordered younger men to shift their arses and bring me to where it was obvious I needed to go. I didn't open my mouth, just nodded, knowing instinctively where I would be led. 'This is *the Soudan*,' I reminded myself and *that* was how it was.

The mechanic was tucked away in the welcome shade of a back street, his workshop a toolbox at his feet. The boys had wished to bring me to a more established 'proper shop', but I could see the man with the box was good. So after a cinnamon *chai* and a pidgin English chat, pointing to this and that on the bike, then another *chai*, I felt almost home. He dived into the transmission with an enthusiasm I didn't have, as I greased cables and trued the wheels. Not a word was said. We knew what to do and, I thought to myself, no matter what his fee, it would be worth every cent. By the time I was rubbing oil into the saddle (a leather oil which he had sent a kid to procure from somewhere), there must have been twenty other kids around. 'We should do this everyday and charge them for the entertainment,' I said. The joke, not being understood, was shrugged at, but that was okay. We shook our greasy hands and bid each other farewell.

'Sudan will test you my friend.' The forewarning of the history-loving Egyptian gentleman with his shiny shoes outside the Aswan cafe returned. I remembered him, sitting there smoking and smiling as if he knew something which he could never hope to explain about what lay ahead for me in his neighbouring country. I smiled, thinking of him, imagining that surely now I knew a little of what he might have meant.

What did I feel as I crossed from Omdurman to Khartoum over the same bridge I had ridden across that first arrival day, stopping at the same place to gaze again at the meeting of the Niles? Exhausted, overwhelmed with experiences, achy to the marrow, appetite-less…yet glad to be back. I wished to rest and be still, but, unbeknownst to me, I carried a liver full of virus. And yet, for the first time in the journey I felt seasoned, well-seasoned, 'salt-and-peppered'—yes, I felt well and truly *travelled*. Despite the exhaustion there was a lightness. Slowly the legs turned the cranks toward the hostel-campsite with a single thought turning in my head, 'Don't complain, don't even think about it. You're one lucky bastard.'

★★★

Two days later Geoff left for the UK. 'Take care of yourself, mate, you've a bit to go yet. See ya in d'Emerald Isle…yeah, must get over there sometime.' Out the gate he strode, one of the spunkiest Englishmen I had the privilege of happening upon. His parting gift was his money belt, graciously donated to my cause; a proper tough leather trouser belt with a secret zip on the inside (and oh what drama that would play on the Malawian border four months later). I wore it first to the Zaire embassy, thinking a visa could be picked up easy. Silly me. The four day visa-wait was outdone by a ten day *insha'allah* airways ticket-wait to Juba. Sudan Airways was having 'issues', none of which I was privy to, but John Garang's second and serious civil war down south probably had something to do with it. The flight *would* depart but only if Allah willed it. *Insha'allah.*

There's nothing 'civil' about a civil war. All things civil are sacrificed on the altar of the binary. There's no place for politeness or courtesy. People die, simple as that. Fighting in South Sudan is long in the tooth. The first North-South civil war began in 1955, two years before I was born. The second took off in 1983, two years before I got there, lucky me! So, giving war no further thought, I went to the tent to rest for the afternoon and mull over a 'shit-load' of travel stuff. It was a cool 38 degree Celsius. I lay on the cool groundsheet to keep my dripping sweat off the sleeping bag and day-dreamed of double-mangoes in the cool of that evening.

Travelling-waiting, travelling-waiting, travelling…then waiting some more. Sooner or later there's no choice, you wait, just wait. Wars, borders, visas, tickets, bad timing, illness, broken parts or hearts, hitches, glitches, robbery, no money, loss, even love and a dozen other vagaries of the road well travelled—all or any can do you the favour, often unappreciated at the time. Fine and dandy when it's expected and factored in, but when ten days of it hits you in the wrong place, wrong time…well, it could easily feel like a life sentence. But then Beckett came to the rescue.

From student days, I remembered *Waiting for Godot*, and waiting in Khartoum brought it alive. Before *Godot*, I thought waiting was a passive exercise at best or a thing to get agitated about at worst, but those tramps had taught how it's anything but. They played the game of mental gymnastics in *their* here and now, while their creator drove a stake through the heart of 'waiting'. He had killed what I imagined it was all about— some fruitless impatient banging against the wall of wanting to get on, move on, be on, gone. I wouldn't admit it, but my head was full of momentum, and the journey as a consequence was all about movement, moving on to the next to the next, until hot sticky stifling Khartoum came as a handbrake, and I went screaming to a halt.

Travelling was transforming me. I looked down to my broken shoes, to my clothes, but this was more than mere garments, this slow descent to a basic state, this slow dissolution of the hero I had imagined I was becoming. Becoming a sickly tramp, was that irrevocable? For ten days I dug in, letting bits of impatience evaporate in the heat and letting the sprawl of Omdurman-Khartoum open her sweaty arms to take me in.

On the Sunday I was an 'alien' drowning for hours in sweat and red tape. The broken fan at the official Aliens' Section hung motionless, but I waited in hope. Without that special Juba Travel Permit there was no going on. On the Monday I felt a little Irish again, but Saint Patrick's Day came and went. A Dane told of a party, but I was too sick to go. He had a red beard too, so I told him to go as me. 'They wont care, honest,' I said. 'Anyway, everyone's Irish today.'

Sleeping little, sleeping late, dreaming of gorillas and eating rice like there was no tomorrow, wandering the town and always via the Sudan Airway's office. I would enter with a smile, say two words to the clerk and wait his routine response. 'Juba flight?' 'Ah yes, sir, perhaps tomorrow, *insha'allah*. We cannot say yet, sir. Please come back tomorrow.' After five or six days, the 'sir' was gone, and all I got was a curt 'No, no flight today.'

I walked the wide and narrow streets, visited the capital's amazing mosques, bought rice and dates in the Omdurman Souk, cycled past the Mahdi's tomb, drunk enough juices for ten lifetimes, said 'hi' and 'goodbye' to too many fellow travellers and finally, sick as a dog, went to a doctor the day before the flight, to be told, 'Yes, you have a bad dose of Hepatitis A.' After that I felt great, just great! So I took *The White Nile* down to the muddy banks of the Blue to read it again and remember my heroes.

Samuel Baker was one. He was a real hero-cum-true-traveller, but Gordon got the kudos. Across the river, beyond those men in their fishing punts, on a balcony of that tired-looking whiteish building, General Charles George Gordon waited and waited, like Jesus in the Garden. He looked north, down-river and felt the 'oppressive heat'. He was trapped and he knew it, and in my own little personal predicament I imagined a whiff of it, but at least I would not die. From where I sat, give or take a hundred yards, the Mahdi's men crossed over and Gordon was speared and beheaded. Roll on Kitchener and the Anglo-Egyptian control of Sudan until 1956, the year before my birth.

To be fair, sitting there in the heat, with Moorehead's book upturned on the burnt grass, it was hard not to be pulled in by the scene, by that particular piece of history. It had all the classic ingredients for a true myth. I was old enough to remember *Khartoum*, the myth-making-movie thriller of the sixties. 'Where the Nile divides, the Great Cinema adventure begins,' said its innocent blurb. Charlton Heston as Gordon, falling off those steps. Laurence Olivier as a boot-polished Mahdi, rubbing his hands in victory. As a kid I thought it great, but could never have known how Gordon (who was probably gay) was an odd lost soul with a martyr complex. With his death, ten thousand others swiftly followed in the Mahdi's bloody aftermath. His beheaded body was never found, tossed down a well so the story goes, 101 years ago, over there in that set-back building.

In 1885 it was the Governor General's Palace, Gordon's residence. Today it is the Presidential Palace of one Omar Al-Bashir, wanted for war crimes in The Hague. The new 'empire makers', China, will build him a new palace nearby to be officially opened on 26 January 2015, the date Gordon was slain. And so the Mahdi's ghost lives on.

★★★

The ticket to Juba was issued on the first day of spring. The clerk took his pen to change the date to one day sooner. I could have kissed his hand. At that moment, two no-happier persons were in all Khartoum. 'I hope you meet your gorillas, sir, but please do not stay long in Juba. It is not safe these days. There is a guerrilla war there.' He broke into a smile, hitting the ticket stamper hard and my heels lifted off the floor stretching over the high counter to seal the deal with cash—265 Sudanese pounds to be precise. I was certain he was happy to see the back of me, and certainly I was happy to be taking 'his' flight into that zone of civil war. No more would I castigate 'Insha'allah Airways'. They had come good in the end, thanks be to Allah.

Sleep and Sudan still don't harmonise well in my memory. Some countries just keep you up all night. The Juba flight would lift off at 6.30am, and cycling along a silent, dead flat Africa Street at 3.15am should have been easy. Yes? No! The hepatitis ensured that every downward push drew every bit of remaining juice like final steps on Everest. When we finally rose above a light-speckled Tuti Island my eyes closed but my brain was full-on.

Five visa days remained to get out of Sudan. Two hundred and twenty kilometres of rutted, potholed, bombed-out track separated Juba from the Zaire (DRC) border, (the preferred option). Did I have the energy to ride it? I doubted it, and what to do about hepatitis in Juba? Where to rest and which way really should I go, Zaire or maybe Kenya? My address book threw up the name of a friend of a friend, a hospital aid worker in Lodwar, Turkana. Surely she would help with some R&R. Yes, that made sense, head south-east to Kenya. We gained height and I played with the options, the-at-times conundrumous Rubik's Cube of the traveller. As it turned out, as it often does, I needn't have bothered.

Through a sleepy eye I watched the breakfast trolley come. 'Breakfast, sir?' Her beauty and whiter than white teeth lifted me momentarily from conundrums. There are but three ways with thinking, forward, backward or neutral-none at all. It seemed all my forward thoughts beyond Juba were a web of unknowns, so I said no to breakfast, re-closed my eyes (to her surprise) and went backwards to Baker. It was easier. Our flight would take two hours. Two hours to do what he and others took weeks to do one hundred years before. Two hours to let my mind off the hook of my personal what-ifs, buts and maybe-this-maybe-that.

Ten thousand metres below our flight line, down there in that vast swamp, Baker's toughness, patience and skilful skippering of his craft would have pushed the best trained modern commando to the limit. For weeks on end he and his men hacked and dragged through dense vegetation, in crocodile, hippo, water-buffalo, mosquito-infested waters and that was the easy part. Dealing with death, disease, suspicious tribes, slave traders, robbers and his own untrustworthy men, all tested his days. Yet the reason he was on my hero list was a far simpler one. He had his wife beside him and they took every step together. Every other male traveller, if they had a wife at all, left her at home, but Baker and his Missus were inseparable. That's what I liked about him; he was different.

> I never either saw or heard of so disgusting a country as that bordering the White Nile from Khartoum to here…the luxuries of… malaria, marshes, mosquitoes, and misery…and as far as the eye can reach, vast treeless marshes, perfectly lifeless. I do not wonder at the failure of all other expeditions in this wretched country.

That was what he wrote in 1863, in his book *The Albert N'yanza,* and those 'vast treeless marshes…as far as the eye can reach' — *that* is *Al-Sudd,* 'the barrier' as the ancient Arabs christened it. It is an ever-shifting labyrinth of vegetation, immense floating clumps the size of counties, dense masses of water plants and tall grasses, here today and gone tomorrow. Channels open for a period then close off, blocking progress in one direction but allowing it in another, a navigator's nightmare. He later wrote:

> There is no more formidable swamp in the world than the Sudd. The Nile loses itself in a vast sea of papyrus ferns and rotting vegetation and in that fetid heat there lies a spawning tropical life that can hardly have altered since the beginning, as primitive and hostile to man as the Sargasso Sea. Crocodiles and hippopotamuses flop about in the muddy water, mosquitoes and other insects choke the air and the Balaeniceps rex and other weird waterbirds keep watch along the banks—except that here there are no ordinary banks, merely chance pools in the forest of apple green reeds that stretches away in a feathery mass to the horizon.

That *formidable swamp* could swell to the size of Ireland with seasonal rains

167

from Diogenes's 'Mountains of the Moon'—today's Rwenzoris. Incredibly, half the water flowing in never flows out, and those clumps would rise and re-shape, squeezing river craft like arctic ice. Al-Sudd took many explorers to it's depths and even the hearts of single-minded missionaries were severely tested, but Baker and his wife got through. Oh, if ever there was a test of a marriage!

What caused the greatest distress for them was not 'the malaria, marshes, mosquitoes, and misery', but rather the real 'White Nile Trade', the reason why for millennia Egypt kept its foot in the door of this land, the reason why Khartoum of old had prospered and why many had made their fortune. Sadly, as it is today, so it was then. For in and beyond the desolate Al-Sudd was the source of that most sought after commodity, not ivory…but slaves and women, and children in particular.

Baker, though he campaigned for change, was ahead of his time, and in his day Al-Sudd symbolised the gap between an ordered coherent European world and the seeming untameable world of Africa. It was a god-forsaken, good-for-nothing quagmire and a headache on the way to fame. How could he have known then that he was hacking through the very pumping 'heart' of the Nile? Anthropocentric thinking as always was loudest, and even the brave and bright were still some distance from grasping how swamps, seas, glaciers, rivers, jungles and all suchlike planetary ecosystems are in fact one almighty One.

For me, I would never set foot in it, would never push or pedal the bike there and now I was leap-frogging over it. Friend's would later ask, 'So why mention it?' Why? From North Cape to Cape Point, Al-Sudd was always destined to be the missing link, the piece that would get away. Every other kilometre from top to bottom I could account for, but Al-Sudd…I could only press my face against the round window and imagine what lay below those scattered morning clouds. For that alone it was as much part of the travel as any other, and in an odd way more special for being put out of reach. Gondokoro too was out of reach, and that was a pity.

Chapter 8

Sounds of war

O f all the names on my African map, Gondokoro
was as full of mystique for me as Timbuktu. It
was a place which witnessed more than its fair
share of the dark side of nineteenth-century Africa. After Khartoum, Gondokoro was a key nexus along the
Nile route where exhausted explorers arriving up from
the south would meet the hopeful expectant ones coming
down from the north.

Here, on 13 February 1863, Speke and Grant, flushed with
their discoveries, arrived in rags to meet Samuel Baker and
his wife Florence. Here also streams of collared slaves came
in from the villages and went out to the middlemen on an
endless conveyor belt in the business of human trafficking.
Mrs Baker would have poured tea during her gentlemen's
discussions on tribal rivalry, bribery, attacks, disease and, of
course, the 'Source', while all around them hung the world
of slavery. One hundred and twenty five years later I would

★ The part of
Sudan referred to in
this chapter is now
the Republic of
South Sudan

have gladly walked the few kilometres up river from Juba to Gondokoro, just to stand there and look around, but the civil war put pay to that. 'Sir...please, sir, fasten your safety belt.' I had dozed with *The White Nile* closed between my knees. Gondokoro was underneath us now, and minutes later came the thump of touchdown. Juba, 7.08am, an end and another beginning.

Outside the flat-roofed airport building a group of European UNHCR people passed by. They looked in my direction but said nothing, which said everything. Did I look like a refugee? I was the only *other* Caucasian on the flight, and I guess to them, in their spruced-up spotless attire, I looked a bit worse for wear. I knew Ben, the US backpacker, would arrive the following day and though I didn't really know him, I was glad. There are situations when travellers need travellers, and this was one. In those pre-technology days information was a bitty, fractured business, especially in a war zone. Travellers would pick up scraps along the way, like stray dogs on the prowl, then regurgitate for their fellows in truck parks, bus parks, hostels, even at the side of the road. It was all so wonderfully collegiate, full of sharing and mutual support. 'Yes tomorrow,' I thought, he and I would pool our scraps...two heads and all that.

I laid what was left of an old T-shirt on the ground, a ritual to protect the Brooks saddle. The bike was flipped over onto the shirt, wheels locked in place, transmission checked, cables fingered, spokes twanged, and then it was flipped back again for panniers to be clipped on and a final look around. So this was it. I was here on the edge of the 90,000-peopled capital of a future South Sudan. My legs were leaden, there was nothing for it but walk the bike the mile to town. (Juba today has a conservatively estimated population of 700,000!)

The settled dust and the earth itself were redder, the trees greener. Gone was the glare of the North. Gone the aridness. Gone too the months of Arab paleness. Here was skin so wonderfully seriously black, I loved it. William and Mary in distant Dongala came to mind and all the things they said were different about their beloved southern home. 'You will see our *tukels*,' William had said, but there were none to be seen, only ordinary single-storey brick buildings with corrugated roofs and not the iconic cone-shaped grass roof of the *tukel*. 'Must be out in the countryside,' I thought.

Along a line of pine-scented eucalyptus trees I followed my nose to where the buildings seemed more densely packed. There would be no wild camping here, and anyway I was in no position to be fussy. The triple dictates of illness, exhaustion and safety drew me to the first 'hotel' I saw. Other possibilities were further down the street but '...not another step, buddy, just get in and lie down.' The Africa Hotel was a simple six-room, no-frills brick building with pots, pans, a water bucket and a timber bench as a self-service kitchen out back. Perfect! I was led through the rear doorless entrance, down a corridor and into its cheapest box room, bare but for a military style bed. The bike leaned against a peeling pink-painted wall, and I flopped face down onto the wiry mattress.

Hepatitis A equals rest, feet-up-rest, no drugs or alcohol, no fry-ups or greasy *chapatis*, nothing to upset the liver, just black tea, bland food, time and rest. That was the plan '... ah *the plan, ah yes, the plan?*' Face down, with semi-conscious dribbles seeping from my mouth into the military pillow, I mumbled about there being barely two months to get well again. J would arrive into Nairobi, and I counted the days and prayed the virus would be gone. My eyes were dry, yellow and tired, my liver swollen and fatigue felt deep down cellular. I slept the sleep of the dead and woke abruptly into twilight and the sound of drums...drums and one lone bastard mosquito. I tracked its high-pitched drone with the light of a candle then bludgeoned it to the wall with my shoe. The peeling pink paint had now a streak of red blood splattered there, my blood! I stared at it. More than likely it would remain there for years, until another coat of paint or change of colour or perhaps a bomb to demolish the building. I swore to be more vigilant with the net and I knew that that inconsequential smudge of me and mosquito would remain as splattered inside my head as on the bedroom wall.

The thunder of drumming rolled in through the window, *badum-badum-badum-badum-badum-badum*, on and on, sporadically broken by very definite gun fire. They could have burst in for all I cared. I lay in a limbo state, looking at candle flickers dancing on the ceiling and dreaming of Kilimanjaro...*and no one else knew bar an Irish nun, whom I hardly knew, and she would be there too on top and it would be the perfect place and the journey would change thereafter and it would all work out, of course it would and*...rapid machine gun fire in the distance shot through the romantic visioning, and I raised myself on an elbow to listen. It was then I felt a mini hunger pang and wondered what to do about it.

Outside sounded more like a rock concert than a civil war. The drumming rhythm had changed to a *badum-dumdum-badum-dumdum-badum-dumdum*. The hotel matriarch bellowed to her young son in answer to my query about the

171

nearest food market. It was the first time I heard the word *mizungu*, as she in-structed him to take me there. So, I was no longer a *khawaja*, I was a *mizungu* now, and the little lad led me and left me by two huge bark-less eucalypti, the gateway giants marking the market entrance. I walked between them into an open sandy compound where parallel lines of stalls faced each other. Round each stall people in tight pods were busy buying their fare and I threaded through, getting the odd curious look and occasionally hearing again that new word *miz-ungu*, but all of us were there for at least one common purpose, our basic human sustenance. Tilley lamps hung from the branches and cast a yellowish hue on the produce and merchandise—the rice, breads, peppers, chillies, onions, greens, eggs, meat, soaps, candles, shoes, clothes, cigarettes, batteries, and god-knows what else and, of course, here and there pockets of watching soldiers. I came away with a sweet potato, an onion, two large tomatoes, one fistful of lentils, three of rice, a pair of candles, a battery, but more importantly, information.

Were those khaki-clad guys government or John Garang's? It didn't feel ap-propriate to ask, but their Kalashnikovs were black and very real. The one who looked at me first got my question. 'Excuse me,' I asked, 'the way to Kenya, is it a good road?' He laughed, turned to his colleagues said something in his language and they laughed. I wondered what was so funny about 'the way to Kenya'.

'You will not go that way,' he said. 'That way is mined, but tomorrow we drive cattle to take them out.' They laughed again. 'Boom, boom,' he said. 'Tomorrow there will be many beef steaks in the air, haha, boom, boom.'

'Boom, boom,' I repeated back, letting him know I completely understood.

So, they were government troops after all. I had heard Garang's men had mined the roads, but never in my wildest did I think cattle would be used to remove them. All night and for a long time thereafter, every time I saw cattle I saw bloody chunks of beef flying through the air—grotesque imaginings that lingered.

(Three months later, in Tanzania, I stood straddling the bike, on the road to Mount Meru. Before me, screaming Masai cattle drivers waved their arms and spears towards a fearful truck driver. Moments before, his truck had ploughed into their herd crossing the road. I stared at the guts and gore and felt what was coming. For fear I'd cause offense and quite possibly be struck by a Masai stick, I rode on apace. The bloody sight let loose a stored-up world of images—cat-tle blown up, cattle mowed down, elephants lying tuskless, butchered gorillas, captured okapi's, stone throwing pygmies, crackpots with guns, women safer as prostitutes than harvesting in the fields, refugees fleeing hither and thither to yet another place of mayhem—it all erupted in me and fits of laughter came until I nearly shat in my pants. A mile or so further, it released itself in a fit of tears which held, I knew well, many other witnessed things. I rode that straight road to Mount Meru with a welling sense of our human derangement, knowing I too was as crazy.)

★★★

Back in the Africa Hotel, under a sole kerosene lamp, culinary experimentation went out the window. I peeled an oversized onion straight into a bubbling pot of rice and lentil. It would simmer away into a 'kiss' meal…a keep-it-simple-stupid pot of nourishment. At seven the sun was gone, and someone took the lamp, so I went to my box to lie in candlelight beneath the muslin net. The war drums rolled for half the night, pounding me in and out of slumber. The mosquitoes whined but I left them do there worst, until in that hour before dawn…silence! The drummers and those whining bastards were asleep, and just as I too was about to drift away, birds in their hundreds twittered and tweeted from every tree outside. Bird song yes, but there was something missing. 'Ah, of course, no *adhan.*' The Muslim morning call to prayer had been so embedded, like a wake-up call, but that was over now for a while, and *that* was the moment the journey shifted, changing to something completely new. At last I knew I was in animist Christian Africa, or at least in my naive, schoolish vision of Africa: a vision full of the stereotypical stories—dictators, wars, corruption, famine and imponderables galore, like why a Muslim North Sudan wished to hold a Christian South. Perhaps the old British idea was the right one, to let the southern part join with Uganda, since they had more in common. But what did I know? What I *do* know is that it would take a further twenty-five years, thousands of deaths, countless refugees and heartbreak beyond measure for this region to assume the official name of South Sudan among the world's list of nations. But names are nothing. I knew something about civil wars. The Irish one split families; South Sudan's is classic tribal.

★★★

Soldiers were everywhere but thankfully not interfering. There was rumour of a curfew but the hotel matriarch said 'No', as if it was she who ran the town. Then

Ben arrived with more bad news. Over milky *chais* in the tea-house next door, I listened to the scraps he'd picked up on the way. There would be no rambling up the riverbank to Gondokoro, no riding to Kenya, no leaving Juba without a permit, no going anywhere, it seemed, bar in an escorted convoy of at least two trucks south to Yei, then into Zaire (today's Democratic Republic of the Congo). At least my wish to see gorillas was still alive, and as for Ben, his wish to climb the Rwenzoris was still a runner. His invitation to join him was warmly accepted, but he could see it would be a while before I'd be climbing anything.

The news came too that two soldiers had been executed. Changing sides, it seemed, was a risky business, deserting government forces for the Sudan People's Liberation Army, John Garang's army. I recalled Dr Essam in his Moshu Hospital and our talk of revolutionaries. 'They all get killed in the end, John,' was the good doctor's view. Now I was here and the killing close. 'Imagine,' I said to Ben, 'if we really wanted to see Garang, we could.' His desire to be a journalist was strong, and the thought of a one-on-one with a real revolutionary excited him. 'Gee, what a scoop that would be,' he said.

Garang was killed…eventually. A mysterious helicopter crash in 2005 spread rumours of treachery. Maybe Dr Essam was right, but regardless, no one doubt's today that John Garang was *the* most influential leader in South Sudan's history. At that time he was on the lips of everyone, friend and foe, so for me it was easy to glean a sense of the man, and as I prepared to leave his country I felt I had I found a new local hero. But Juba was volatile, unpredictable and surrounded by his men. That both Ben and I would consider this kind of unstable situation to be what our respective journeys' needed was…well…daft, but we were youthful, carefree whites and at times reckless in our travel; like all on the long road, we searched the best of ourselves…adventure yes, but beyond that, to lose ourselves and find our edges in such crazy places.

'What would your family think?' I asked him.

'I don't know what they'd say, probably that it's completely nuts to be here but then of course they would, they'd never understand. But you know there's nothin' like guns and soldiers to add spice to your travel.' I tuned in to his east coast US accent, certainly a change from Geoff's south coast of England English. 'Look,' he continued, 'they're all goin' thru' Ethiopia. For shit sake, man, down here is where the real action is.'

He was right, though since he was American, I considered him more at home with gun-toting than I, yet most other travellers I'd come across avoided South Sudan and Zaire, and it wasn't simply due to the price of the no-choice flight over the Sudd. Did they know something we didn't? 'Spice up the travel,' he had said. Indeed. Four days later and over the border we witnessed enough spice to flavour and scare anyone's journey. 'Up there', in Ethiopia, the kids might fling sticks and stones, but I doubted they would have poked a machine gun in your back. Such and more awaited us in the jungles north-east of Zaire, where ironically we saw more guns, madness and violence than when we were in Juba amid a civil war.

★★★

The furthest I got from the Africa Hotel by dint of shank's mare were the few hundred metres to the White Nile. I told Ben it had to be done. In a quiet spot my arcing stream of hepatitis piss looked as dark as a Smithwick's beer. The yellow bubbles floated and popped, and now finally I could write to my brothers to tell them 'I'd done it', my wee contribution to the Nile! That this was the same river Eamon and I had strolled over in Cairo, almost 4,000 kilometres back, was hard to fathom. Above the Valley of the Kings I had looked down on its glorious ribbon-like spectacle, felt its colonial history above the Old Aswan dam and listened to its latent power above Lake Nasser. Somewhere in Nubia I had washed my pot in it, crossed it twice in Kermah, stood lonely on its banks in Al-Dabba, mesmerised by its slow steady flow, and then, in what had felt an end, I felt uplifted on that Omdurman bridge where its two arms became one—cameo moments in a shared, lengthy drama. I shook my penis dry and about-turned to the Africa Hotel, wondering if even a molecule would make it through the Sudd and to the sea.

Sometimes long solo travelling is crazy. It breaks you up, overflows you, cuts into you, mirrors you to you and slowly shatters the conceived and preconceived notions of your age and time. It can make it damn difficult to ever go back to the 'life' you knew. It can be a one-way ticket and often is, but I knew nothing of that then.

Outside my city flat, tinkering with the bike, Brian dropped by. 'Ah, yeah,' he said, 'so you're headin' to the real open university.' He watched me kneeling, fumbling with tools. 'No, no, the eight mil, use the eight mil.' 'Okay, okay,' I'd say, embarrassed at using a wrong tool and annoyed at being instructed, but he was a pro. Brian Murphy, Walt Whitman look-alike, veteran cyclist, veteran thinker who had always stood outside or way outside the box, unwittingly inspiring people, not that he cared a whit if they acted or not. All he ever said when he knew I was ready, was, 'go for it, sure you're crazy but you'll be fine. And come back. I want to hear all about it.' I was going anyway, but to receive that from him gave an extra pep to the push off.

Now in Juba, Ben told of just how 'crazy' travelling could be. I never knew he knew Geoff. Two years previous they had met for the first time on the east coast of Australia. Six months later they met again by chance, on its other side. The two years passed, and not knowing where in the world the other was, they met on a dusty Khartoum street a few days before Geoff and I boarded that Nyala train. 'We're like billiard balls,' said Ben, 'bumping into each other on a world-sized table.' Yes indeed, inexplicable bumping to some, but to the seasoned traveller they were ordinary, almost to be expected.

'Out on the road, we move in a different time space, don't you think?' he said, '…a different dimension.' A different dimension, I liked that. Scale, immense in one dimension, but like one's backyard in another.

★★★

The two UNHCR trucks would depart early to bring refugees from somewhere to somewhere. If we wanted a free ride, we 'had better be there'—so we were told, and so we were. I stood at the rear holding the cross-bar above my head, watching the earth road stream like a dirt-brown conveyor belt from under the chassis, out into the eucalyptus-lined distance. Following us, the jeep full of government soldiers rode shotgun, making Ben ponder what his mother might think. 'Couldn't be safer, Ma,' he shouted back to no one while waving to the soldiers. His gesture was returned with guns in the air. And what of my own mother, dead six years, what would she have thought? Her sick son bumming a ride to the Zaire border with warnings of mortar attacks from his 'hero's' men ringing in his head. What *would* she have thought?

On the truck floor a real flesh-and-blood mother held her baby tight, cajoling her truculent other child not to climb up the sides. Up front, some men happily hummed some song. The day was warm and bright, and this rutted road to Yei was not as bad as I had imagined. It was even cycle-able had that been allowed, but standing for six bumpy hours made jelly of my legs.

We were just ten kilometres from Juba when the truck was halted. Spanning the track was a tree trunk resting on two barrels, as innocuous a checkpoint as one could imagine. From the adjacent tiny hut stepped two semi-uniformed guards, one a 'shorty', the other a 'lanky', like Simon and Garfunkel. In a truck full of dark-skinned locals we were easy targets, and they made a bee-line to us, making Ben mumble what was already in my head, 'Oh fuck, the permits, the fucking permits.' We had completely forgotten to get them.

It was a civil but no-nonsense affair. The convoy would go on but we and the few other permit-less unfortunates would have to stay. No permit to leave Juba, no way on, that was how it was in what is now South Sudan. In hindsight, Ben should have rode my bike, but I was asleep to the reality of my illness. He remained behind to protect our gear and I took off behind our 'lanky check-point Charlie' on his Chinese high-nelly bike.

He was a tall, lean, jovial bloke, chuffed at dragging a European back to the permit office like a bounty hunter bringing in his convict. I christened him Art after Garfunkel, and he insisted we had to get there before it closed for the day. Of this he was adamant. The fact that he was escorting me at all was quite extraordinary. I could never imagine a European official getting on his bike and saying, 'Now sir, follow me so I can assist you in getting your permit!'

Art rode like the wind, dodging the ruts and holes as if he knew them personally. Those long legs were too long, making his knees stick out and his right-side crank-arm made a *clickedy-clack-click-clack, clickedy-clack-click-clack* noise, which drove me nuts. I had ridden from the very top of Europe, had bulging *recti femori* as hard as elephant tusks but nearly died attempting to keep pace, and to rub salt into that embarrassing wound, I was fairly and squarely outrun by a pair of secretary birds.

Art was well ahead. He had disturbed the duo. They took off running parallel and easily passed me out. It was without a shadow of doubt the weirdest bird experience of my entire life…trying to out-pedal a pair of secretaries. *Sagittarius serpentarius,* an Archer like myself, but then I was no killer of snakes. There they were, something out of Africa's misty past, two four-foot high, red-faced, long-legged, eagle-headed, prehistoric-looking birds clipping along in high savannah grass, their quill-like head feathers flying, passing out a head-down red-faced white man…on a bicycle! I lost the race but at least got up-close to the very emblem of present day North Sudan, where ironically I never once saw a secretary.

A feverish hepatitis sweat drip-dripped and a body-mind screamed. Had I had more sense, I would have said 'fuck-this-for-a-game-of-cowboys' and got off to walk. It was *the* toughest, 'painfullest' ride I'd ever done. 'And what *was* your hardest day's cycle?' some would ask years later, presuming it to be some sweaty mountain pass or a torrid desert piste or a long-into-the-night-into-a-bitter-cold-headwind-uphill-drag, but no, it was never any of those, though they too are sweetly remembered. No, the hardest day's ride of two years on the saddle was all of that twenty kilometres, there-and-back, back the way we had come, back to Juba, back for those two fucking permits.

By the time we returned, night was well bedded down and the two pieces of officially stamped paper were safe in the handlebar bag. I saw that tiny hut among the high trees by the faint beam of Art's Chinese lamp and in those final few hundred metres I could have been forgiven for the all the ego-thoughts that flowed, for a sweet touch of imaginative delirium had set in… *was it 'The Long Valley' or 'The Lions Den'?…I was back home with friends and those creamy heads of beer were settling and I was telling of a night-ride in a place of war when I rode behind a lanky checkpoint Charlie with his clickedy-clack-click-clack noisy crank….*

★★★

We slept, or attempted to, on the ground by the gable of the hut. Art lit a fire and we *mizungus* bathed in a sea of melodic Nilotic languages. Around the flames the sheer complexity of Sudan, let alone Africa, made both of us feel silly with our northern hemisphere understandings. Several languages crossed over and back as Art threw on more wood. Sudanese Arabic may have been the dominant tongue but, as I was to learn, over one hundred others hold their own in the country's huge mix of peoples. The African continent has almost 2,000 languages, Europe about sixty, America a lot fewer. But whatever the language we all had to get by and get on, and getting to and through the border was everyone's concern.

Nothing slaps the senses awake more than the rancid taste of vomit. In semi-darkness behind some trees, the hot mush of freshly puked beany-rice looked just like it did when Ben poured it into my bowl a few hours earlier. He had done nothing wrong—in fact we reckoned it had been one of his 'one-pot wonders'—but my hepatitis stomach was acting independently. Out of habit, I peered deep into the regurgitation for any sign of movement but thankfully all was simply 'plain 'ole bean and grain', as he had described his culinary offering. I wiped my mouth with leaves from a tree, then pulled some more, letting them fall to cover the heap. 'The ants are going to have some feast,' I thought. Back beside the hut, all was silent. In the far distance, vertical flashes of light made no sound. Being in a war zone I presumed they were artillery blasts, but Ben woke up and explained. 'Naw, not bombs…heat flashes, saw the same in Oz.'

'Gee…wow,' I muttered with absolute disinterest before crawling back inside my bag.

In the morning another convoy arrived with two jeep-loads of 'khakis' front and rear, guns everywhere. Was it that we were whites? Inexplicably, we were loaded up, but others were left behind, and then the half-empty trucks took off for Yei. From the rear I saluted Art, fellow cyclists that we were. He stood head and shoulders above the others, watching us leave. 'They want to get us out of here,' Ben suggested. Get the whites out, into Zaire, where it's safer! How naive was our thinking.

Yet, bar the guns, all seemed as it should, normal life carrying on. Even those who walked or cycled waved as we passed, and the passing scene became greener and greener. 'Lush,' I heard myself say as we spoke of the changing landscape. Never had I imagined 'lush' and 'Sudan' in the same sentence. In a forest of eucalyptus trees beehive tubes hung like pendants from the highest branches. Some were of woven dry grass, others from hollowed out trunks. 'How the hell do they get the honey down,' Ben wondered. 'Hardly by ladder,' I offered. 'Maybe ropes and pulleys.' But get down the honey they somehow did, and like every mouthful of local natural food it was delicious. With the remaining piastres I bought a half kilo. It was the last item purchased in Sudan. I peered through the glass at two bees suspended like fossils in their own hard work, and we asked ourselves how much this authentic bee-in-the-jar-honey would cost in Dublin, London or New York? 'Multiples of multiples,' we agreed, acknowledging the embarrassing pittance I had paid.

There were no signs of a civil war, no burnt-out vehicles, no dead bodies lying around, but then this 160 kilometres from Juba to Yei was the 'safe corridor'.

'You are going to Little London?' asked the guy squatting beside me. His question was confusing. 'Little London?' Apparently the name was coined to give Yei a cool credence as a place to do multicultural business in those halcyon inter-civil war days (between 1972 and 1983). Even the weather, he told us, was not too dissimilar. Stretching things a bit, I thought, but then just as the outer humble looking limits of Yei loomed, the rain came, wonderful, cool, wet rain, falling gently, but more a West Kerry drizzle than a London downpour.

The trucks and jeeps lined up neatly outside the police station. Those of us going on to the border were told bluntly to wait. The drivers walked off and the soldiers went to eat with the police, so we waited and waited, watching the rain get heavier.

'Five months,' I said to Ben, 'five months of blue skies and not a drop from the heavens.'

'Geez, must have been bliss for an Irishman!'

'Hey ,watch it buddy…half the States in America get more rain than where I come from.'

'Yeah, I'm sure, but some place has to carry the can!'

We bantered like schoolboys, our mouths opening to catch the drops, getting soaked and knowing we'd be dry in an hour. By dark we were well dry but still going nowhere. The message from on high was simple, to ' stay put 'til the morrow', but when 'the morrow' came there was still no news of moving, so we strolled into Little London.

I liked the town. I could see why some smart-ass local latched on to the title. We ambled down and back on the dusty main thoroughfare, gaining a fuller perspective with every step, not solely of the town but the entire region. As Khartoum is a tri-partite city, Yei, it seemed to me, was at the heart of a tri-national, multicultural complex trade block. There were Sudanese of all tribes, Ugandans of all tribes, peoples of North Eastern Zaire (DRC), Kenyans, Chadians, Tanzanians, Ethiopians, Eritreans even Pakistanis, not to mention European NGOs, UNHCR people and the few vagrant passers-through like us, all toing and froing over 'those bloody awkward borders', as Ben put it.

Along with all the differences, there were tribes, culturally, linguistically and ethnically the same but living across from each other on either side of political lines on a map—lines arbitrarily drawn by European powers in the early twentieth century, and it went without saying, but must be said, that this carving up of a continent was neatly wedded to a profound arrogance, a jockeying for power and a decent dash of good old colonial greed. The half-baked ideas I had of Central Africa, indeed of everywhere before leaving home, were, of course, too coarse, too simple. Reality, as much as it can be entertained at all, was far more nuanced, rich and diverse. It was in this deep south of Sudan that I first understood how the decisions by distant powers from a bygone era reverberate down the generations, onto the streets, into the markets, into new and uncharted consequences. It was no surprise that being there made me reflect on that other 'Border' between Orange and Green. And so it goes; you travel to travel, only to better understand your own Place, Nature and State.

It is a timeless old story, and old stories are either remade or forgotten. In my handlebar bag the creased-worn, finger-stained Michelin map of Africa had all the contemporary borders drawn, but who knows which, if any of them, would have made it onto the map if Europeans had been enlightened or had not interfered as much. That was the question we mulled on as we walked about in sunshine along the red dusty side streets of Little London.

At a corner under a massive mango tree, three young girls sat by their mango pyramids. With the skill of surgeons they cut mango 'hedgehogs' in seconds and proffered them up to us with angelic smiles. Had they asked thrice the price, we would have paid, for mango when its good, is 'awesome', as my American partner muttered, with the juice drooling down his shirt. In mango-tree shade, we sat beside the giggling girls sucking at the big fleshy stones and prognosticated on the war. 'If it ever stops, this would be a great place to throw a party,' said Ben, '... a party for Africa.' What a great idea, here in the relative cool of Yei. (But the war didn't stop. It dragged on for twenty-two years until 2005, up there with the longest civil wars on record. Today (2018) it continues within the new nation, with more civilians dead than in any conflict since the Second World War.)

A runner came running, a young boy sent to find us, to haul us back to the police station. The convoy was readying itself. Within the hour it would depart for the Congo border. It was a 'goodbye, goodbye' to our mango angels and a goodbye to Yei as we swiftly followed our young running guide.

★★★

To Kaya then Buzze, a typical split village straddling either side of that border line. That's where we were headed, and for the final time in Sudan, the bike was lifted up and strapped down. I followed and stood in the half-filled truck, enthralled by all the quizzical looks at my mute machine. When I laid claim to it, with a hand on its only bit of leather, all the looks came to me and I smiled and bowed and stroked the saddle, then stroked my rear-end. This got everyone on-side with fits of laughter. I had sensed a tension, justifiable I guess with all that was going on, and gauged that a little lightheartedness would go down well, and so it did.

It had been said many times en route, by many travellers, how an Irish passport was 'a real good one to travel on', and how the Irish were good travellers, not only in not ruffling too many local feathers but by their general easy blend-in nature, moving through with humour and without being overbearing or falling into the trap of comparing the local scene to how it was at home. I wondered was I unconsciously playing to this perceived tune of the 'jolly Irish rover', dispensing his jocularity ad lib. I didn't think so. I liked to think that those unconscious quirky traits were as much on the side of national character as on any personal idiosyncrasies.

How differently I saw the bike to them, not as a piece of expertly welded tubing with pedals, carriers, brackets, bars, not as a clothes-horse for my wardrobe, bedroom, kitchen, toilet. I saw it as a hill farmer would his loyal collie or an Egyptian *fellah* his old donkey, this well built Mercian machine, this unsung hero. What it had been through, and *we* were only half way there! I was one hundred percent attached to it now, like Flann O'Brien's *The Third Policeman*, enough at least to have some private chats, which were many—'When will we ride again, in thunder, lightning or in rain?...It's been too long my friend. Bloody hell, if you could talk.' I longed and dreamed of cranking up the pedals to the limit on a long straight road with a cool wind on my back—'Surely one is coming, somewhere out there in Africa, surely.'

★★★

Things changed from Yei on. It got lusher still, and more people were on the move, by foot, bicycle, even the occasional motorbike, but unlike Sudan's North there were surprisingly few donkeys. Yet the signs of conflict grew—a burnt out jeep, then another, a torched village and checkpoint after checkpoint, each taking an hour or more to pass. At one, a bare-chested teenager knelt behind the guard hut, his arms outstretched with a fist-sized stone in each hand. The soldier sitting on a chair before him was unmoved by the cries of sheer muscle agony. He merely raised the boy's drooping arms with the barrel of his gun or struck his stomach hard if they dropped too much. It was difficult to watch. The squatting man beside me said the boy was an orphan, had been in one of the SPLA camps and was being tortured for information.

One lone tortured orphan teen kneeling in the dirt, and I knew absolutely nothing then about the thousands like him. That whole bloody civil war was just one damn awkward obstacle to my own personal little trip, and though his pained face flashed briefly across my own, I was in another microcosmic world.

But travel reaches into the future and it caught up with me, and I went back to remember him when the tragedy of all the wandering orphan children was fully told. Other harrowing scenes would also crystallize and over time they would surface and resurface again and again to hammer home that I, and too many in the West, 'live in a world a million miles away from the rest of the world'.

War is one thing, nature is another, and the war at that point had still not inflicted crisis-wounds on the wonderful animal-bird diversity in a region the size of France. To travel through without birdlife blowing you away would, to say the least, be pitiful. The love of seeking them out slowly shifted my mind from torture to the trees. Our convoy stopped at the last checkpoint before the border. The soldiers stood about talking and smoking. Others, with their guns slung low, looked at papers and permits. Then out of the blue, out of nearby acacia trees, came a raucous burst of calls: 'Go-away, go-away, go-away!' It was a husband-and-wife pair, the infamous white-bellied go-away-birds with their stiff protruding head-tufts like Mohican head-dresses at a Goth party. From branch to branch they hopped like squirrels, screeching 'Go-away, go-away, go-away'. Eventually we did go away, but their cackles followed us, and we debated if they really *were* telling us to go, or if the wife was simply telling the husband to bugger off.

In such a fraught land, birds would lift anyone's spirit, and they certainly lifted mine. A silent red-crested cardinal woodpecker clung to the side of a dead-looking tree, probably feeding on ants or termites. A bunch of dazzlingly bright northern red bishops flirted in the long grass, a strutting paradise whydah, a few black-headed gonoleks, two green pigeons high on a branch, and higher in the thermals were the birds of obvious prey, gracefully gliding and spying on us all. There were little innocent fellows of all colours and none, all darting about, making my head spin with scribbled notes to myself to remember…a futile task, but fun.

Yet the bird which took the biscuit was a lone male ground hornbill, black in the yellow grass with his bright red pouch under his chin. He turned to look, as if to check what was going on, then cool as you like, seeing we were of no interest, turned and strode calmly into cover to disappear. I pointed him out to Ben, but he wasn't into birds…not that kind anyway.

There were so many exquisite 'exotics' that I let go of the scribbling to see them for what and where they were in this tortured land to which I knew I'd unlikely ever return. Just like her Egyptian sister to the north, Sudan too gave me more…far more than I bargained for. I had ridden in to a dusty-deserty Wadi Halfa, feeling like superman, and now at the other end of the huge country I walked feebly out into a damp and steamy jungle, proud, defiant, but in truth like a spent docket and that, I supposed, was how it was meant to be, for back then there were no easy rides through Sudan.

Chapter 9
Being disturbed

★ Now known as
the democratic
Republic of the
Congo

Bar one gorilla-loving woman and a long dead Irish nationalist, I had no heroes in Zaire, and President elect-for-life Mobutu Seso Seko just didn't qualify. More anon about the others, but Mobutu…ah Mobutu and Zaire, such great-sounding African names. Yet that is who dictated and that is how he re-branded 'his' country until his overthrow and exiled death in 1997. Whether Zaire then or the Democratic Republic of the Congo now, the country was way too big to get my head around…and big? More than half the area of the European Union is I guess, big.

I entered it's most north-easterly and dangerous corner at Buzze, and to re-trace for those in the dark about where this might be and to where I was headed—from Juba to Yei to Kaya to tiny Buzze to Bunia to Beni to Kasindi and on to a spit of a village on the forested shores of Lake Edward in the heart of Parc National de Virunga. In truth, and more than in any

other part of the journey from Cairo to Cape, this section should have had a
sign saying, 'Beware, beyond here there be dragons!'.

Back in the safe world of my father's kitchen, his pot of Barry's Tea brewed
like stew, I would tell him for the umpteenth time to 'get rid of that aluminium
tea-pot, will ya!' and he would grunt his widower's grunt and stand there unperturbed, looking over my shoulder, cup in hand. He looked, as my finger traced
the map, running smoothly over South Sudan and Zaire in a millisecond, on to
the 'easy' asphalt roads of Kenya and beyond. 'Hold up now,' he said, 'that's the
Congo your going through', but his words of warning came out of the sixties,
some story of Irish troops besieged and outnumbered, of shooting and looting
and other nebulous dangers. 'Ah, come on, Da,' I replied, 'that was years ago,
there wont be any problem, get a grip.' But he had a 'grip', and more than I
knew, for some things and some places don't change despite the decades, and
some…some get even worse.

'Would you like to go for a beer?' I asked him. So we drove to Murphy's East
Ferry Pub and sat on the wall in the sun, across the river from a mansion which
had always brought the Great Gatsby's yearning to mind…that gaze across the
water to a dream on the other side. 'This dream of yours,' he said, 'it'll work out
fine. Once you mind your back and mind your pocket, you'll make it.'

'Hope your right…tell you what, if I do, we'll come back here to celebrate,
okay.'

He had a habit of saying 'right so, right so,' and that's exactly what he said,
'Right so, right so.'

During that easy afternoon we spoke at rare length about the stuff of his
early life, much of which I had just a hazy idea of. In the long solo months that
were soon to come, this new insight would nourish a new understanding of the
man, and I would forgive him and myself for all the battles we had. I had little
idea how often I would replay that afternoon as I lay in the tent at the edge of
so many back roads and dirt tracks…but that too was part of it, I guess, part of
what it was all about.

We chatted about the proposed route, through a corner of what his generation still called 'The Belgian Congo', which naturally enough for an Irishman who knew his history brought Roger Casement into our conversation.
There can be few Irish who do not know of the sacrifice Casement made for
his country's independence, and yet, according to my father, few knew that his

turning to that cause had its roots in what he witnessed in this turbulent part of 'Darkest Africa'.

A journey through a country is *the* opportunity to peel back the layers of its history and peer into its hurts and if, in doing so, that peeling reverberates back onto one's own place then all the better and richer it will be. It was my father who first made me aware how Casement became a more fervent Irish nationalist having first witnessed the savagery and injustice of King Leopold's personal rubber plantations in the jungles of the Congo. On returning to Ireland, Casement saw more clearly the injustices of his own country's incarceration 'to another Empire'.

My old school history book painted the Dubliner as 'a British Diplomat' and a humanitarian turned gun-runner who—as the larks climbed high to sing on that Good Friday dawn, 21 April 1916—strode happily from the breaking surf at Banna beach, straight from a German submarine. He was summarily arrested for treason, branded a traitor, stripped of his knighthood and hanged in London's Pentonville Prison three months later.

After an unusually sun-kissed afternoon, enjoying a beer with my father, I preferred to see Casement as a traveller, a sensitised archetypal traveller, returning home to contribute something real out of what he had seen so far away. He had travelled, and the travelling had profoundly changed him. That he carried a hidden and private sensitivity to the complexities of being human certainly helped in his reporting of inhumanity. Some think him the 'father of human rights investigations', and indeed those in Irish Amnesty know his colours well.

My father was full of historical tit-bits, and if one had the patience to tap into a seam of his interest, gems would fall to the floor. I learned how Casement met Joseph Conrad, that they shared rooms together, that they even looked alike. 'But they were troubled men,' he said 'and became doubly troubled by what they saw out there. Conrad? Oh yes, he went on to fame all right but Casement, he went to the gallows.' That was his opinion and I was in no position to disagree. Now knowing a little more, I think it was a fair summation of what eventually happened.

The Heart of Darkness was one of those books that left a definite mark on me. I had read Conrad's classic long before my travel dreams manifested. 'A bloody good book,' my father had said but never did he contemplate a day when his son might go ride a bike through its landscape. The book is dark and sinister, and even after more than a century Conrad's words still have a weird hold on foreign sentiment toward this vast, jungled central African country. As the Belgian Congo, it had been pillaged and plundered under Leopold and suffered 'the horror, the horror'. Today, it sadly continues to make its own.

Marlon Brando in *Apocalypse Now* didn't make it any easier for Westerners to disentangle the real from the myth or the ordinary person from the witch doctor, the voodoo, or even Mobutu in his leopard skin hat. Though the movie was set 'in and about' the Vietnam War, everyone knew it came out of Conrad's Congo experience…and then, as if someone had pushed the fast-forward button on my tape of life, I found myself holding onto the roof bar of a bouncing truck, closing out the tail-end of Sudan and edging ever closer to the green tangled mouth of it's southerly neighbour. I could do nothing to stop those images of Conrad and Casement sipping brandy in a jungle hut, swapping colonial stories into a noisy drumming night, or Brando's mad contorted face, or Dian Fossey's face beaming to the camera from the undergrowth with her friend, Digit, a monster male gorilla sitting close by, or those misty *National Geographic* pictures of pygmies that I'd once stared at in a dentists waiting room…but above them all came my father's voice, 'You be careful there.'

★★★

Two dusty cowboys in a western, that's what we must have looked like, Ben strutting just ahead to the barrier marking the border to Zaire, our passports like six-guns at the ready. 'Borders, a fucking pain-in-the-ass,' he said. Above the customs shed a sea of climbing creepers clung and dangled from the trees. 'Some change from Sudan,' I said from behind. We stepped up and innocently entered, and after the usual formal checking of passports the informal back-room 'negotiations' began. It's happened to thousands, but when it happens to you, it's more 'pain-in-the-ass' than the borders themselves.

I came out of their inner sanctum exasperated and with no passport. 'The bastards,' I said to Ben, who had the same befall him. We sat on the step refusing to go down the *baksheesh* road and were prepared to 'play hardball with those fuckers', as my American friend bluntly put it. His French was better than mine and he went in again to let rip. The two junior officials who hoped to make their killing got his wrath full-on, '*Mais on a déjà payé ton putain de visa!*' he said, but to no avail. '*Les passeports,*' would remain '*dans ce bureau, monsieur,*' he was calmly and coldly told; a machine gun rested on the desk of said bureau. There ended that brief exchange. Fifty metres, that's all it took to enter a different world, so we moved into sunshine to watch the locals pass, some shaking their knowing but helpless heads at two more misfortunates.

'Bienvenue au Zaire,' a bloke called out, smiling his white teeth as he peddled by. I gave him a thumbs-up. 'At least they have a sense of humour,' I said.

But who here is the real misfortunate? Me, with 400 dollars stuffed secretly round my waist in Geoff's money belt and more dangling down the down-tube in a plastic bag? Me, with a probable job to return to and an upward trajectoried life ahead? Or those border officials who hadn't been paid for months while their 'Helmsman', Mobutu, lived beyond the wildest dreams of the wildest despots? He once asked his soldiers why they needed to be paid at all, when they had guns, and rumour was he had his private jet about-turn over the Mediterranean, back to Marseilles, because Madame Mobutu forgot a magazine. After I read that, I had another take on coups.

Ben went to walk off his exasperation while I sat flicking dirt and letting the 'situation' sink in, reminding myself as logically as I could that this was part and parcel of the travel game. Whatever else, at least the sun shone, it was peaceful, and the women in their bold and brilliantly coloured *liputas* walked elegantly by, some carrying heavy loads on their heads. The freshness of moist air was a tonic, and I began to settle into this new and different space. Moments later and very near, an explosion jolted us all.

The women came first, followed by some men. They ran in the same direction, down a path into the trees. There were shouts, people calling to each other, pointing, running, calling. I had no idea what was going on until a man came bounding back onto the road carrying a young boy. Half his arm was gone and what was left swung bloody and limp. A second man followed screaming, carrying another child with its clothes covered red and its head hanging.

We got our passports back through the good sense of a senior officer. We had seen him storm into the shed just minutes before the explosion and heard him bellowing at his minions. Obviously some influential passer-by had tipped him off. That we should take 'les transports' to Bunia because of the 'les combats' was his advice to us. '*Quels combats?*' I enquired. I thought we had left the fighting behind in South Sudan. But no, Idi Amin's legacy of mayhem lived on through his loyal men, who lost no opportunity in raiding across the border from Uganda on all those lucrative convoys coming up from Dar-es-Salaam carrying food and humanitarian aid. The Zaïrois commandos had been sent to protect the convoy's, but for the traveller *they* were even worse, extracting their own pound of flesh. Not being paid by the government, they took Mobutu's advice and raided their own people and anyone else who passed through their web. It was a crazy, no-win situation.

Half an hour after that tragic incident we pulled away from Buzze, away from the grief and the wailing at one more child maimed for life and another dead. Fahmi-Hassan, the driver of our Bunia-bound truck told what happened. The boys had found a grenade in the undergrowth, picked it up and…boom! 'They come in the night and leave them there,' he said. 'Who?' we asked. 'Ugandan guerrillas.' he replied 'They come from across the border. They are from Amin's tribe. This truck you are in, *my truck,*'—he shouted the words—'it was captured by them. I had to pay one thousand dollar ransom to get it back…to get my own truck back. This is how they work.'

'Fuck me, this is going to be a rock-n-roll trip,' muttered Ben. 'You bet,' I said, 'you bet.' Barely in the door of the country and already a first harsh lesson about the Congo—one moment you're in paradise, watching the women's vibrant colours, the lush green growth, exotic birds, lively talk, jiving music and then…in a split second that life-filled surface-life shatters. You never knew what or when, and often the locals neither.

On to Aru—100 kilometres on a dirt-red rock-n-roll jungle road—by night! It snaked inside the border to Uganda and was at times barely the width of a railway track. Fahmi drove to loud music courtesy of Lionel Richie's 'Can't Slow Down' album. The cassette was turned over so many times I thought the tape would wear out. The only track I knew was the ridiculously appropriate 'All Night Long'. That got us all going, and though it helped make the physical rocking and rolling less tiresome, it made it all the more surreal. 'Why by night?' I asked Fahmi. 'To avoid check-points,' he replied. 'They are many by day and at every one I have to pay.' It was true. In those first few hours to midnight we were halted at no fewer than five, and at each he paid his token *baksheesh* to some senior commander. 'Half my profit go to them and *they* are here to protect *me!*' At each, we too were checked and double-checked to the point of incredulity, but thankfully at Ariwara, Fahmi would drive no further.

From Ariwara to Aru was different. It was a notorious stretch of good old-fashioned banditry over an inconspicuous and porous border. Fahmi made it abundantly clear that 'these guerrilla guys don't care who gets hurt.' So for dirt money we settled in for the night in our safe cockroach-filled hut with six bottles of Primus beer standing to attention on the earthen floor. Fahmi had given a bottle each to his young Ugandan helpers. They were to sleep in the back of the truck – 'to keep it safe,' he explained. 'One bottle is okay for them, but two, they would sleep too quick and my truck would be gone in the morning.'

As for me, I wailed inside. From Aswan down all I heard from northbound travellers was just how good Zaire beer was. In beer-less Sudan there were parched days when a swollen tongue stuck to the roof of my palate and I dreamed of beer—dreamed of a first cold sip in the shade of some evergreen, and now there they stood within easy reach, tormenting me. 'Dream on, baby,' said Ben in jest. 'Damn this bloody hepatitis,' I half roared, half laughed and reached for a bottle. 'Don't worry, it's worth it,' said Fahmi, and indeed it was. The neck was divine but probably any neck of beer would have been in such circumstances, but I couldn't finish it. Outside, I poured what was left into a bush and looked to the sky, pondering my congenital compromised hepatic system. What did the consultant say again, was it Dubin-Johnson Syndrome or Gilbert's? I couldn't remember which.

Back inside, Ben and Fahmi were deep into conversation about the 'Rumble in the Jungle'.

'Did you watch it too' Fahmi asked.

'Of course I did, the whole world did,' I said.

'Those two certainly put this place on the world stage, that's for sure,' Ben added.

'Did you know,' said Fahmi, 'Mobutu executed so many gangster people before that fight, Kinshasa was to be the safest capital in the world, and it was.'

It was, we all agreed, the most famous bout of boxing the world had ever witnessed and we all had seen it in our respective countries. Fahmi raised his bottle of Primus in a toast to his own hero, Muhammad Ali, who in beating the hot favourite George Foreman that sweaty night in a Kinshasa stadium probably, at least according to Ben, ' did more for Afro-American, Black-White relationships than anything to do with what went on inside the ring.' Fahmi and Ben savoured every last drop of Primus, and I watched them both with not a little envy. Fahmi talked on nostalgically of his memory of that fight night when a bout of boxing shone a bright light temporarily into the dark turbulence of his adopted country.

Night came down like a shutter. Strange bird calls from the forest, drumming from the distance, insect scratchings on the earth floor and above our heads, in the thick grass-frond roof, the nightly rat expeditions had just begun. It was enough to test a saint but my mind had gone elsewhere…on to meeting J in Nairobi, on to gun-toting guerrillas and leaf-eating gorillas—the ruthless and the oh so gentle. I woke early, the rats and cockroaches having won the war, and indeed it was that type of place where it was wise to check before placing feet on the ground. Sure enough, a monster cockroach rushed passed Fahmi's shoe, making a bee-line for the cob wall. 'Shake out your shorts, buddy,' I thought, 'just in case.' And yes, with the first flick, out shot a young 'roach', hitting the ground like a bullet. It scuttled off unscathed. My companions slept on so I stepped quietly out into a muggy Ariwara morning. It had lightly rained in the night, damping down the dust along the main drag. A few people hung about at an 'eatery' so I headed in that direction. The smell of eggs and fried cassava tempted but I passed, knowing I'd soon be eating Fahmi's promised cassava porridge—some special recipe of his mother's.

Smells of cooking drifted from the rears of red tin-roofed huts and blended like incense with the an all-pervasive smell of forest growth. Like a lush green Irish spring morning, I thought, only by a factor of a thousand. Behind the huts, the trees were full of birds, chorusing their symphonies. There were *'tweeee-tweeee, tweee-tweees', 'zuaa-zuaa-zuaa-zuaas', 'chippa-chippa-chippa's', 'kwoa-kwoa kwoa,kwoa's'* and much else besides. That good-to-be-alive feeling that at times hits the traveller hit me and that familiar new country feeling came. A man and woman, happy together, holding hands, entered a cafe. It had been a long time since I'd witnessed such normality and it made me reflect how I'd found the segregation of the sexes in Sudan and other parts of the Muslim world hard to swallow.

Like Yei, Ariwara had a good name for trade. It was busy even at that hour. It seemed everything and anything was up for sale—trucks, engines and parts thereof, down to the single nuts and bolts. There were bicycles, bongos, bananas and cassava tubers by the ton, food enough to feed an army, designer clothes, fake 'Rolex' watches and enough kerosene to blow up the town several times over. I was certain that behind the street facade, beyond those first line of trees,

I could have purchased any amount of assault rifles, bazookas, grenades, anti-aircraft missiles, poisonous pea-shooters, voodoo dolls, you name it…and for all I knew, maybe even people. At the outer limit of my amble down a side track off the street, two trucks were being loaded with wooden crates. It was not the crates which drew my attention but the sounds emanating from within them. Crates, large, small and tiny were being lifted into the covered truck. I stood by a corner, seeing movement through gaps in the wooden planks, hearing grunts, squeaks and bird calls.

I had never seen an okapi, but it had to be. There was no mistaking those zebra-like legs and rump. It was pushed and yanked by rope, up a ramp to disappear into the second truck. Later, over Fahmi's cassava porridge we asked lots of questions. 'They are smuggled over the border to Arua,' he said. 'Those lunatic guerillas will get their cut and will pass them up the food chain…for export to private collectors or a zoo somewhere in the West. There is big money in this, but, my friends, if *you* think rare animals are the smugglers' prize, you know nothing. Everything is smuggled here but the *real* money is not in animals or even weapons, it's in marijuana and minerals. Tin, tungsten and gold, oh my friends, this country is cursed with its riches.'

We climbed into the cab and he was still talking, enlarging our understanding of where we thought we were. 'Borders mean little here and few care about countries…there are people from everywhere and you survive how best you can. If that means helping smugglers, then you do. The routes out are the real arteries for business.' He told how the 'corridors' are like conveyor belts, moving merchandise secretly out of Zaire and they are protected by militia groups, a murky dangerous business. He painted a picture of a long chain of people from the teen with his machine gun in the jungle to pin-striped men in high glass offices scattered across the world. 'The militias, oh yes, it is they who keep control. For them and their bosses on both sides of the border, the corridors are more important than the countries.'

'Are they in the pay of people in the West?' I asked. 'Who knows my friend, who knows? Nothing would surprise me here, nothing. Zaire has always been bleeding, Africa has always been bleeding. Why do you think with so much gold, so much of every precious thing, there is so much poverty. I believe the roots of the wealth you see in Paris or London or Brussels and other cities there, was pulled out of Africa a long time ago and it's still being sucked away. That is what I believe my friends.'

The conversation waned with the noise of the truck and we swayed side-to-side in silence. All I could think of was my father and what he had said about Casement and Conrad and the same-old, same-old....

I was fast adjusting now to this new and very different place, but it would take awhile. The contrast from moving by day in Sudan through desert or scrub in dry sweltering sun to moving by night through a humid and dense canopy of trees was enough to contend with, let alone deal with the can of worms Fahmi had opened up for us. Yet in the back of my mind it was my personal state of health which was foremost. 'Maybe,' I thought 'maybe this change, this greenery, will help ease the hep away.' My eyes were still a cross between a pair of lemons and two blood oranges, my urine was dark brown and my body weak and achy. Recovery would take awhile.

By afternoon we reached the Catholic Mission in Aru where we holed up for a second night amid so many refugees from so many places that my grasp on what I had imagined Africa to be began to crumble. 'But I am refugee too,' said Fahmi. 'My parents came to Uganda from Iran a long time ago. I was born there but had to flee when Amin went too crazy. Now I and my brother share this truck to survive. I drive from Bunia to Buzze and back again. I take whatever needs to go, sugar, coffee, plantain, generators, fuel, timber, people and yes I have taken the animals too. For six years...up and down through this madness. I want to go home. I want to go home to Arua but it's my way now, what else can I do? My whole family are strung out along the road, from Butembo to Aru but we are the lucky ones, we had money to begin. Most you see here have nothing but a bag of rags. What will they do, where do they go? Some are better off dead, and don't ask about women and children. All I will say to you, my friends, it is more dangerous to be a woman here than to be a soldier. Do you understand...but how could you? Don't think about these things too much, you would only get upset. You are on your journeys, enjoy and have good time.'

'And have good time?' Christ, after Fahmi threw that grenade, I couldn't sleep and used half the battery writing the diary. Fahmi never meant it, but his throw-away comment put me more firmly in my place than anything else said along the way. I knew what he meant. His life had been torn apart and he had escaped from frying pan to fire, from one dictator's chaos to another's, to rebuild and make ends meet in a place as corrupt as hell…and as for women and girls…as he said, they were being raped wholesale, and I…I would simply pass through 'having my good old time.' Of course in reality it was not the sweet and smooth 'good time' a traveller dreams of, for there were days when… but then again, I knew what he meant. As for travel, what does it mean? That night I wrote in a vain though full-hearted attempt to purge confusion with words.

Outside I hear the close-and-distant sounds from the forest, the night calls from the canopy. It's very late or very early and a little realization dawns, a little explanation why…why I travel, why perhaps we all travel…in the end …

I travel to be disturbed—to be shaken and woken from a kind of sleep. To be disturbed on the way to a mere taste of real freedom. In the beginning, in those first days through Ireland, Wales, and onward, the rush of false freedom, of innocent freedom swept all before it. Joyous and innocent because the real 'travel' still remained cocooned in the dream. Every kilometre from my father's house to Sudan was a beauteous warm-up, and if Egypt before it enmeshed me in humanity, Sudan followed with it's very physical demands but Zaire… Zaire feels emotionally my boiling pot and is shooting so many holes in my travel dream that it's deflating thankfully into the seedy state of raw realism.

In our limited personal 'capsule-time', we travel and we do so within a cultural framework-time, infused with all that infuses the social history-space of our era. We act and interpret, perceive, imagine and discuss…ceilinged by the roots of our own upbringing, our culture and the multitudinous limits of being a human sand-grain in an ocean of extraordinary unknowable experiences. What can I do with what I am being offered? What do I do with this experience? Where do I put it? How will I tell it? Where will it take me?'

★★★

The head-beams bounced up and down, reflecting off a never-ending tunnel of trees. Fahmi had turned his music off, thankfully, and shook his head. He was disappointed. The deer had got away. We had come so close to catching it. It had sprung from the bush onto the track and took off ahead of us, confused like a rabbit in the beam. And to think I even had my foot on its leg in the undergrowth and didn't know. It had lain so still, then bolted again. Ben and the Ugandan boys had tried to corral it but '… c'est la vie,' as I said to Fahmi. He was really hoping to bring home a surprise to his wife, and we felt we'd let him down. It was the least we could have done for his service to us.

We were all too tired to speak, and then round a bend our collective hearts sank yet again. The lights shone on another barrier. It was 1.20am. Two flaming barrels and some lanterns lit up the space in front of several military-looking guys. As toughened and travel seasoned as Ben and I were, every time we rolled up to these 'Russian-roulette stops', as Ben called them, it always sent a shiver. There may have been fewer barriers in the night, but they were far more dangerous. Young, bored, tired, drunk or doped soldiers…an explosive cocktail.

Fahmi did as usual, stopped, greeted, got out, showed papers, told them of us and his two Ugandan helpers, brought them around the back, lifted his tarp to show his empty truck, bar my bike. We watched this from the cab and just like before waited to be called, but there was something menacing about their faces. We were ordered out, pushed against the truck side, frisked, then told in French *not* to move. Giddy laughter and the smell of booze told me this was different. The young Ugandans were unceremoniously dragged and kicked to the ground. Fahmi called out. I turned my head slightly to see him held back. 'Where were their papers?' They had none. Fahmi began to plead. '*Oui, oui,*' he would present them next time. The boys' shirts were ripped off and used to tie their arms behind their backs. They were forced to kneel, slapped in the face then prodded hard with the guns. 'Jesus,' Ben mumbled. 'Say nothing,' he added, but I had already called out 'Hey, hey, easy on', stupidly thinking I could defend them. I felt the nozzle of a gun in my back and was told to '*ferme ta gueule*' (shut my mouth) and to look at the truck.

Bar the odd word, I could not follow what was being said. Fahmi was working hard now. He climbed into the cab, grabbed something then climbed out. Whatever it was, it brought more laughter. (Later we discovered it was his day's pay.) On a roll now, they turned to us. Ben, his hands held behind his head, was frisked again and his passport extracted. '*Américain,*' they called out, '*Américain*'. Then his reading glasses were held up and were about to be taken or crushed. '*Non, non s'il vous plait, non,*' Fahmi said, explaining how Ben needed them to read, that they were useless to them. In the end he was lucky to be relieved of an expensive Swiss army knife and some small money in his pocket.

I felt a hand push the middle of my back, keeping me pinned to the side of the truck. '*Irlande? Un Irlandais!*' he called out, holding my passport up like a trophy. They were used to French, Americans, British, Germans, but an '*Irlan-*

dais,' that flummoxed them for awhile, but I was frisked regardless and held my breath as the hands ran down over Geoff's thick leather belt with all that cash inside. The hands continued almost to my ankles then came back up slowly and I was certain he'd feel it, absolutely certain,…but they kept going, up to my chest and I let out the deepest breath. We helped the bleeding Ugandans into the truck and drove off, Fahmi muttering how he was glad we had not caught the deer, for they would have taken it for sure and *that* for him would have been a worse pill to swallow.

We drove through the town of Djugu in the night, no one saying anything much. To the east lay the Blue Mountains and beyond them lay Lake Albert, where Samuel Baker was certain the Nile rose. In my 1984 Michelin map No.154 it was called Lake Mobutu Seso Seko, as was Lake Edward further south called Lake Idi Amin Dada. Such was that time and such those dictator men.

I was just beginning to get my bearings when suddenly we swung left off the trail into thicker jungle and I was as lost as ever. Twigs, tendrils, even an occasional night bird whacked the window. The trail deteriorated to mud. Another deer shot across and a grey fox disappeared beneath the chassis. Bats swooped into the headlights then vanished. Through breaks in the trees small homestead fires dotted the hills. Finally the truck roared into a clearing where the dawn light lit our next load: ten bales of hardwood planks, thirty sacks of coffee beans and two guys looking for a lift to Bunia. Fahmi was tired too, so spoke only in French and reassured our drooping heads, 'Ne vous inquietez pas, mes amis, on va rester à Bunia, chez mon oncle.'

In some village, not on my map but half way to his uncle's, we took a mid-morning break in a café. Half way into that break shouting erupted from down the street. Kids sprung from nowhere to sprint downhill to where the action was. 'Quickly, get in, please, get in,' Fahmi ordered. He drove fast and seemed to know what was going on. Dead ahead a large ring of people had gathered around some as yet unknown activity. They parted like a wave as he drove through them to the centre…and there, like a scene from a wild west movie, three men, then four, were pummelling one of the guys he had given a lift to. The crowd seemed incensed. Fahmi jumped out and prevented further beating before listening to the angry men. One of them faced him, pointing a finger into Fahmi's chest, after which he went straight to the rear of the truck, threw the guy's bag to the ground then quickly climbed into the cab. The guy ran to the driver's door, pleading not to be left there but we drove off leaving him to his fate. I looked back to see the ring close in again. He had robbed a toothbrush, toothpaste and some money and had tried to slip away without paying for two beers. 'I know this guy,' Fahmi explained. 'I took a chance taking him. I warned him not to bring me trouble. They blamed me for bringing him to their village. This is a hard country. They will beat him hard but they will not kill him, but you can get killed for less.'

We reached Bunia. Seven hours of a bone-shaking, Lionel Richie-filled trip that would have blown the head off any rocker. The following day Ben set out to hitch onward to Beni and his long-standing dream of climbing the Rwenzoris. Fahmi left soon after with ten tonnes of sugar back to Buzze and I sat drinking coffee on a old mattress outside his uncle's small tin-roofed house. His uncle, also a driver, was sandwiched between nice neighbours. To his right was the much bigger home of the thick-necked 'controller' of a nearby gold mine, to his left an equally large busy brothel, paid for by the controller himself, each girl with her own door. It was April Fool's Day, and I lay sweating on the grass in the shade of some exotic spreading tree, day-dreaming of that very day one year before—how friends had waved farewell before mounting their bikes back to the city, J staying the night, my father, coughing in the morning, leaning into her red Fiat engine when it would not start and then…then a little later, that final, forever-frozen hand-shake moment before the corner whipped me away into *that* dream, into *this* unheralded adventure. And for some odd reason I re-called the drizzle just two hours from home, sitting against a crash barrier on a hill outside Dungarvan, devouring the cheese and onion sandwiches which my father had made. He never made sandwiches, never, but that day he did…and now on another Fool's Day, sitting beneath the lilac flowers of that spreading tree I listened to the sounds from the brothel.

Bunia, capital of Ituri district, was not a small place, even then. Today (2018), perhaps 400,000 people reside in its sprawl, but when I rose in front of *chez oncle* to tinker with the bike on that Fool's Day, 1986, it had but a fraction of that number. To this day it's still seen as a safe haven for UNICEF, UNHCR, UN, and NGOs of all kinds…safe amid surrounding zones of militia control. Thirty kilometres to the east lay the blue of Lake Albert, but out beyond to the west the Ituri Rainforest undulated into a green and vapoury distance. 'They hide deep in there,' Fahmi had said of the militia's ease of disappearance beyond reach into the bowels of the jungle. Robin Hood and his Merry Men came to mind but these guys were no do-gooders. Apparently they felt safe in the Ituri, and why not, it being twenty times larger than even the largest primeval forest in Europe, so vast and easy to disappear in and so easy to control the gold mines and the forest villages, to capture okapis and other rare animals and, for the few, to be as Mr Kurtz was and hold the whole rain forest to ransom.

What militias did or didn't do or where they hid was altogether academic; what I needed was a seamstress. When I found her and lifted up my 'job' for her to see, she shook her head but, seeing my disappointment, got a girl to take me down a backstreet to the best cobbler in town. The long overdue stitching of cycling shoes was executed professionally for cents, but I had to plead the case for my frayed and tattered shorts. The thick lambskin chamois bought in an Amsterdam flea market had been well sewn in and had kept the original crotch in place and kept the Brooks from grinding my manhood to bits, but now there was little doubt it would require a cobbler's needle. The old codger of a cobbler, with his bird-like laugh, went outside and raised the multi-patched garment for all his codger friends to see. Like the seamstress, he shook his head but eventually, with the promise of a bonus and, I guessed, the 'ah go-ons' of his mates, he went back inside to sit at his table.

There he became a different man, sharp and focused and true to his worthy profession. With the skill of his awl he gave to the shorts all the attention they hardly deserved. When the job was done I slipped his due plus bonus into his leathery left palm, shook his right hard, bowed to his mates and walked off with the biggest, best-sewn patch of the journey. It is still there today, stretching one ass cheek to the other, a magnificent piece of patchwork if ever there was one and an everlasting reminder of Bunia.

The evening before I departed for Beni, I sat alone in Uncle's garden. Between my feet the pot simmered with another 'kiss' meal, a *mélange* of bits of this and bits of that, a gruel of cooked rice, okra, chopped cassava leaves, half an onion, a piece of unknown fish (that just *had* to be cooked) and the last of my cumin. Above me the cicadas chirped in the spreading tree, the fruit bats zig-zagged and sex-driven mine workers to-and-froed on the path. I stirred the pot as they bee-lined past me for their fill of pleasure. The laughter and lights went on and off as I ate, but my mind was concentrated on preparing itself for the following day's ride. It would be my first time on the saddle since Khartoum, where I had arrived so shattered. How different the worlds they were, that hot dry, seemingly sexless one to this utterly 'other'. Different, yes, but the same could not be said for my continuing depleted physical state. The bike was ready, but was I?

'*Venez visiter, venez a moi, venez.*' She stood squarely in her doorway, a big-breasted mature woman, beckoning me, inviting. I passed up the offer, feeling safer spooning gruel. Later, in the tent, listening to the eager footsteps, I wondered would I too have gone if my energy had been brimful with vigour and glory. I tried to grasp what Fahmi had said: that those women were safer in that house than many of their sisters in the villages.

There were two well-beaten paths, one straight from the controller's house, the other rising the slope from the public thoroughfare, the latter trodden over the years by the tough boots of the mine workers and those of the jungle militias, the flip-flops of the truck drivers and the good shoes of the horny male aid workers. I admit, like a shy sex-mad teenager, I peeped for awhile through the unzipped zip of the tent bell. That night it was mostly the men from the mine who strolled past the tent to their chosen woman at her door. The doors would open and close, open and close so frequently, I wondered how many guys were billeted over there. Or were some returning for seconds? It was the first and last time I ever pitched by a brothel. What a night…a night for old and new imagination, a night for hard reflection about who I was in this too often god-forsaken world. Twenty-five years later Margot Wallstrom, the UN's Special Representative on Sexual Violence, spoke of the Ituri region as being 'the rape capital of the World'. When I read that, I wondered what Conrad and Casement had really seen one hundred years before. Did they see a real 'heart of darkness', a thick psychic lanket of pain that let no light in, no crack to allow the soul or mind to breathe…keeping the spirit of men as twisted as a climbing tendril or an open festering sore in the clammy heat, growing more corrupt with the generations? As to the seeds of torture and mutilation, how many decades before were they set? I was no expert, but *they* were the thoughts that arose out of the pain of later reflections.

★★★

It felt good, real good, to saddle up. The load was pared to the bone. In the front pannier, one spare litre of water, along with the three 500cc plastic ones hung off the tubes. The larder was down to two tins of pilchards, a few sweet bananas, a half bag of old dates from Juba and a plastic tub of cooked cassava leaves, which Fahmi suggested I chew on as I rode. My appetite was pretty shook but I knew in my gut I'd be fine. Food and water had rarely been an issue anyway. I rode off with that feeling of uplift one gets from doing the right thing and letting go a little. I'd given a pair of unwashed T-shirts to two boys who had hung around the tent from day one. They cared little that the shirts were way too big for them, and as far as I can recall they were the only lads in Africa to proudly wear the bleached and unwashed mementos of my passing.

At Uncle's door I passed over a five Zaire note (Mobutu Seso Seko staring up at us both, like the good dictator that he was)—that, and half a kilo each of rice and lentils and other bits, making Uncle's smile a happy one. He pointed to the dirt road out of Bunia and his rapid-fiing Swahili sounded like he wished me well. The track was red earth, like a farewell carpet laid out between the green grass margins. Few vehicles passed and I shared the way with those who walked or went by bike. The *jambos* and *bonjours* came by the dozen, and I would respond instantly with a *jambo* or a *oui, bonjour* or a *bonsoir*. Occasionally someone would call out in Swahili *pole sana* and I'd reply *asante sana*. It felt like I was one of the family and despite physically feeling thirty percent, I was as happy as Uncle and mentally pinched myself to look hard at every tropical-looking tree, every multicoloured swooping bird, every passing smiling face…for here I was riding in the Congo at last.

The big leafy equatorials filled out the background, and palms of one kind or another stood among them, their trunks naked as telegraph poles. Sometimes the vista opened up wide to reveal the rolling distance with wispy grey smoke-funnels rising here and there out of the green. Banana and coffee trees grew higgeldy-piggeldy, and occasional square patches of pineapples always made me salivate when I stopped to look. Bushy cassava plants were everywhere, or were they cassava at all? Cannabis or cassava? It was hard to tell. I presumed that, given its importance as a food, the plants were the latter, but then I'd smelled a fair deal of weed along the road. Regardless of what they were, there seemed to be no order or method to the growing, as if they were planted at random and in hope. Probably a grossly unfair observation on my part. Yet what did look true to my passing eye was how hard the women worked, how they carried, tended, harvested and tilled the earth. I wondered what the men were doing. Yet from a people point of view it was so, so different to Sudan. Here there was no beckoning or hailing me back to join a communal bowl of beans, no ease of interaction. The people were friendly, they smiled a lot and helped where they could, but you'd pay for everything else. In Zaire I realized how Sudan had spoiled me and, indeed, many a traveller.

Sometimes the forest foliage closed in tight like a tunnel, and sometimes I'd stop at nothing more than a coloured cloth at the edge of the road. I would see it up ahead with it's attendant women in their equally multicoloured *liputas*—not as bold and bright as those in Bunia but still so completely and wildly incongruous for the setting. I would draw closer and they would point at their pyramid piles of bananas, their baskets of pineapples enticing me, but they should never have feared that I would not pull over. Pineapples alone were reason enough, for to sit on the red earth and gorge in the sun, the juice seeping through my beard and knowing that I was the cause of all the sudden animated talk...what a cherished pineapple-memory that is. I'd gorge way too much, then ride again, willing the sugared energy down into two slow-pedalling lethargic, legs. The humidity must have been eighty and I thanked the puff-clouded blue heavens that the rain was falling somewhere else, for it would surely have turned the red earth to a sticky goo.

Yes it felt good to ride...for a while. At ten kilometres it was all systems go, at fifteen still okay, at twenty the legs began to ache, at twenty-five the struggle began, and by thirty the mind-over-body game was in full swing. Hepatitis sucks and I cursed it, but hep is hep, and if it gets in there's no easy out. The strung-out village of Niakunde couldn't come fast enough, but Niakunde, at least that part of it by the side of the road, hardly existed. I went on until a stall-full of buxom brash *liputa*-clad women came like manna from beyond. They even had tea and tried hard to sell me the last of their oily dumplings, but my yellow eyes were fixed once again on their whooping great pineapples. It was a pity for their piles of leaves and tubers, but I had no interest. '*Trois pineapple, s'il vous plait et une kilo de bananes. Merci beaucoup!*' Behind their stall I cat-napped, then rose like Lazarus, wondering if pineapple juice could really resuscitate a virus-filled system. Amazingly I felt light and bright and knew I'd make it to the infamous Komanda junction before dark.

A few good cycling hours later, I stood in the heart of that town and saw where the dirt road split. Straight was the way to Kisingani, all 640 kilometres of it, and from there a further...yes, a further 1,200 kilometres to the capital,

Kinshasa. The Congo is big, Africa is big, very big, especially when you're in the middle of it. I swung left to Beni, thinking the 125 kilometres a dawdle in comparison. Ah yes, 'to dawdle', *to go somewhere very slowly, taking more time than is necessary.* That sounded just right. I would dawdle to Beni, and what a dawdle.

In Komanda Ben popped up again. He had his own story to tell, which he told as we ferreted out a place to place our heads. Perhaps it was inevitable but no other alternative could be found except another decrepit mission-hut in which to sleep another zombie-like night. Mission? The word lends itself to vocation, dedication, cleanliness, even a trajectory to godliness but no one told the rats. Truly, they were the largest either of us had ever seen, fattened by the fact that the local church used the hut as a grain store. They came in hoards and pushed the merely annoying ticks, cockroaches, mites and mosquitoes to the ha'penny place. It was a mission hut straight from hell, and only for borrowed candles burning all night, Ben's regular swishing of the floor with the hut broom and my swiping at the them with my bicycle pump, the devils might have eaten us alive. Poor Ben, he choose the softer grass bed, threw himself down, then shot-up like a lightning rod. The sudden high-pitched squeaks came from a whopper of a fat furry mama. He kept his cool as she shot straight out to leave her tiny offspring in the nest, and I just cracked up laughing. The strange thing is that we were mentally long prepared for encounters like this; it was all to be expected. We had gone 'native' so to speak. 'Of course they're pissed off,' I said, as we gathered up the wriggling rats and chucked them to the bushes. 'Rats sharing *our* space? Shit, man, it's we who have gate-crashed into theirs.'

Dawn brought an end to the onslaught. 'At least they didn't get this,' Ben joked, holding up his right thumb, 'I'm goin-ta-need it today.' Indeed, soon after a breakfast of *matoke* we left the Komanda fat-rats behind and he stuck it out at a passing Beni bound truck, but it drove on, already top heavy with its human cargo. I too made my way, turning once in the saddle to give him a thumbs up. 'See ya in Beni, buddy,' he shouted, his cupped hands round his mouth. 'For sure,' I yelled back, 'race you there.' It was one of those cameos that cycling travellers will know: when, to be on a bike, to be independent, to be able to move however slowly under one's own steam was to feel the brush-stroke of freedom. By noon, however, I was well spent, and he had long passed me, waving his glee with a perfect grin from the back of a pick-up.

If Fahmi had not suggested Mount Hoyo, God only knows where I might have slept on that second night to Beni. 'You will like it up there,' he had said. 'The view (over the Ituri) is so, so good.' He warned that the sign could easily be missed, 'it' apparently being 'a small one'. Through dense forest and open forest and at times no forest at all, the road wound its way, passing the occasional village and the odd cluster of pygmies. All the while I kept a watchful eye for that Hoyo sign. Just as well, for when it did show itself it was almost completely obscured by grasses, but there it was, 'Bienvenue. Mount Hoyo Hotel et Reserve' in tidy hand-written script. The stone-strewn track took off up a steep hill and I admit I rode not a metre of it. Upward and onward I pushed, wondering what kind of 4x4 tourists came here, what the nightly fee would be and if I could afford it. Head resting on the handlebar, face facing the ground in front of the front wheel, I was practically in the swarm before I saw it.

There dead ahead, on a rising hairpin bend was a veritable wall of bluish butterflies. They blocked the way entirely. The swarm was immense and appeared to quiver in the filtered forest light bouncing off the fluttering mass of wings. Nothing like it I had ever seen. It hung there, like a single entity as if to say 'Hey, mate, you gotta go through us first if you want to go on!' I froze. 'Nothing to fear here,' I thought 'they're butterflies not bees.' Yet, to be slowly enveloped by thousands upon thousands of them is not something one easily forgets. I inched closer, then stood motionless and let the swarm swallow me, a loose but massive teeming cloud. Some explored the handlebar, some the saddle, some the back of my hands, my head, shoulders, arms, and all the while a strange soft sound whooshed around, as if I was being fanned by a host of fairies. It was surreal, absolutely surreal, but the word fails, absolutely fails. The swarm drifted off in slow motion, leaving me open-mouthed, half wishing to re-enter to be blessed again, half to let it be and let it go. Here and there stragglers hung on to bits of me, but one by one they too let go and flew to rejoin the mother cloud.

The butterflies gave fresh energy to my legs and I reached level ground with a *joie de vivre*. Earlier a thunderstorm had bucketed on Mount Hoyo. The grass was wet and the air had that earthy smell of growth, tinged with the incense-like resinous smoke from a nearby pygmy fire. In these parts the word 'hotel' can well deceive but I was pleasantly surprised. Before me, facing out onto a green grass lawn, stood a simple single-storey concrete structure with its claim to fame waiting timelessly to reward the visitor. The Mount Hoyo Reserve Hotel may have been basic and decent enough, but it was superbly situated overlooking the sea of the Ituri rainforest. (Sadly the hotel does not exist anymore. It was plundered and destroyed long ago, years after I spent that memorable night there, when it played to it's best.) I rolled passed the 4x4s and the beer-bottled tables of fellow visitors, their gazes following this curious sight, on to a low parapet where I let the bike down gently and took in the view, and what a view. The Ituri stretched from the far horizon to the parapet where I rested my foot, a vast matt green canopy of tropical trees beneath a blanket of gunmetal cloud. Out there, down there, in there, I imagined the militias, holed up around some Mr Kurtz, waiting for their next onslaught and, of course, the pygmies, for whom it was home.

In his classic book, *The Forest People*, Colin Turnbull tells of his three years with the Mbuti pygmies, three years which changed his life forever. Everyone of that era, including me, whether they read it or not, unwittingly knew of pygmies because of it. That night up on Mount Hoyo, the 'tourist' pygmies danced. They danced and drummed and sang and then came round for *cadeaux*…cigarettes mostly or donations, but I was the wrong kind of tourist. I gave a dollar, not nearly as much as the mix of French, South African, American and German real tourists with whom I shared the space, but the pygmies did not differentiate. In their small round eyes I was a mean white man and got no brownie points for having arrived by bicycle instead of a flight from Paris, Munich, or New York. Yet, to be fair, they did seem bemused by my tent, pitched with permission and for half the price.

Bar the Mbuti and me, everyone was on Primus. That it was near double the price at the bottom of the mountain mattered nothing to the real tourists but I was counting every cent. From behind the glass door of the diesel-powered fridge, those brown beer bottles looked out at me and for once I was happy to have hepatitis. It kept a tight rein on a limited purse and, of course, the health of my liver. If Sudan was Pepsi, Zaire was definitely Coke, and if beer was out then my sole treat would be a cheaper chilled bottle of the latter. So, with that iconic curvy bottle in hand, I gazed over the gyrating heads of the pygmies, out over their vast homeland. Coca Cola's ultra-sharp PR department would never know, but that evening they missed a rare advertising opportunity. It was certainly not I who would have made their executives dance a jig, but two pygmies resting on the parapet, sipping their coke bottles against a stupendous backdrop of a golden sun sliding smoothly into the darkness of *their* Ituri home…what a dream shot for the adman. As I wondered how much those pint-sized pygmies might have received for such a shot, a hotel worker came over to whisper, 'Do not look at them or they will come to you for more money or cigarettes.' True enough, I had already seen the hassle and carry-on, so I gulped my last and looked away to the east, where a host of glow worms blinked and danced in the dark.

Down hill the following morning I pumped the brakes with a head full of arrogant chatter, '... bloody tourist pygmies...rich bloody tourists!' I wondered was it possible for a 'real traveller' to meet 'real pygmies?' I rode into thicker jungle with some naive hope. I did see them later that day as the wheels rumbled over a narrow wooden bridge. The band were ten metres below on the river bank, their dugouts tied up nearby. I waved down, then made the god-awful stupid mistake of pulling out the camera. A stone came flying upward and I knew by the angry shouts that I was being told where to shove it. Yes, I was late, late by years and years for this type of flippant passer-by photo shoot. I took off fast for fear they'd come up and I'd get a poison dart in my ass.

By late afternoon Beni lay before me and I knew for sure that somewhere here I would rest-up for as long as it took. The tank was empty. Turning west towards the centre of the town and looking out for some cheap hotel, the sight of the Rwenzoris took the last of my breath away. It was a visceral shock to the system—a snow-capped mountain range rising out of equatorial forest. The sight stopped me dead and I straddled the bike. If Sudan's deserts had offered their expansiveness, and the Congo's forests their sense of contraction, what stood before me now, rising to the sky, grounded and centred me as only big mountains can. They lay deceptively low on the skyline and appeared as if just beyond the town, but scale created its illusion. White clouds and forest covered the lower slopes with snow just showing. These were no Alpine or Himalayan dramatic jagged peaks, but with Mount Stanley at over 5,000 metres, Mount Baker at 4,844 and four other peaks at over 4,600 these were no piddly little hills. These were Claudius Ptolemy's *Lunae Montes*, the 'Mountains of the Moon', part source of the mighty Nile. Not much prepares you for snow near the equator, but then not much can prepare you for anything in Zaire. There was nothing for it but shoot the camera. No one cared or bothered me; people stood about chatting in the warm pleasantness of evening, a guy cycled passed, a big red truck came towards. I was left to my own devices, alive and in Beni, and that felt good enough.

★★★

Restaurant-Boulangerie—two faded French words high on the gable of what would become my Beni convalescent base camp, two words that conjured up old French memories of morning sticks of fresh bread, a spoon or two of confiture, the smell of Camembert and oh, that first gulp of a good Bordeaux. Sure, I was hungry, and memories of times in France played in my mind but my senses swam in a world so remote, so different and though the French language was in the air, it wasn't enough to span the enormous gulf. Was I surprised that France, though not my culture, felt close and familiar? Not really. Given the metre-by-metre hard-won-experiencing of the distance between them, even Europe itself had morphed into a sense of home, leaving my Irish umbilical looser than it had ever been, and as for 'home' what did that mean anyway? I had both far less and far more of an idea of what it meant than ever before.

The Hotel Lualaba would be home now, its roughness matched by a homely, friendly atmosphere, and just as in Juba, the *petit chambre* I was offered was like a prison cell. On the threshold of that little room I blew out a deep breath, surveying the spartan space and knowing that for several days this was it…and indeed *that* was it, a world so remote from today's, a world of no internet, no texting, no uploading or skyping, no easy phoning, nothing…nothing but the isolated, insulated mind and where it went with what it saw. Never did I write so many postcards and letters, only to grasp later, a long, long time later, how that writing was as much about me writing to myself as communicating to those who knew or half knew where I was.

Into that hard-working world at the rear of Hotel Lualaba, under the wing of a caring 'mama', I was blessed to be welcomed—as if she had not enough to do with a toddler and a baby hanging off her without a sick *mizungu* to tend to. Yet, as so often was the way throughout that vast continent, she batted not an eyelid. For five days I was tutored under her watchful eye—peeling and chopping cassava, cutting greens, kneading dough for the daily bread or watching her white fish simmer. She would show the best way to hold a knife, and the knives were many and they were large. (Knives in Sub-Saharan Africa, like guns in America, are so easy to grab if you are angry and wish to do damage.)

Knife in hand I chopped vegetables…carefully, then Ayuba came to help.

He was different to the others; for one, he was Muslim, proudly wearing his crocheted *taqiyah;* for two, he had a certain confidence, for he felt he owned the place and, as I was to discover, he almost did, or should have done. I hardly saw his knife blade for the speed with which he chopped, not even looking to his fingers as the diced pieces flew away as if from a machine. It was the skill of years, and he laughed at my slow, careful chop-chop.

'Yes,' he said, 'my father was Belgian, my mother from Congo. He came here to invest, to buy things. He bought a coffee plantation and this hotel. He took my mother and they had my brother and me. Later we found out that he also had a Belgian wife and three children there. During the rebellion in the sixties he returned to Belgium and my mother fled with me to Uganda. After the war he returned but was killed in a car accident near Bukavu. All his land and this hotel was seized by government soldiers. We have no papers to prove anything. I have tried to contact my half-brother in Europe…but nothing. I think they do not know we exist.'

I read the letter he had written in French, to be sent yet again to an eighteen-year-old address in Switzerland. I hadn't the heart to tell him how unlikely it would be that it would ever be reciprocated, even if it made it out of the country. 'Why do you stay here' I asked. 'I stay because my mother stays. We stay because we have no place else. Maybe one day my half-brother will come with papers and show that our same father did own this hotel. Then I will become the manager, but for now I work here just like the others.'

By day two, I was just like 'the others'. Mama would ask for wood or water to be fetched and I was happy to do so, not having to think, just follow her instructions. In the cool of evening I would stroll to the edge of Beni to gaze at the Rwenzoris. That, of course, brought its own mix of awe and regret. I imagined Ben and his guide up there somewhere scaling the slopes of Stanley. On the way back to the Lualaba I would bemoan what 'might have been' then swiftly counter that there are no 'mights' on the long road. No mights or shoulds or maybes; they do not exist. Fate had swapped for me five days of an arduous mountain climb for five of mundane tasks at the rear of a hotel, but if fate allowed I would return from Nairobi with J and we would climb Stanley or Baker, or both, together.

(But Fate had other plans. Ninety metres is all that separates the heights of Mounts Kenya and Stanley, the second and third highest mountains in Africa.

How it would have changed my mood as I looked longingly at the Rwenzoris had I known that not three months later I would stand in snow and almost at the full height of Stanley but on Mount Kenya, fortunate to be part of a mini Irish-British expedition to attempt its summit. That bit of luck lay ahead, but would be hugely dampened by what awaited me in the Kenyan capital.)

As a weary convalescing *mizungu*, I was not the only soul that Mama looked out for. One young woman rarely if ever left the hotel. I noticed how she would sometimes venture briefly into the rear yard to join in some chore but only if Mama was around; otherwise she would remain within. She never looked me in the eye though I tried my best to be cordial. From her window she would secretly look to see the white man chopping vegetables; I pretended not to notice. Once I waved, but she withdrew. 'Why is she so shy?' I innocently asked. Mama was blunt. 'If what happened to her happened to you…you would not leave the safety of your room either.' That's all she wished to say on the matter, and I enquired no further. I'd been in the country just about long enough to get the gist.

Outside the door-less rear door, an outcrop of grey granite rock was used as a seat. On it the girl would rock herself gently holding Mama's baby in her arms, humming a soothing ditty in her own language. Love and pain were etched equally on her face; the thought of snapping a photo came and went in a flash. I had neither the skill nor experience, nor courage, for hers was too intimate, too raw and too personal a space to be invaded by that. The grief of her life was plain enough to feel, and not until the hindsight of years did I realise how she was but one of thousands and thousands of grieving women who had the good life bled from them.

That night rain thundered on the tin roof with a ferocity I had never before witnessed or since. In less than sixty seconds the pitter-patter turned torrential and then turned to what could only be described as violent. I sat up in complete darkness, for there was no electricity, wondering would the roof cave in. Then, as sudden as it began it stopped, like turning a tap off—just like that! I went outside to pee, to see an amazing clear night sky. Where had the rain come from? There to the west, above those tree tops, the guilty hulk of black cloud slunk away like some behemoth from a Tolkien story, and there also, just where I had left it draped on a rope to air my sweat away, was my sleeping bag. 'Oh shit!' What a great idea to hang it out. Even at the equator it would take weeks to dry. The feathers never got over the soaking shock of that night. They stuck together in a clumpy state until the bag finally disintegrated towards the end of the journey. There were, however, other, bigger issues on my mind.

Every cyclist knows that 'road less travelled' dilemma, that fork-in-the-road feeling. Mine was a mental one, turning slowly in the night, weighing the pros and cons. For five Beni days I batted the options over-and-back and over again—Beni-Butembo-Goma versus Beni-Kasindi-Lake Edward. The latter had always been ahead in the betting, but Butembo now beckoned with a 'new' address and, of course, an easier dirt road for legs still in convalescence. To go the Kasindi way was far tougher. It involved negotiating the Virunga National Park, crossing the Semliki river, then crossing the full length of Lake Edward from Ishango to Vitshumbi to arrive into the gorilla zone near the Rwandan border, and from there...I wasn't quite sure what to expect but knew at least it would be a challenging onward route to enter Uganda at Bunagana, a small border post at almost 2,000 metres in altitude.

In the end it was the gorillas that swung it. The thought of being up close to them, high in the Virunga hills, just wouldn't let go and anyway, as for many of us in the eighties, Dian Fossey was a hero. She had devoted half her life to them and was the genuine reason why I took the Zaire rather than the Ethiopian route. 'Maybe', I used to muse, 'maybe I might even meet the woman.' So with mosquito net suspended over my face, I drifted off, knowing it was a *fait accompli*; the Virunga-way had won.

On the morning I saddled-up to leave, Mama sat as usual on her rock, her baby blowing sleep bubbles on her shoulder. She had prepared hot milk for me and a feed of *matoke (cooking bananas)* followed by sweet bananas. Then, as if on auto-pilot, she continued to peel big chunks of cassava into her big aluminium pot, her baby's sleeping head bobbing up and down as she worked. She had seen to it that I got what I needed, mainly rest, and for that I was grateful. To have given her a farewell hug would have been a 'nice' gesture but the cultural gap was too wide. As I pushed the bike round the side of the hotel she rallied the others to follow, curious I guessed to see more the 'how' of my pedalling away than to actually wave. Not that I cared, for it was always a pleasant boost to be seen off by a few, even if they just stand there and gawk. They giggled as I rediscovered my legs again, but quickly I was gone, curving round a tin shack-cum-grocery store on a corner and I left them to get on with their lives. It took all of two minutes to get out of the Beni that was then and to hit the red earth road heading south-west toward Kasindi.

That day's ride of about eighty kilometres is at least up there among the top twenty best, partly because I thought I was leaving illness behind, partly because I was back on the Brooks saddle (I had missed it!), partly because my mood was so buoyant with the *bonjours* and *jambos* of the many passers-by, partly because the air was so fresh, the sky so blue, the hills so green, partly because I felt at last I was heading to where the gorillas lived but mostly…mostly because the dirt road snaked all day due west of the Mountains of the Moon, the Rwenzoris, and *that* like any dream fulfilled felt really, really good. 'Bloody hell,' I mumbled several times, 'there they are, here I am…fuck-me-pink, if Da could see me now.' On the opposite side of that same road, which ran on to Kasindi, lay one of the most biologically diverse game-parks in the world, and as my journey through Africa unfolded I would see nine of them in all—Masai Mara, Mount Kenya, Ambosseli, Mikumi, Zambezi, Chobe, Namib-Nauklift and Etosha, all amazing, but none gave me the 'hit' that Virunga did.

Chapter 10

If our brother gorillas could speak…

Stanley, Baker, Speke and all the other peaks in the Rwenzori clouds ran down into the twists and folds of their foothills, down to the green aprons at their bases. I rode past the tin-roofed homes and the strung-out habitation, the clumps of trees and small fields of crops. After Nyaleke (I think!), I was officially in the Virunga National Park, but after crossing the Semliki River I was out of it as quick. I didn't care; I was in the saddle and that's what counted. Not far from Beni, the Semliki introduced herself below me. It was one of those rivers that those Nile-source hunters were so keen to track down. From a bridge I watched the skin of my sweet banana fall into the swift brown waters. The Semliki drains Lake Edward into the much bigger Lake Albert, at the northern end of which the enormous Lake Victoria adds her considerable volume through the Victoria Nile. What departs Lake Albert is called the Albert Nile and flows on as such to Nimule on the border with South Sudan. There the beautiful sounding Bahr-al-Jabal comes into being…the White Nile. Strictly speaking the river does not 'get white' for another thousand kilometres, where the Sobat joins in at Malakal with all that white sediment from Ethiopia, and not until Khartoum, at the confluence of the Al-Mogran, do all these names settle down to let the Great River flow on into everyone's consciousness as simply 'The Nile'.

Cloud hung over the summits, but they came and went in and out of view. As for riding a bike with hepatitis, it was like riding while roped to a dirty great boulder behind. All the fine vistas, all the *jambo* waves and the happy little reflections could not overcome a deadening ache. All was glorious all around but it dragged like an anchor. I was the donkey and the only carrot dangling before me were the images of Fossey and her gorilla friends. I imagined an upward trek in the undergrowth, on the slope of some volcano, the searching, the heart-pounding at seeing the bulk of a great silverback, followed by the shock and awe. I ran the whole imagined scene from beginning to end, and it kept me going almost as far as Mutwanga.

Mutwanga, half way between Beni and Kasindi, is a one of the villages in those Rwenzori foothills. It is a little off the main road and there was no reason to go there but I needed a boost of something, so I swung the handlebar left and headed slowly up a stony trail. Too slow. The pack of kids who trotted alongside pissed me off. The older ones slapped and pushed at the panniers and the younger ones cackled their '*Donne moi un cadeau, donne moi un cadeau, donne moi, donne moi.*' They annoyed the hell out of me, until I jumped off and erupted like a lion, 'For fuck sake, fuck off, would ye. . . .' The little buggers ran. They may not have understood a word but they certainly got the anger.

The bike rolled in to a village heaving with the od-songs of 'Praise the lord' and 'Jesus heals' and 'God will save us all from sin' or was it 'God will save us from all sin…if only we let him.' I can't recall which, but if some angel saw the scene from above, she would have assumed that the visiting truck-load of missionaries singing 'god songs' to the accompaniment of the local mini brass band had gathered there to welcome me…but no, they and their swaying, clapping, chanting village-entourage were too lost in the divine to notice the arrival of a most Jesus-looking guy, despite his vitriol.

Behind the missionary truck in a dappled shade, I listened to the Lord being praised while working my way through a bunch of those small sweet bananas.

'Who wouldn't sing praise, living in such a Paradise,' I mused but then remembered how brutal life can be in Paradise. A few teens came snooping round, checking me out, so I tossed them a few bananas to keep them sweet and on my side. They were bemused by this very earthly looking diversion to the hard-core religion which they didn't seem too taken by...and then Evan came. The first thing I noticed, for it caught me off guard, was his camera. Encased in brown leather, it dangled from his neck. This, along with his cool baseball hat, a matching top-and-bottom blue uniform and the fact that he spoke a rudimentary English made me sit up and take a bit more notice. He saluted the teens, and by their response it was obvious he had their respect.

Straight to the bike he went, but unlike other casual onlookers he looked it over with a keen eye. When he pulled out a pen and notebook to jot down the brand names of bike, pannier, saddle, derailleur, even the faded name on the plastic water bottle, it was I who became bemused *and* impressed. 'That is a first,' I told him. 'Oh yes,' he answered, 'I too wish to do a journey with the bicycle. First to Beni then Butembo then Bukavu and with the help of God all the way to Bujumbura.' Above the heavenly din of brass blowing and hymn singing I tried to tell him how there was no magic to it—'Just grab your bike and go for it'—but the din was too much so he took me first to a backstreet cafe, where he insisted on paying for the *chais*, then to the market where he explained how unusual it was for a 'Congo man to be doing the shopping', then uphill to his home where waited his wife and two lovely toddler daughters. She was a petite woman, a nurse who worked in Butembo, and although I was completely unexpected she gave me a welcome befitting any Irish home.

Not alone did Evan buy the produce but he helped his wife prepare it. I'd not seen that before! I liked the guy, he was certainly...different. I noticed too how his black Chinese bike was polished spotless, putting mine to shame. 'They think me a fool cycling around taking photos and going to the market to buy food instead of my wife, but it does not upset me.' He told how he had departed the Catholic flock to cross over and swell the armies of Seventh Day Adventists—they who await the second coming—and then I re-considered why he might have descended so quick to my picnic spot behind the truck. Perhaps a teen had told him that a 'missionary looking guy' was scoffing bananas there? Who knows, but I wasn't so surprised, for in Africa no one gets too far from some god.

215

Over the meal I told of the plan to cross Lake Edward from Ishango to Vitshumbi and on into the gorilla zone. He was surprised by the route, then concerned but then came a glint of enthusiasm. 'It will take a long day to cross the lake,' he said, 'if they will allow you, but if you pay I am sure some fisherman will.' He explained how the *pirogues* had only outboard engines and were narrow and small. 'If you can find someone to do this it will be very, very special for you, Mr John. You will see Virunga from the centre of the lake and see the fishermen fish. Maybe I will return this way after I go to Bujumbura.'

I also told how my girlfriend would arrive to Nairobi a few weeks later. 'Then you must not visit the gorillas,' he said. 'No, no, you must wait and see them together.' Of this he was adamant. 'It is a thing you will want to share. You will never forget it and after you visit them you can visit me. It is not far.' As he spoke I was already nodding inside at this unexpected proposal. 'Why not,' I thought, 'yes, bring J to see the gorillas, then cross the lake again to Mutwanga. Wow, she'd like that.' It all made perfect sense.

To get back into the Virunga National Park, Evan wrote a letter in French to give to the Warden at the barrier. That made good sense too, and so Evan, unwittingly and in a very innocent sort of way, played his part in my own little drama. Later, when his wife and girls had gone to bed we stood naked—black and white—outside his rear door sharing a cold bucket to wash ourselves. Above us, on the roof of the Rwenzoris sheet lightning lit the sky before clearing north to reveal a night so studded with starlight it seemed the whole of the *Via Lactea* was showering down on us. And there, standing wet and naked, I saw for the first time both the Northern Plough and the Southern Cross at either end of that heavenly spectrum. It was a memorable night and in hindsight even more so, for the journey ahead was to take three terrible twists, all of which would combine to ensure I would never return to sit by the gorillas. Unknown to me, back in Ireland, the first twist had already occurred, for on another though far lesser mountain J tripped and fell into the soft purple heather. She grazed her knee harmlessly on a stone but *that,* like the proverbial flap of a butterfly wing over the Amazon, lit the slow fuse of a storm which would scupper the dreams of innocence.

★★★

True to his form, Evan rode a little way, his camera dangling as ever round his neck. We even swapped bikes, but he found the weight of the front panniers tricky to handle. 'I will travel light to Bujumbura,' he laughed. He laughed too at the dozen or so 'Donne moi' kids who cheered us along—they not daring now to touch my bags while he was beside me. We straddled each other's bikes and someone took a photo and that was it. 'Bon voyage et bonne chance, Monsieur John.' 'Merci Evan, merci beaucoup de votre assistance.'

Bonne chance…bonne chance, indeed, I needed it. By opting to cross Lake Edward I knew I was making one hell of a detour to get into Uganda. Straight down the road, just beyond Kasindi, a straight-forward border-crossing lay waiting, it was that easy, but adventure is adventure and as someone somewhere said, 'If you're going a long way to the city on a shopping spree, then go the whole hog, including the taxi!' My 'whole hog' was simple: get into and through Virunga, get onto and across Lake Edward, get out of Vitshumbi past the Gorilla Zone and over the border at Bunagana into Uganda. A piece of cake!

Evan was right. At the Ishango turn-off, where the barrier to Virunga National Park stood, I was not allowed to enter. The bike alone befuddled a bemused Warden. He chuckled to his junior, then turned to me and said with some incredulity, 'Avec la bicyclette? Non, Monsieur, il y a des animaux dangereux dans le Parc, Monsieur. S'il vous plaît, Monsieur, continuez vers Kasindi pour obtenir votre autorisation.' No permit, no entry, and even with a permit I would not be allowed to ride. I crossed my fingers and handed him Evan's letter.

Do travellers get a perverse pleasure on seeing an official's eyebrows rise? I did. I watched the Warden's face brighten as he slowly read the letter. He turned it over to see if there was more on the reverse, then looked at me and grinned, as if suddenly I'd become one of the team. It was a moment of childish glee, when you know you have (with the help of a local) slipped in behind the normal ring of official steel. Evan had written a volume but the nub of it was pretty simple:

> Monsieur le gardien, mon ami, M. John, est un naturaliste, qui aime beaucoup les gorilles et la nature…il voudrait se rendre à Ishango, pour voir les pêcheurs…et il voudrait traverser le lac vers Vitsumbi, pour voir les gorilles. Merci de l'aider. Evan Mafuta.

At the Warden's instruction his junior raised the barrier. 'Wow, I'm in,' I thought, yet it became clear I may have been 'in' but I wasn't going to Ishango. The Warden beckoned to a driver who had come through behind me. He showed the letter, pointing in my direction. Their heads nodded. A deal was being done on my behalf, the result of which I would pay 500 zaire shillings ($10 at that time) for the 'transport service'. What cut the Warden got, who knew, but he deserved it. I was loaded up with handshakes all round and off I went, not a clue in the wide world where in Virunga I was going. The Warden stood clear as the pick-up pulled away and called out, I guess to reassure me, that same unintelligible word he had said earlier, but it meant nothing. Late that evening after a doubly bumpy ride I understood what he was trying to tell me. '*Kyavinyonge, Kyavinyonge,*' he had shouted, '*Pas Ishango...Kyavinyonge.*'

Hardly a hundred metres from the Warden's hut a warthog family, tails erect like antennae, tore along in single file. I lit up when I saw them, how could one not? It was love at first sight. They are odd creatures and won me over easily for they exuded a sense of not giving a damn for anything else going on around them. Plucky, confident little buggers they were, their faces so warty and horny one could only love them for being brave enough to come out into the world at all. Forget beauty and grace, if you're looking for character you're on to a winner. Any animal that reverses home into a hijacked or 'borrowed' burrow deserves to be taken note of.

It was my first time too to go bumping through a national park. If I knew then what I know now about Virunga, I would have enjoyed it all the more. Most of Africa's famous Game Parks rolled easy off my tongue—Serengeti, Ngorongoro, Maasai Mara, Mikumi, Amboselli, Chobe, Zambezi, Krugar, Etosha ...but Virunga? It seemed that those other parks had a cooler brand name. They could be spoken of separate from the lions, elephants, giraffe, zebra and other big game within their confines...but Virunga? For far too long it was a mere footnote to the chaos of power struggles, of civil-war, of fighting or indeed Dian Fossey's fight for the plight of mountain gorillas. It seemed as if such tragic happenings were always spoken of first and Virunga second...to the point that beyond the circles of conservationists it was hardly known about. Yet how often does Africa hold her prize jewels tight to her bosom?

Virunga is such a jewel, a place of unparalleled biodiversity among the long list of the continent's parks. It was the first and is the oldest of them all, decreed as a park by King Albert of Belgium in 1925 to protect the gorillas. How *incroyable* that half the plant and animal species in Africa are represented within its domain—truly a naturalist's utopia, and all due to the unrivalled variation of its habitats: savanna, jungle, rivers, marshes, mountain slopes, snowfields, permanent glaciers, even volcanoes, of which Mount Nyiragongo is without doubt the more (in)famous with the planet's most spectacular lava lake bubbling in its caldera. No other park comes near, but tragically no other park has been under the cosh of so many diverse and well-armed bands of poachers, competing militia gangs, charcoal-making syndicates and civil war. In a word, no other park has been as dangerous.

Into this volatile Virunga mess, who would dare grab hold of the reins of stewardship? That it would be Dr Emmanuel de Merode is so fitting, given his blood connection to the very king who initiated Virunga in the first place. In 2008 he accepted the onerous responsibility to re-stabilise Virunga from the Congo government. His role as Chief Warden and National Park Director was, and still is, perhaps the most dangerous one in the world of conservation. In April 2014, two days before the New York premiere of the documentary film *Virunga*, he was shot and severely wounded in an assassination attempt. He survived and was back at his desk within weeks.

His team of park rangers daily risk their lives for a cause felt deeply in their hearts. It is not a job for the faint-hearted. Up to now (2018), more than 175 of them have been killed. They protect the park's integrity, the people who live there, the elephants *and* of course the last remaining mountain gorillas on Earth. The attacks on them and the park come in many guises—even, amazingly, an oil company given rights to drill in what is not only a zone of volcanic instability, but a Protected World Heritage location and arguably the world's most precious reserve of nature. Are we insane or what? If our brother gorillas could speak, surely they would beat their chests and roar across the jungle, 'Oh yes, my short-sighted half noble comrades, you are, you are.'

★★★

Here and there wisps of smoke rose from the vast blanket of trees on distant hills. Those who have travelled here will remember the innocent-looking plumes which I naively assumed came from a home or a hunter's campfire. Later I would learn what they really were. Charcoal kilns are now deemed the number one threat to the gorilla habitat: too many people, too many mouths to feed, too many cooking stoves consuming vast quantities of the charred wood. Right through the continent, I witnessed the results of its voluminous production, its roadside sale and many, many times its daily usage, often to my own personal and hungry benefit. Chunks of forest get cut, animals get pushed into ever more receding enclaves, and sometimes even the animal itself is cut down too, to be cooked over the charred remains of its very own habitat.

Yet the terrain now passing by was all of what I had imagined Africa to be. 'Goddammit, this is it, this is what I came to see' —the jungle, the expanse of sky, those wispy smoke-funnels on the hills, African buffalos, African hippos, African antelope, the rear ends of two African elephants, mother and calf trundling into undergrowth and, of course, the occasional perky line of those oh-so-African-looking warthogs. Focussed? You bet. I didn't want to miss a thing, and as we approached the Semliki my attention was directed upward to a great black and white bird gliding toward the river, its head and snow-white chest sandwiched between huge black wings spanning two metres or more. With a flick of its wingtip this African fish eagle angled down to the river, hidden behind the trees. Sometimes a sense of having once been privileged rises up in retrospect…sometimes years after the fact. Not that day. I was blasted by it and it rose in me as the pick-up bounced me along. I didn't care that I could not cycle, and although the bike at my feet was suffering the terrible vibration of potholes, I revelled in what was all around.

By the time we reached the Semliki River we were five in the back, all going to the lake-side fishing village of Kyavinyonge. To cross the river, two metal *pirogues* had been lashed together with timber and rope to make a catamaran-like vessel. Planks were fastened on top to form a transport platform, and up onto this the ferryman drove the vehicle with consummate ease. We stood aside to watch; watching too was a herd of curious hippos, their eyes peering barely above the surface. The unconcerned ferrymen took their long poles and pushed us out. The hippos responded with indignant snorts and submerged under us like so many submarines.

Kyavinyonge sits just south of where the Semliki leaves Lake Edward, as picturesque a location for a village as you will find, there beside the blue lake with hazy mountains close and distant. Five rows of reed-thatched homes greeted the eye, and on the roofs of many of them marabou storks stood like wizen old field marshals surveying their precinct. If I'd thought the span of the fish eagle was something to behold, then the marabou notched me up to a new level. They are big, up there with the albatross or the condor but with an added 'don't mess with us' demeanour. They strolled in and out between the homes as if they owned the place, and one look is all it took to understand the reason for their nick-name, 'the undertaker bird'. Scavengers they are, of carrion and any frail looking creature nearing its end. With that powerful long bill, a carcass would be ripped to pieces in seconds, and when I was subsequently told that 'only the bones remained' of some poor guy who had fallen unconscious somewhere beyond the village, my respect for them doubled and I gave them a wide berth. Apparently for marabou, flesh is flesh. I even saw them eat shit!

If the 'undertakers' owned the roofs above and the streets below, hippos and pelicans owned the water's edge. There they chilled in the sunshine, as village kids kicked ball on the bare grassy pitch beside them, while thirty paces along the shore their fathers mended nets and tweaked at their outboard engines. Women pounded and washed clothes and carried water back to the homes, keeping a sharp eye on toddlers toddling and splashing in the water. Everyone smiled at the bearded visitor and 'he' was made more than welcome. If ever there was a place which brought the Biblical Paradise to life, Kyavinyonge was it, but then again, that may well have been the mood I was in to make it so. As to the place itself—within a national park, of mountains, jungle, water, vast sky with per-haps the illusion of happy families mingling unperturbed among content wild animals—it certainly looked the part and seemed the perfect place to hang out while waiting for some fisherman to take me onward.

Above the only tin-roofed brick-built building in the village, the flag of Zaire flapped it's Olympic-like flame in the breeze. It was an ubiquitous flag in the country then, with its pale green background and bright yellow sun, in the centre of which a brown arm held a torch with a red flame. It was part of Mobutu's *retour à l'authenticité* programme where all things colonial were ditched so as to return to a more African-local way. Coming from where I did, I 'got' that, but to change the nation's name, to prevent citizens from taking Euro-pean Christian names, to insist on a new dress code...I wasn't so sure. At least the 'Helmsman' himself led by example and changed his own name to *Mobutu Sese Seko Nkuku Ngbendu Wa Za Banga*, a mouthful meaning 'The all-powerful warrior who, because of his endurance and inflexible will to win, goes from conquest to conquest, leaving fire in his wake'— which he did until he finally fled to Morocco from the forces of Laurent Kabila. A few months later the 'all-powerful warrior' died of prostate cancer.

Mobutu's flag signalled an apparent peace over Kyavinyonge, and I felt for certain nothing much would happen here, bar a quiet though indefinite wait for a *pirogue*-ride to Vitshumbi. Outside the home of *le gerant* (the manager of the fishermen), my sleeping spot was 'arranged' on a raised wooden platform, and there, in boxers only, I stretched out for the first of four of the most extraordinary nights. The marabou, silhouetted by a half moon, cackled and shuffled on the roofs, fighting for some prime position, fencing each other with their sabre-like beaks while at ground level the village dogs came to bare their teeth. Thankfully *le gerant* barked at them from his window and they scattered. Then everyone and everything settled for the night…until the hippo procession began.

It was past 10pm when they lumbered from their watery home, their awesome nostrils drawn by the sweet smell of juicy grasses beyond the village. Each night they did so, the same routine, the same paths followed between the houses. To say I was a little scared that first night would be not to overstate the case. The hulks trundled so close to where I lay I could have reached to touch their backs, their puffing, blowing breathing was that close. That I was aware how hippos, especially older cranky ones, could crack a human in two with one jaw snap made it none the easier to relax into what was otherwise a wonderfully close encounter.

The hippos made their way through the village to the grass plain beyond, and then, somewhere between midnight and 1am, antelope came cautiously in the opposite direction to drink their fill at the lake. As for trying to sleep, maybe half an hour came before dawn, before the hippos returned and the antelopes quietly tiptoed away. They would pass each other in this nocturnal musical-chair drama to resume their daytime positions, and partly due to this 'drama' I had let my guard down on the one creature in Africa more dangerous than any other. Perhaps after four nights of being enthralled by these comings and goings, sleeping half naked and stupidly uncovered, it was too late. It is almost impossible to pinpoint exactly when one is infected with malaria, but everything, from its incubation period, checking the dates in the diary, to that only time I had dropped my guard in a 'high probability area'…all pointed to one of those bizarre nights in Kyavinyonge. I was certain it was there that a simple silent bite of a lone female anopheles mosquito caused the dreaded *plasmodium falciparum protozoa* to visit me.

★★★

He wore a blue-white hat, a clean but too-tight white shirt and pink pin-stripe trousers, more in keeping with a flamboyant city salesman than a Congo fisherman, but *he* was the 'skipper'. '*Je n'ai jamais pris de vélo dans ma pirogue,*' he exclaimed proudly and loudly to the crowd. '*Moi aussi,*' I said, '*je n'ai jamais été dans une pirogue avec mon vélo.*' I never shook so many hands on a beach, and a farewell cheer went up as skipper revved his outboard to take his small craft and this, his most unusual cargo, away from Kyavinyonge. On board, his three fishermen mates, their huge net, barrels, markers, petrol, food and one probably infected *mizungu*, his baggage and his bicycle—and not a life vest in sight!

Lake Edward, the smallest of Africa's Great Lakes, is seventy kilometres long. We travelled twenty-five to the fishing spot, and there, somewhere on the Zaire side of that watery border-line with Uganda, the throttle was set to idle. Out went the net, out and out and out while the outboard chug-chugged us along. Over went the fifty-gallon drum—splash—then more net until the drum disappeared. It was well beyond dark when the skipper cut the engine. He shone his torch to arrange the floor boards, for with an extra body a little more thought had to go into the sleeping arrangements. I got the narrow bow, they the slightly wider stern. He passed around the food bag, and each man's hand dipped in, then my own, pulling out flat breads and dried fish.

Soft light from a half-moon fell on his white shirt, and as he spoke to his men I couldn't help but think of Jesus chatting to his fishermen disciples. Their Swahili dialect may as well have been Aramaic, but he translated *en français* for my benefit, saying how they hoped the net would do a good job and how they prayed the wind would stay away. But nothing is straight-forward in the middle of a Rift Valley lake at night. Murphy's Law, like a devil, swooped in and ensured the weather changed. First a little wind, then a little swell, then a little rain, light rain, then not so light rain, then more wind and then, as if to try and drown us all, the clouds let rip. The fishermen got under a plastic tarp, one popping his head up as if to say, 'Hey, why are you not underneath?' He popped under again and the sky came down in buckets. Under I went and we held the edges out over the vessel's sides to keep the rain from coming in. The wind would whip the tarp from our hands and we would wrench it back. Lightning lit the low Ugandan hills as thunder rolled over Edward. It was wild and I felt wildly good in that edgy-nervy way. I thought of J and wished she too was there under the tarp. Then that last desert-day in Kordofan came to mind, holding another tarp on top of a truck, keeping the *haboob* sands out. What a déjà vu that was, and just as then all I thought of was the bike.

The *pirogue* rocked and the skipper bailed with his pot. The crew laughed as the heavens opened wide. From beneath the tarp I reached forward toward the bow, moving my hand from side to side in the dark, feeling where the bike was, but there was nothing. The rain pelted like a hellfire and I panicked. If the bike had tipped over to the lake bottom what the hell could I do, but the mere thought made my mind reel. Without thinking for a millisecond about my own safety I stretched full-out over a barrel…and oh, sweet Jesus, the relief to touch the rear wheel. The bike had shifted to the very bow-tip and was now dangling over, the front wheel baptising itself in the lake on each alternate roll; with one water-filled front pannier dragging it downward, sooner or later it would certainly have gone over, but I had it now and it wasn't going anywhere.

There is a old *pirogue* joke: how some are so sensitive that if you are chewing gum and you move the gum to the other side of your mouth, the vessel will lean to that side. Thankfully, unlike those *pirogues*, the one we were in was more stable but, bloody hell, did it rock that night. For the landlubber I was, with the wind punching us hard, the scariest thing, bar a hole in the bottom, was being in one at all. The wind whipped the swell and the swell got 'swellier' until it rocked us silly. In the stern I huddled under the plastic for what felt like hours, gripping the rear wheel like a vice. The others had no idea what was going on and it was pointless attempting to involve them. Maybe they had Jesus on their side and weren't too scared, but for me, after a year on the road, this was without doubt the craziest test of nerves by a long shot. I held tight and may have said some words to my maker, but can't recall.

Nothing indeed is straight forward. We were not the only *pirogue* on the lake that night. At 1am the high winds abated and the arduous job of hauling in the net began. We pulled and hauled, tossing the odd fish to a bin, until the skipper raised his hand to be still. Off to starboard a barely audible voice drifted from the dark. He cupped his hands and shouted out. The voice responded. From out of the mist, like the witches of Macbeth, another *pirogue* emerged and it became clear that we, like them, had been hauling each other closer and closer. The two nets were hopelessly entangled and Jesus must surely have wept or burst his sides laughing. For two hours they failed to disentangle them so both were lashed side to side, and despite the continuous bumping everyone tried to rest. At 5.30am the work began again. Fishermen are not fishermen for nothing. They found a way, and by the time of a red horizon we were free. Dawn does not remain red for long near the equator. Red changed to a burning yellow as we hauled in the two kilometres of net, tossing tilapia and other fish to the bottom of the boat. By noon, the skipper, his white shirt now wide open, gripped the tiller and we began to reel Vitshumbi in like another big fish.

Even for those seasoned fishermen it had been a rough night. They looked at me, smiling and shaking their weary heads. '*Trois heures*,' the skipper called out. *Trois heures*, that's what remained of my lake-faring adventure. In the distance, behind where Vitshumbi must surely have been, the dull green wall of the Kabasha Escarpment butted in to the high rolling landscape which rumbled south for a hundred kilometres, through the land of volcanoes and on to Lake Kivu, truly one of the most dangerous lakes on Earth.

Kivu, one of Africa's Great Lakes, sits on the border of the Democratic Republic of the Congo and Rwanda. It also sits on top, or rather its very deep bottom sits on top, of a Rift Valley being slowly pulled in opposite directions. A lake sitting on a tectonic plate at the foot of an active volcano is asking for trouble, and Kivu has been described as akin to 'a big keg of soda-water sitting on a cracked keg of explosives!' It has so much methane and carbon dioxide dissolved in its waters that an eruption would mean catastrophe for life and the million plus inhabitants of Goma and Gisenyi on its shores. Two hundred and fifty six cubic kilometres of CO_2 is one gargantuan soda-bottle.

The skipper was in full throttle mode and the narrow bow rose and slapped the surface, sending spray flying. My back was stiff against a barrel, my arse cold and wet, my hands sore and raw *and* never did I feel adventure more. If it's to end out here, I thought, or on that approaching shore, it would have been worth everything…and then I knew, knew more clearly than the rawness of where I was, that there *are* things worth living for, things that can rock the life into us, and often, all too often, *they* are the very things we either fear or can't ever imagine ourselves embracing, but they wait, it all waits, until we arrive one day to find ourselves where we never dreamed of being, right there in the unpredictable, unfathomable heart of our own adventure.

The *pirogue* bow was now splitting the choppy waves, splaying them aside. Before me, leaning safe against the port side, as if leading me on, was, as ever, the bike. It was the symbol of the un-nameable in the journey, yet out here in the

225

middle of the lake I felt my graspable, well-calculated adventure had vanished in front of my eyes. Instead, adventure's unpredictable wild child had taken over and something in me had shifted. Fear had become friend, and I knew even if this 'symbol' had been lost to the depths, I would go on.

To port side were Uganda and the low hills of Queen Elizabeth National Park; starboard and dead ahead were the higher mountains of Virunga. The sky was a mush of whitey grey, as fitting a sky for a January day off the Kerry coast as anywhere. The lake was a dirty brackish brown, and just ahead a pod of pelicans glided in like big cargo planes. In my nostrils the smell of fresh fish and fresh petrol blended with the old embedded fishy smells of net, gear, tarp and timber. We were all tired from the nights exertions, yet these guys would do this day in day out to earn a measly wage; their generosity of spirit was humbling. Five hundred metres from the beach I saw the long line of people watching our approach. The bustle of Vitshumbi drew close. Shirts, trousers and clothes of all colours could be clearly seen, then gradually the faces became more and more distinct, until all the smiles and excitement showed. We drew closer and closer, down to the last yard and the crunch of bow on the shingly shore, and then I began all over again to find my way.

★★★

On the beach I hooked up the pannier bags. The skipper came over and hung three fine tilapia off the handlebar. '*Merci beaucoup pour ton aide,*' he said. '*Et merci, monsieur, de m'avoir amené ici,*' I replied and meant every word. He shooed away the smallies who clamoured '*Bonbon, bonbon*' and whistled older boys to come. They were given instructions to 'help the *mizungu* prepare and cook his fish'. I was led away by an excited team of teenage chefs, already deep in the negotiations of who would do what. At first they didn't interfere, just eyed my 'fish-ability', but their giggles made it plain: I was no adept at slitting and cleaning tilapia. The older, confident one had seen enough. He held out his open palm toward the knife, suggesting I had had my chance and it was time to hand it over to a professional. His pals began the fire, and privately I was glad not to be making a bigger eejit of myself. 'Let them at it,' I thought. *Samaki* is the Swahili for fish and it tasted good, they tucking in to one and I the other, as tasty a *bienvenue* to Vitshumbi as I could ever have hoped for.

There was one beer hut in the village and though I knew I shouldn't, I did. 'Oh come on, hepatitis? What the hell, after last night…you deserve a beer.'

I stooped to enter the low door, into a dark shoe-box space. The few older fishermen in there fell silent and looked up, as any bunch of locals would in any out-of-the-way drinking hole in the world. Straight off I could see there was a queue and I dared not jump it. Sitting centrally, beneath a paraffin lamp, with her back against the main roof-bearing pole an older woman was in charge of doling out the beer. Under her voluminous skirt was her economic mainstay—a full bucket of millet *pombe* and another, a kind of banana brew.

Using her jug as a measure, she'd pour into whatever vessel her customers came with, and God help the bloke who tried to lift her skirt! There was no argy-bargy. She could only dole so fast and each man waited his turn.

I came empty handed but, being the only *mizungu*, that was certainly not going to be a problem. An array of fancy calabashes, a small pot, a cut down plastic container, even a bean can with a fancy handle, were thrust at me by as many hands attached to a bunch of welcoming, chummy-looking locals. Which vessel to accept was a subtle diplomatic decision. Not wanting to offend any of my future drinking partners, I opted for the calabash belonging to the oldest looking face in the group, and for that unwittingly wise though innocent move, a chuckle went round the room. I was in.

In dry and dusty Dongala, 2,200 kilometres to the north, William's younger brother Abraham had told how it was the women who made the beer. Their home might become 'a pub' for a night or two, where village adults could gather and carouse. Now here in humid, cloudy Vitshumbi, I was in such a home. I sipped her brew and tossed a nod of appreciation. The 'older face', who as it turned out came from the other side of the Congo (a distance from Dublin to Rome away!), was proud that I drank form his spare calabash. He motioned me to follow his lead and flick beer drops to the floor. He was dumb, but the young guy who came in and sat beside me explained his meaning. '*Pour nos ancêtres*,' he said. 'Ah, for the ancestors, right, okay, I'm into that,' so I flicked drops across the dirt and hoped to get some blessings from my own forebears.

Mama's brew wasn't bad at all and sensibly, before launching into a second gourd-full, I considered where to sleep. '*Pas problem, monsieur*,' said the guy beside me. His slicker dress told me he was no fisherman and he was too quick to answer, as if anticipating the question. He let it be known that whatever I wanted, he could provide. I took that with a grain of salt, but as the night and the *pombe* wore on, I noticed him speak a few times to a young woman. She began rubbing some sort of butter-like substance over her arms and legs and I began to get his drift. Accepting one more gourd for the road, I watched her as she slicked the glistening creamy paste on her limbs, massaging it in and giving me a coy eye. I tried to deflate the guy's obvious game-plan, wagging my finger with a '*Non…non, ce n'est pas nécessaire.*' He grinned, '*Oui, oui, mais elle est tellement bonne.*' He was too pushy for my liking and I felt like telling him to piss off into the night, but diplomacy, often not the best of my traits won out, and I kept my mouth shut. On the road, one never knows when even a pest might come in handy.

My pushy friend led the way to the village guest hut. It was, or so he said, on the far side. Thankfully, the young butter-lathered woman was nowhere to be seen; she had left the shebeen sometime before us. We crossed the alleyways between the rows of homes, then without warning he grabbed my fleece from behind. With karate reflex I swung, thinking I was being mugged, but no, he whispered words of alarm, 'Kiboko, kiboko' (Hippo, hippo), and pushed me against the hut wall. No doubt, his ears were well tuned. Seconds later an old slow hippo sow lumbered passed. '*Elle est très dangereuse,*' he said, as if he knew her well. I let out a relieved, expletive-filled breath. There was too much *pombe* in my system. I would have walked straight out in front of her.

Travel long enough and sooner or later someone will be in your bed before you. Sometimes that's an easy pleasure to deal with, sometimes it's an awkward sticky point and sometimes…sometimes you don't know what to do, you just stand there, numb and dumb and wondering what shape your next move should be. A paraffin lamp was already lit. Its yellow smoky light fell across a glistening naked young woman, stretched out and waiting in the only bed in the room, 'Oh, Jesus-fucking-Christ!' Drink was no excuse, but it made it too easy for her, and too hard for me to change the inevitable. She took me by the arm and down I went. Like some birds, it was over before it began, and then she wanted seconds and I wanted out. She was brim to go, to go all night and I hadn't had a decent sleep in days. It was game set and match to the woman from Vitshumbi. There was no discourse. She had no French, I no Swahili, so I went outside to feel the night, to breath, to take a pee and to do what…I wasn't sure, just stand there naked, looking at the marabou shuffling on the roof. The *pombe* began to kick my head in and I was certain they were all cackling at me. Then I thought of J and my mouth opened wide but nothing came out. Back inside I asked her to leave. It was gone two in the morning. She shook her head, made signs that that was impossible, that it was too dangerous, some animal, not hippos but something else. I didn't push, so I lay on my karimat on the dirt floor while she snored in my bed, and that was it. What a day, what a night.

In the morning she was gone, and slowly like Humpty Dumpty I gathered my pieces. Cycling was not a possibility, as I was still within the national park, but a truck would depart for Rutshuru early and 'damn it' I mumbled to myself, 'I'll be on it.' I wolfed down the last of the rice along with tilapia number three, then headed to the far side of the village where women were busy loading the truck with fish-laden baskets. En route, my lady of the night caught up with me, along with my friend or rather her friend or her pimp to be precise. He made sheepish demands for his money. I told him where to get off and pushed on. She, though, was more forceful. Everyone around (and there were many) knew what was going down but thankfully they stayed neutral, bar the truck driver who, as we roped the bike to a fish-basket gave me the inside track on who was who. My friend the pimp was the girl's brother. *Mon Dieu!* He too was a passenger on top but gave up hassling me for fear of *un fracas*, but she…she continued to hurl her venom from below, and as the truck pulled away she trotted alongside, pointing her forefinger at her other hand, making a strange twisting gesture.

The route out from Vitshumbi to the main Beni-Goma artery was, to say the very least, rough. The landscape at this southern end of the lake was low-lying savannah, with pockets of forest through which our narrow route cut its way. We ducked the whacking branches, the creepers and all kinds of growth whizzing over our heads, only to break out every now-and-then into a prairie-like vista where impala and gazelle, ears erect, stood motionless to look. There were potholes, of course, but it was the scale of them! Rivulet upon rivulet had joined forces to form road-eating torrents. They burst from the forest to wash great chunks of track away. In the places where the road was gone, the driver eased his load of fish and humans and two broken outboard engines down into the great chasms then up the other side. Families of baboons barked and scampered alongside. Hippos huffed and puffed in a chocolate-coloured river and, close-by, three wooden crosses marked the graves of three drunken unfortunates who had been chopped in two by their jaws. Buffalo too glanced up, then continued their grazing, but my real friends, the warthogs, didn't seem to give a toss about our passing. Tails up, they hot-footed-it across the plain, going about their business in their own special warthog world. Oh, I loved them.

I was now between the lakes, Edward to the north, Kivu to the south, and south was where Virunga's eight volcanoes pushed their latent fiery heads to the sky. In 1977 I was 20 and remember news of Nyiragongo's eruption, when lava swept down at 100 kilometres an hour, incinerating villages and people. If it ever 'decides' to erupt for real, Goma and it's million plus will be another Pompeii. Virunga comes from the Rwandan word *ibirunga,* meaning volcanoes, and it is on their slopes that the last of the mountain gorillas have chosen to make their last stand. They have no place else to go.

The cloud cleared, and I imagined I could see some hazy peaks, but whether or not, I knew that at Bugayo, not far from Rutshuru, I would turn west and away from them. The north-south Beni to Goma artery forked just beyond that town. The bigger leg ran straight south to Goma on Lake Kivu, the lesser leg hobbled on a rocky trail to the quiet border crossing at Bunagana, my doorway to Uganda. That was the way I went. I postponed seeing volcanoes and the gorillas on their flanks until after Nairobi, when J would come.

We reached the fork at four but at the equator it gets dark at six. It was too late to ride on. Anticipating that this might happen, I had struck up a conversation while on the truck with an older, grey-whiskered man. '*Ça va?*' I had asked, making that universal tent shape with both hands. Would it be okay to pitch the tent in his *jardin*. '*Pas problem,*' he said, '*pas problem*', but, as if fate was playing games, who should he turn out to be but the father of the pimp who had pimped his own sister, his father's daughter. Well bloody hell!

In any journey, all kinds of situations are experienced in the homes that welcome, all kinds. From the ordinary cup of tea in the hand to the extraordinary canopied four-poster bed, from sublime or sacred moments to ridiculous 'I-want-to-get-out-of-here' situations, and then, of course, there are the easily forgotten 'welcomes' and the ones hard to forget. That night was firmly there among the latter. The shock on the son's face when I followed his father into their space told me everything. His look set up an awkward poker-faced evening. He was terrified I would spill the beans, but how could I? If I did, I'd also have to admit I'd been in bed the night before with the daughter of my host. I guessed the old man was unaware of his offsprings' entrepreneurial efforts and that his *mizungu* guest pitching tent in his mud-filled yard had fallen prey to their

230

trap. Then again, with three wives and eighteen children, the old man, if he was told the whole story, might have merely shrugged his shoulders in indifference, had a good laugh and poured me another tea. Who knows?

By his son's look and certainly for my part, neither of us wished to take that chance. I wondered if any or all of his wives knew. They probably did. The senior, older wife came with food. She rammed a chair as a table into the mud outside the shelter. On it there was barely room for three small plates and a paraffin lamp. In that meagre light we discussed, of all things, the weather, and while his father apologized for the mud and rain, son and I kept our mouths occupied with fish and manioc and our lips sealed in a silent, eye-averting, private understanding.

I left them very early and struck off up the stony rain-guttered way, feeling real good that my shit was solid, and pondering, pondering, pondering, my mind flitting back and forth between a buckled rear wheel and what some have to do here to make ends meet...how would it pan out for them, brother and sister? Did they pimp each other? Did their other siblings depend on monies from their sexual exploits? Then as I sweated up that hill, a kind of guilt came and weaved its way into a corner of a befuddled mind and stubbornly would not let go. 'You're a mean bollox, why didn't you pay her? It didn't matter that you didn't know. You knew in the end, didn't you? You should have paid, paid what she asked, no matter the extortion.' Such were the thoughts until about noon when the clouds broke and the sun came down on my uncovered head like a thundering brick.

Near the equator, a hat for a red-haired white man is as vital as his visa. At one degree south, the sun, when it got its chance, made no mistake in reminding me where I was, and I was rightly cheesed off to discover that one of the fish-helping boys in Vitshumbi had helped himself to my cherished blue hat...as 'payment' of course! I'd grown surprisingly attached to that shrunken bleached bit of head cover and was taken aback at a kind of sadness that came at its loss. Fatigue had now seeped beyond my legs. Sunstroke came to mind. I pulled out a greenish T-shirt to wrap round my red mop, giving the passing women with their own heads burdened with wood piles or branches of bananas something to giggle about. I'd no sooner arranged my head-cover when the cover of trees loomed ahead and the green sweat-soaked T-shirt was shoved back into the handlebar bag. I coasted down the smooth earth surface, not a bump or corrugation to be seen, breathing in an air infused with fragrances of such diverse tropical life. In the valley below the trail, a raging stream raced ahead. Uganda was now just a few kilometres away. It was already throwing shapes, and I was already adjusting to a new transition.

Banana plantations were everywhere, organized and productive looking, and in the settlement of Jombo I purchased a bunch of small sweet ones from a pair of squatting, pipe-smoking women. They put their pipes down to clap with laughter as I mimicked a monkey popping bananas whole, like daisies to a bull. Their laughter attracted attention. Two guys ambled over to explain (*en français*) that it was 'only' 600 zaire shilling to see the gorillas. '*Êtes-vous interesé?*' they asked, but I had made the decision. '*Je reviendrai ici,*' I answered. I must have looked ravenous, for an old man sat down beside me on the earth bank and from his soil encrusted hand passed over a maize cob. '*Kula, kula* (eat, eat),' he said, but the cob was filthy. I nibbled a few token corns then looked at my watch and mumbled about having to catch a new country before dark. I shook his earthen hand and took off. Terrible to say, once out of sight I flung the cob into the undergrowth.

Not far from that cob-throwing spot, I pulled the brakes. There it was, a small sign at the edge of the trail, two foot long, one foot off the ground, a hand-crafted hardwood signpost with fire-branded lettering, *Parc des Gorilles*. It had a simple black-and-white-painted gorilla hand, with thick index finger pointing toward a narrow tree-covered way. For several minutes I looked along its length as far as it would let me, and I honestly wavered. I had dreamed of arriving at that very spot, of going down a trail just like that, and now I stood there. In a shaky, lip-biting instant, recalling what Evan had said about returning as a duo, I flicked the pedal, pushed hard down and went on, comforting myself for a few hundred metres that I'd be back. 'Yeah, it all makes perfect sense', but somewhere in the back of my mind I knew I was already bending backwards to believe it.

I often wondered how going down that forested trail might have gone. Would I have seen gorillas or would I have walked into a poacher's hornet's nest? What is for certain is that I would never have met Dian Fossey. Four months earlier, on 27 December 1985, as I was packing the panniers to leave Cairo and savouring those final pre-parting days with my friend Eamon, Dian Fossey was butchered to death by machete. They came in the dead of night while she slept in her hut, high on the Rwandan side of those Virunga hills. She had no chance and in the poachers' eyes had to be disposed of. Not until I reached Nairobi did I hear that terrible news, but by then for me everything had changed.

Twenty years is a long time to hang around gorillas in the chill mist of the mountains. She devoted every ounce of her life's worth to them. When her favourite, Digit, was beheaded seven years before, part of her died inside. She needed no one to tell her about 'the heart of darkness', for she had seen it many times and must surely have felt 'the horror, the horror' more deeply than anyone. She took her stand against the poachers and those who would have sold a gorilla hand as an ashtray on the black market for a few dollars. She even disliked the wildlife tourism to her beloved gorilla sanctuary. The locals called her *Nyiramachabelli*, 'the woman who lives alone on the mountain'. The final entry in her diary reads, 'When you realize the value of all life, you dwell less on what is past and concentrate more on the preservation of the future.' How we need such 'crazily' focussed visionary minds as hers today! Dian Fossey is buried at Karisoke, Rwanda, at the Gorilla Research Centre she founded in 1967. She was laid to final rest next to Digit and the many other of her other gorilla friends killed by poachers.

A year or so after I returned to Ireland, I watched the Hollywood movie on her Virunga life, *Gorillas in the Mist*, in which Sigourney Weaver played Fossey so well. Though I was with friends, it was nigh impossible to stop the memories… of brothel doors opening and closing through the night; of Evan and gospel singing in Mutwanga and lightning on the Rwenzoris; that first time seeing the Plough and the Cross and a night of rock-n-roll with four fishermen in a pirogue; of the misty world of mountain gorillas whom I never saw and the bloody imaginings of machetes in the dark. They asked questions and I tried to share something…maybe tried too hard, for it didn't take long for that glazed look to come to their eyes, leaving me with a lonely isolated feeling, perhaps familiar to many who have returned from the long road.

Chapter 11
Death's door onwards

If nothing else, it was intriguing that I should leave Zaire (DRC) through yet another split village. On the way in, Sudan Buzze to Zaire Buzze, and now on the way out, Zaire Bunagana to Uganda Bunagana. Yet there was something I found even more intriguing. The customs official, who had no reason to, invited me to join him for what was to be my final farewell meal in his country—a plate of *matoke* and what he called 'Irish' potatoes—not '*pomme de terre d'Irlandaise*', no, 'Irish' potatoes! He looked at my passport and had no idea of where *Irlande* was, so I told him straight how good was his gesture and that for me at least he had balanced the scales for his country. On the other side of the border, as I was soon to discover, such 'Irish' potatoes were on everyone's plate, and everyone knew where Ireland was.

With passport stamped and a belly full of 'Irish' spuds, I crossed into no man's land and turned about to look—back beyond the customs post as far into Zaire as I could, and nodded to no one but myself at something I had read about the country, that it 'never stops fizzing you up then pummelling you down until you don't know what's for real or not, that it's not a straight-line place.' True as hell, I thought, and for me then it felt I'd just come through a physical, visual, emotional washing machine on fast spin. It was and is an incredible, unpredictable place to travel, and as that Khartoum traveller put it, 'You won't need to get stoned there, the place itself will stone you!' Facing forward, I rose up on the pedals and cranked myself out of no man's land towards Uganda, the original of Africa's 'Switzerlands'.

Who could blame him his siesta, certainly not I. It was a late soporific afternoon and the Bunagana crossing was quiet. When I eventually found him, snoozing in his home, he loudly lamented, 'You disturb me again. Why do you keep coming through this way.' What could I say—sorry to wake you, but could you please stamp my passport! I waited while he laced up his boots, thinking 'What does he mean *again*? Have I been through here before?' But of course it was not me personally he was referring to, it was anyone, anyone at all who came through during his off time. He cheered up no end when I enquired where I could officially change money, knowing full well he'd bite. We did our mutually beneficial deed with a few bananas thrown in, and I rode away happy, thinking that these are the kinds of border crossings to raise the spirits: get fed at one, change money at the other.

It was 10k to Kisoro, to the Traveller's Rest and to a 'No! No tents here, sorry sir,' from the burly manager. 'Try the Police station down the road. Oh, and welcome to Uganda!' The police, however, weren't having me either, and one of them kindly marched me back to the Traveller's to plead my case. Reluctantly, the manager pointed to a dark corner at the rear, but later he too saw the light of opportunity. He came all meek and mild as I stirred my pot in the dark, enquiring if I wished to change dollars. We did the deal and he ambled away grinning down at a twenty dollar greenback, Andrew Jackson grinning up at him, and then he turned about. 'Hey, mister,' he called, 'I will tell my man to patrol this area.' And to be fair he did, for on the hour until I fell off a cliff-edge of tiredness, I heard a pair of hobnail boots tramp the nightly vigil, and I knew at least I was safe. What a managerial turnabout, but before the morning sun had peeped I was already long gone, almost 10k to Kabale, leaving him no more evidence of my being there than a faint impression on his bare goat-nibbled grass.

The way began to rise steeply, so down I reached, gripping the gear lever between thumb and forefinger, shifting it forward a fraction. The chain responded, slipping smoothly off the bigger sprocket, dropping to 'mister low-low', with that special springy sound of a derailleur adjusting to the sudden slackness. Ah, 'mister low-low', that child-friendly name. It had stuck, stuck all the way from Rovienemi on the Arctic Circle, where a young boy whose family I had stayed with had nicknamed it so. What would I have done without mister low-low, my favourite gear, the bikes '28 to 32' lowest transmission. Low? The chain went round the smallest front sprocket with its twenty-eight teeth, to the biggest rear with thirty-two, a less than 1:1 ratio. Thus under so much less strain, mister low-low had single-handedly hauled me up some awfully steep gradients.

Yet, as I rose up the Ugandan hills, even mister low-low would have forgiven my weak down-strokes and my 'getting-offs' at any opportunity if 'he' had known how my red cells harboured a rampant cerebral malaria. Slowly, round and round the chain went, and round and round in my overheated head went the same thought, 'Look, it's heat exhaustion, okay...put a pinch of salt in the water bottle and keep drinking, okay?' I convinced myself it could not be malaria. Had I not been popping prophylactics since Sudan? Had it not begun soon after that Vitshumbi kid took my hat? 'No, no, it's got to be the heat. Come on, drink-up and lets go.' And that's how it went along those truly eye-watering high roads.

The sun was warm and I nodded to the nods of passers-by. Up ahead the way thankfully levelled off and there, even at that early hour, a bunch of industrious young lads were preparing a fire to roast their mother's corn-cobs...and I hadn't had breakfast! They hailed me over and I told them I'd wait as long as it took. When the cobs came they were juicy sweet, but it was the vista behind where they stood which had me captivated. It looked mythical and magical and made a pathetic pale nonsense of that notion of my own so-called 'Emerald Isle' with its forty shades of green. 'You will see how green my country is, just like yours,' said John Azambi. He was so, so right, and I raised a yellow cob to him, stuck as he was at Station 14 in the yellow deserts of far-away Nubia. 'Jeez christ,' I reflected, 'to have been forced to leave *this* for *that*!' I could barely fathom then the forces at work to drive people to such measures. I remembered him fondly, wished him well and hoped he got that promotion to Station 6 where at least he'd have water enough to wash himself and dilute his *aragi*.

Directly below the trail lay the growing-plots of intensive agriculture, all neatly laid out in terraces, each descending, level by level, to the valley below. Down there, in the foreground, a large blue lake was bounded on one side by forested hills. Beyond the hills in the far, far distance, six misty-green volcanoes were just then undergoing a creeping baptism by the sun's first rays. Even their names sounded mythical. Furthest, in Congo's Virunga National Park, Mount Mikeno was almost completely shrouded, but Mounts Muhabura, Gahinga, Sabyinyo stood clear on the boundary with Rwanda. According to my map, Mount Sabyinyo sat right on the juncture of the three countries, Congo, Rwanda and Uganda. On top of its highest peak, at 3,650 metres, one could do a jig, stepping in and out of the three neighbours. I could not picture a more fitting place for a 'Lord of the Rings' movie. It had it all, from the homeliness of Hobbit-looking homesteads to, in certain parts, the real pillage and terror of war.

There also, straddling the border line, Mounts Bisoke and Karisimbi looked as if they were huddling together like twins. Up there, on a col between their ancient rounded peaks, Dian Fossey had made her long-standing camp, to live as close as she could to her beloved gorillas. On the steep forested flanks they roamed free, munching bamboo leaves, playing with their young until moving on before dark to set fresh nests for another night. I recall standing by those corn-cob boys, chewing toasted kernels and imagining Fossey somewhere way over there on one of those mountains contentedly doing her research, but by then she had been murdered.

'Your country is too beautiful to pass through just once,' I said to a bloke who munched his cob beside me. Then, half jokingly, I complained about the hills. He laughed at my geographical ignorance. 'Hills, hills?' he said. 'You must travel over there for hills,' pointing towards Rwanda. 'Over *there* they have too many hills.'

'Oh, well not this time,' I told him, 'I go on to Kampala.'

'What, you go to Kampala…with this bicycle!? That is too far. You cannot do this.'

There was absolutely no point telling him how it was actually to Cape Town I was riding and certainly no point explaining where I had come from, so I stretched him a bit, saying how I was *only* going as far as Nairobi.

'Nairobi, ah, Nairobi…but that is in Kenya. Ah, that is too, too far.'

238

He was dead right; for the way I felt, it did seem that the thousand plus kilometres to the Kenyan capital was 'too, too far'.

Heat exhaustion, indeed! It may not have sounded as sexy or severe but how naive that was. Heat exhaustion can lead to sunstroke and that's a no-nonsense affliction in its own right. Yet that's what my little red book led me to believe, the eighth edition of the Ross Institute of Tropical Hygiene's *Preservation of Personal Health in Warm Climates*. Not that it was the book's fault, for the symptoms of cerebral malaria can be very different to those of the regular kind and can mimic heat exhaustion, but I was not to know that then and it almost cost me my life. I sensed it was more sinister but was reluctant or just too damn stubborn to admit it, so I kept on pedaling. I rode the rising contours, snatching occasional peeks at those hard-worked terraces down below, with homesteads embedded in them, and it all looked so serene in that butterfly-filled afternoon.

Ahead of the front wheel I spat the uncooked kernels out, just like the sugarcane gobs in Egypt and the date stones in Sudan. The *déjà vus* were flying now, but here was different. Any morsel to hit the ground was quickly whisked into the green margins by hoards of ants as if they were waiting all day for magic crumbs to fall from their sky. A rhinoceros beetle, the biggest beetle I'd ever seen, halted my progress as it laboured to cross the earthen road. It took an age, so I egged it on to safety with a stick. Further on a lone pygmy went by, shouldering a pile of bamboo canes thrice his size. '*Asante*,' he said. '*Asante sana*,' I replied. As I turned to look at him, the front wheel hit a stone, the bike wobbled and down I went. The clatter made the pygmy swivel, his two hands above his head holding the straps. He did a little dance to cheer me up, a dance like an Irish jig with the dead-weight of bamboos on his back. I saluted him and he turned to waddle away, two little bendy legs protruding from a twelve-foot-high mass of dead straight canes, a sight that has forever stuck.

As I sat there, a longing came to share this strange and wonderful world I was coming to know, full of strange sights and spontaneous intimate cameos of people's daily lives, of moments so precious to me and probably so mundane to them. As my pygmy friend rounded a bend and disappeared forever, I immediately knew how innocent that longing to share was, for it was unlikely it could ever come to pass. I was on that solo road for solo reasons that no one else could understand, and the jewels of reward were non-transferable, being too personally embedded, and yet, sitting in that dusty silence there was something else, something I could neither name nor sense, a foreshadowing of something to come. As for 'jewels', Marlow's words came tumbling out of *The Heart of Darkness*: '...no, it is impossible; it is impossible to convey the life-sensation of any given epoch of one's existence—that which makes its truth, its meaning—its subtle and penetrating essence. It is impossible. We live, as we dream—alone.'

★★★

I was clearly not *compos mentis,* and riding hatless up and down hills near the equator was not the sole reason. Had I had a clearer head, perhaps, I might have pulled in to Kabale Hospital. I even saw its sign but sometimes the pull of an address scribbled on a scrap of paper pulls one on in the vain hope of reaching a welcoming door, through which everything would be 'just fine'. Somewhere along Rhona Street, Masaka, Richard and Geraldine's door was waiting, and I kept myself upright and together until I leaned the bike outside it and knocked. I didn't know who this Ugandan couple were, bar Geraldine was sister to a woman I had met in Vitshumbi. Somehow they knew I was coming and could not have been more courteous and welcoming, but all was not well with me, and on the second day, as I sat on their couch with Geraldine's hand stretching out to pass a plate of beans and *ugali* and my hand reaching to take it—that was all I recall—I collapsed on the floor.

Who would wish a passing traveller to kick the bucket in their living room? Richard bundled me into his car, and in less than an hour we were through the gates of the Kalungu Girls' Training School. 'Do not worry about your bike and bags,' he said, 'I will bring them later.' For the first and only time they were not even on my radar. I had in my possession one Irish name in all of Uganda, a Sister Carmel from Tipperary, a dedicated no-nonsense missionary teacher, and Richard rightly thought it best if I died on her watch rather than on his couch. Thankfully she was at the school and after a very Irish welcome, including Barry's Tea, Jacob's fig-rolls and, unbelievably, my favourite dunking Irish digestive, I was shown a bed in the male teachers' quarters. All was well in the world again, but *plasmodium falciparum* is a devious devil.

In the gap between the first bout of feverish sweat and a convulsive teeth-chattering shivering, as if the body lay naked on an ice-sheet, in that gap the delirium came...*Her face was, as I'd last seen it, tight with anger and menace. She ran beside the truck, her hands twisting and pushing a needle into my scalp, then another and another.* My breathing became rapid, a hyperventilating, causing a tingling sensation throughout my body, but in that mental confusion I drifted away in a dreamlike state to a campfire on a chill November night with Eamon, to leaping flames and old camaraderie on the Bulgarian-Turkish border, and then to Emeric and what he had warned me of.

Emeric, former French legionnaire, six-foot-four, larger than life Parisian, had joined Eamon and me that cold November night for warmth and conviviality. He had walked and skied from *la banlieue de Paris* to Tromsø, Norway, *in winter*! From there through Finland's 'thousand Lakes', over the high passes of the Polish-Slovak Tatras and Romania's Transylvanian Alps, across the Danube into Bulgaria, to walk along a lonely twilight hill-road, right to the place where he spied our campfire. His destination was Nairobi, and we laughed together that we were not the lone idiots we thought we were…to have done the 'up' before the 'down'. He was a guy you would listen to and I listened intently as he spoke into the fire of his time near the Okapi Reserve, west of Kisangani, in Central Congo. 'Be careful, monsieur, the voodoo *et la magie-noire* are alive and well there, and some have the power.'

I remembered Emeric in the moments of calm, when the disease's fever-to-freeze pendulum waned and I wondered was this what he meant? Is this the nightmare? There was no doubt in my throbbing head that the woman who had been in my bed, who ran beside the truck looking angrily up at me, looking for her money…she was doing this. She was playing voodoo with a doll of me, and in a half-delirious state I mumbled into the sweat-soaked sheets 'Jesus, why the fuck didn't I pay her, why?'

In the morning Carmel brought me her last Mogadon and some books from her personal shelf. 'They'll keep you entertained,' she said, '…oh, and take the tablet before you read, you'll fall asleep before you turn the page.' She smiled and closed the door gently. I kept the Mogadon until evening and turned the first page of Charles Miller's *The Lunatic Express*. Through a restless appetite-less day, it did indeed entertain. Its pages were full of the turbulence of an older Africa and the almost six 'lunatic' years building more than 600 kilometres of rail line through lion-filled, malaria-ridden swamp and savannah from Mombassa through Nairobi to Lake Victoria. A big part of the 'lunacy' were the 2,500 men who died in the process, and so many from malaria. I turned the pages, innocent to the fact that I was reading a salutary forewarning of what I was about to fully experience, for I *still* did not appreciate how I too was being drained by the dreaded virus.

Convincing everyone about sunstroke was easy, when that was what I believed, but you can't fool missionary sisters for too long; they've seen too much. On the second day, I arrived late and dishevelled to the breakfast table, where six of them had just finished saying grace.

'How did you sleep John?' asked Sister Carmel.

'Not well' I responded,

'Not well, oh dear, and when last did you get a good sleep?'

'... aahmm, aah, a few days ago...I think. I can't remember exactly.'

Their breakfasting more or less stopped and they looked at each other, and then at the dark rings under my eyes. Later, when Carmel visited the hospital, she told me how they were unanimous. It was not sunstroke but cerebral malaria which was taking me down. 'Oh, my dear young man, you nearly left us,' she said. As to why or how *plasmodium falciparum* infects the meninges of the brain and wreaks havoc in one's neurological system is beyond me, and I'm not even sure if it's fully understood, but one symptom is an inability to sleep, leading inexorably to coma and death. At that time three out of four sufferers never made it.

Sister Carmel drove the school jeep hard over the potholes of Uganda's Resistance War, apologising for every bump. She knew well I was on the cusp of coma. Her destination was Kitovo Hospital, Masaka, run by the Irish Medical Missionaries of Mary. Two other Irish sisters sat in the back. I overheard Carmel mutter a clear instruction to 'keep him talking'. It was a jumble of conversations from the kind of bike I used to Idi Amin's fleeing Uganda by helicopter to Gaddafi's Libya, to one of them regaling me with the history of Obote and Museveni's war with each other over Uganda's future, and the other with the pleasures of teaching Ugandan girls and the even bigger pleasure of dunking Jacob's digestives in the staff room...indeed, anything at all they felt would keep my mind engaged. They did a good job, for despite wishing to switch off and sleep, I tried my level best to be civil and converse.

It seemed the Irish were everywhere in Uganda in those days. Dr Bernadette O'Brien from Dublin, another MMM sister, took charge. Though Richard and Carmel played their crucial parts, to her specifically I owe my life. As in all hospitals, much of the action and decision-making happens behind the scenes.

She had read the notes: my liver had just come through a dose of hepatitis; it was weak and the immune system was low. The hard drugs she wished to administer, to take-out the virus, would also hit the liver like a sledge hammer. What to do? She explained later how her decision was made very simple when she looked down the microscope at a blood film. It was, as she frankly put it, 'dense with virus.'

While Dr Bernadette and her team deliberated on the course to take, I honestly thought it was the end of the road. I'd given it my best shot. I lay in a pool of sweat seeping from every pore. Three times the sheets were changed, making me wonder was there a leak in the saline drip-line, but I rallied, enough to piece together a prayer from youth and then, perhaps in answer, the thought of J came and that changed my mental state, which changed everything. We were due to meet two weeks later in Nairobi. It was enough. Her image floated to mind and I knew I would make it. I played out every possible happy scenario of that future meeting and I can say without a shadow of doubt, as Dr Bernadette concurred afterwards, how that singular thought saved me from slipping away. 'You left it very, very late, John, almost too late,' she said as I finally left her care. 'You are a lucky man.'

The MMM had their provincial retreat home in Ggaba, south of Kampala, on the shores of Lake Victoria. They would not countenance anything but for me to go there and rest. 'You need to convalesce,' Dr Bernadette said. 'We have people there who will take care of you.' She would have preferred if I'd taken the first flight home but she understood I had to get to Nairobi. 'You'll not be cycling for a while, John. You have lost a lot of weight. Have a great time with your girlfriend. You deserve it, and she will love Africa, you'll see.'

'Thank you,' I replied, 'thanks for everything. I'll see if I can get that microscope out to you.' Ggaba translates as 'to serve'. Perhaps that was why they choose the place.

Three days R&R was enough, and though I would have gladly stayed, it was already the fifth of May. J would arrive into Nairobi's Jomo Kenyatta airport on the seventh, her birthday. Gingerly, I rode the twelve kilometres from the lake-side retreat to Kampala bus station and took a local bus to the border at Busia. A night bus to the Kenyan capital was not at all the way I had intended to arrive into that new country. Somewhere past midnight, beyond Nakuru, when there was nothing to see but a black window, a face, gaunt and drawn, looked back at me. I had pictured powering down this tarred road through Kisumu and Naivasha with a warm Kenyan breeze in my face, but the cycling journey had grown up to become a mere means to an end, there to serve me on the way *into* and *out of* the vicissitudes of adventure and all its subtle personal explorations. If I could not yet throw the leg over the Brooks B17, then we would walk together like brothers-in-arms until I was able.

A seven-hour bus journey could not rob the sheer excitement of getting to the Irish Embassy where a Christmas-like morning awaited: cards, letters, news of home, brake-pads, patches, tubes, glue and even (I hoped) hard cash in several a brown envelopes. At 5.10am we arrived. I had three hours to wait. A coffee in the lobby of a nearby two-star hotel with the bike parked outside the window was as good a place as any to whet the imaginative juices before the embassy doors opened. Where does energy come from? At five minutes to eight I bounded up the levels to the fourth floor of Maendeleo House, Monovia Street, as if the physical depletions of the previous few weeks had happened to someone else. Sure, it was nice to see the Tricolour's green white and gold hanging outside, but it paled in comparison to the buzz I felt. The secretary stood up sharp when I announced who I was. My name seemed to unhinge her. She looked at me squarely and in a soft tone said, 'Please take a seat, Mr Devoy. I will get the Chargé d'Affaires.'

My gut got the hit before my brain. Instinctively I knew it was dark news. It happens to us all at some stage, when the world turns inside out and you try to keep calm, to keep a straight face while re-reading telegram sentences in that cold, impersonal print, as if chiselled in stone. Half-conscious whispers…'hey, it's all a joke…can't be true', but the Chargé d'Affaires stood there with his hands clasped, politely waiting for some response, and all the while the mind does what it has to, to try to make sense of it. He had indeed handed over two telegrams. One was already two months old, the second barely two weeks. I caught some words of his sympathy and support, 'We are sorry…we tried to locate you…If there is anything…etc., etc.' Yes indeed, they do their very best, embassy staff.

I took the telegrams to a nearby park and sat by a tree to read them again and then again. So, of the two people closest to me…one was dead, the other seriously ill in hospital. My father had died of a heart attack over two months previously. I looked at the date and realised it was close to that strange night in the Khartoum hostel, when my own heart felt as if it would burst or shut down. From the front pannier I pulled out the letter, ready to post to him, telling him of that sandstorm in Kordofan, of the wildness of the Congo which he had warned me of and of course of my recent brush with death, but then he probably had guessed all that anyway. That afternoon I posted it…anyway.

The second telegram rocked me even more. I knew my father was frail, that there was a chance he would not be around on my return, but I never imagined my girlfriend, young and fit, would end up in a hospital bed with an undiagnosable disease. Weirdly, and of course completely unbeknownst to either of us, we had both been in hospital at the same time. She with what turned out to be an extremely rare rheumatic reaction to a yellow fever vaccination, and I with cerebral malaria.

Squeezed between telegrams, I grappled with the new implications. In the days that followed, the avalanche of communication eventually settled and clarified that new world. On the phone I listened to my brothers tell the story, listened to the well wishes of close friends and to J's tears. It made perfect sense to end the journey then and return to Ireland until my younger brother put it bluntly, 'And to do what,' he had said, 'stand by his grave…and then what? He'd have wanted you to go on. If I was you, I would.' There was hope too that specialists would discover what on earth was going on with J's immune system and the possibility of her getting out to Kenya was not ruled out. They would soon decide. She too had said to continue, but I was not convinced.

All the journey's dice were all still tumbling from that first 'throw' on that April Fool's day, and the drama was incomplete. Over several gin and tonics in Mrs Roche's home-hostel in the suburbs of Nairobi, Mrs Roche spoke sense. She had seen more hardened weather-beaten overlanders come and go through her back yard campsite than anyone else in Africa. She had heard all the stories and more.

'You can't walk off the stage, you can't just leave what you've begun.' she said. 'You say its like a 'drama', then complete it, if not for yourself then for the people you have yet to meet. Forget those at home…they're fine and they want you to keep going…yeah?…so you must! There are people out there waiting for your journey to catch up with them, do you know that, do you understand?' She put her glass down on the table and looked at me coldly, 'Do you understand? They're waiting to meet you. Go meet them.'

An Edi and a Philippe from Switzerland, motor-biking from Lucerne to the Cape, a Herfrid from Germany motor-biking back to Berlin from Lusaka, and Pete, a lover of mountains from England (whom I would eventually join to climb Mount Kenya)—all travel veterans, all sitting around Mrs Roche's table, and all of them concurred with her. We raised our glasses and clinked salutes to ourselves, our journeys and what they inevitably had to offer.

Ah, Mrs Roche, Mrs Roche, you liked your G&T and with your wise words I let go once more to fate and serendipity. A week later in downtown Nairobi, still not having an inkling how to move on or to where, I rounded a corner and out of the corner of my eye caught the answer in a travel agent's window. There it was, a full-sized poster of the Great Red Island. 'Dammit, that's it,' I said and walked right in.

Out of her bluest sky, Madagascar beckoned.

Acknowledgements

I wish to acknowledge the following people, whose influence, support, and encouragement, in small or significant ways, helped in making this book a reality.

Dervla Murphy, for her inspiration, hospitality, and that very first cup of tea! Ted Simon, for if Dervla's books opened a door, his *Jupiter's Travels* kicked it down.

David Mitchell who said 'of course you can write, your Irish for heaven's sake!'—but then a long time later sent me back to the drawing board.

Old friends Eamon Wallace and Arie Baas who know all about the long road. Paul Brennan, Peter Sammon, Billy Cremin, Pat Barry, Mary Foley, Cian Ó Sé (RIP) and Brian Murphy (RIP), and to Jennifer Duggan, a warm and special thank you.

To David Bateman, Orla Shine, Orlagh O'Brien, Laura Constantine and Marie and Carol for all the teas and coffees in the corner table!

To Chris Pooley and Mary Myrane for helping on the farm and giving me the time to write.

A sincere thank you to my editor Maurice Sweeney, who with huge and thankful enthusiasm pulled it all together.

My parents May and Thomas Devoy

Finally, I remember Michael McGuirk. He lit the fuse. Without his finger being poked in the author's chest, the many diaries, letters, maps and other 'stuff' would have remained boxed in the attic. He was not afraid to tell it straight, 'Shame on you if you do not write this,' he said. 'You owe it to everyone.' He died six months later. I hope he's smiling, seeing how there is no shame.

John Devoy
Rosscarbery
May 2018

90890685R00150

Made in the USA
Middletown, DE
27 September 2018